T0148286

Fighting for Road Apples

Fighting for Road Apples

a memoir

Erika C. Stevenson

iUniverse, Inc.
Bloomington

Fighting for Road Apples
A Memoir

Copyright © 2012 by Erika C. Stevenson

All rights reserved. No part of this book may be used or reproduced by any means, graphic, electronic, or mechanical, including photocopying, recording, taping or by any information storage retrieval system without the written permission of the publisher except in the case of brief quotations embodied in critical articles and reviews.

iUniverse books may be ordered through booksellers or by contacting:

iUniverse
1663 Liberty Drive
Bloomington, IN 47403
www.iuniverse.com
1-800-Authors (1-800-288-4677)

Because of the dynamic nature of the Internet, any web addresses or links contained in this book may have changed since publication and may no longer be valid. The views expressed in this work are solely those of the author and do not necessarily reflect the views of the publisher, and the publisher hereby disclaims any responsibility for them.

Any people depicted in stock imagery provided by Thinkstock are models, and such images are being used for illustrative purposes only.

Certain stock imagery © Thinkstock.

ISBN: 978-1-4759-3882-1 (sc)
ISBN: 978-1-4759-3880-7 (e)
ISBN: 978-1-4759-3881-4 (dj)

Library of Congress Control Number: 2012912885

Printed in the United States of America

iUniverse rev. date: 8/8/2012

To my children: Patrizia, Claudia, and Monica

Mankind must put an end to war or war will put an end to mankind.

John F. Kennedy

Contents

⚜ ⚜ ⚜ ⚜

Preface

The year was 2003; spring had just arrived in all its glory. I sat in a doctor's office, dazed by the words the man in the white coat was gently conveying to me: "You have cancer of the colon, stage III." My life changed at that very moment.

After surgery, aggressive chemo, and radiation treatments, I retired from my job and traveled to Germany, where I had grown up. I stayed for nine marvelous months. While there, writing a memoir vividly occupied my thoughts, and I enthusiastically began researching places and links to my past. I traveled to the Czech Republic, to Bohemia, where I was born in the foothills of the Ore Mountains. Walking the streets of my birth city, Komotau, memories of my long-ago deceased parents and places they talked about came alive in my imagination and tugged on my emotions. I could feel the connection to my roots, although those roots were cruelly severed by the time I was six years old, and I never got to know the land of marionettes, myths, and Good King Wenceslas.

While enjoying life in Germany, many anecdotes about me from before I could remember told by my parents and grandparents came to mind, and my eighty-six-year-old aunt Klara, a vital connection to my former life, provided oodles of missing pieces to fill the gaps in my memory. Her alert mind spiced with stories and a trove of family photos dating back to the 1880s was an immeasurable resource. By the time I returned to the States, I had gathered much valuable information and felt inspired and highly motivated.

As I sat in front of my computer and diligently compiled my story, Aunt Klara again became an integral part of the project. She never tired of my many overseas phone calls asking questions or clearing doubts while writing this memoir, and she deserves my utmost gratitude.

I am deeply indebted to my husband, my biggest fan, who faithfully supported me in writing the story. He was my voice of encouragement when I was in the dumps and felt frustrated. Thank you, Schatzi!

Lastly, my sincere appreciation goes to my three children. They loved the memoir-manuscript of their mother, who once spoke a different language and lived on another continent in an era gone by. They strongly encouraged me to publish the story, not only for posterity's sake but also to disclose some horrific events that still remain cleverly hushed up after many decades. Most Americans have never heard of the vanished Sudetenland and the brutal expulsion of three million German people from their ancestral lands in the middle of the twentieth century.

Nine years have past since that devastating diagnosis. As I reflect back, cancer has prioritized my life to a different sequence, and writing about my life before I immigrated to the United States of America was high on the list.

Geography

❧ ❧ ❧ ❧

Sudetenland is a twentieth-century name and not a historical region; thus it is difficult to describe a distinct, consistent history of the Sudetenland. Until the twentieth century, the history of the Sudetenland followed the history of Bohemia and Moravia. The Sudetenland derived its name from the Sudeten Mountains, a mountain chain stretching from East Germany to the Czech-Polish borders.

With its declaration as a new state in 1919, Czechoslovakia included an area shaped like a horseshoe around Bohemia, Moravia, and Silesia inhabited mostly by the descendants of the early settlers: the Bavarians, Frankish, and Saxon Germans. They named the area Sudetenland, and these ethnic Germans called themselves the Sudeten Germans.

The shaded areas on the map are the regions that comprised the Sudetenland, where these ethnic Germans lived. The rest of Czechoslovakia had a mixed population of Czechs and Germans, with Czechs in the majority. The Erzgebirge (Ore Mountains) marks the border between Saxony, Germany, and the Czech Republic to the northwest. The cities Eger, Karlsbad, Komotau, Aussig, and

Reichenberg are in the foothills of the Ore Mountains and a part of the region of Bohemia.

The Böhmerwald (Bohemian Forest) separates Bavaria, Germany, from the Czech Republic in the west past the original beer city of Budweis, and it is a part of the region of Bohemia. The jewel of the Böhmerwald is the city of Marienbad. The cities Brünn, Iglau, and Zwittau are part of Moravia and border with Austria, Hungary, and Slovakia. Silesia is bordering Poland in the east; the German cities of Troppau and Teschen are part of Silesia.

MAP OF SUDETENLAND

1

Expulsion From Bohemia

Unruly Soldiers

Violent banging on our door shattered the peace of that crisp, sunny July morning. My *Opa* (grandfather) leaped to his feet and moved cautiously toward our heavy wooden door while the rest of us followed him with panic-stricken eyes, holding our breath. There at our entrance stood four heavily armed Czech soldiers. In broken German, they ordered my startled grandfather to get his family out of the house and for all of us to line up by the open door. Opa called for his wife, his daughter Klara, and me, a six-year-old child. Although scared stiff, we stepped outside as ordered.

Suddenly a noisy gray army truck purposefully smashed through our white picket fence into our courtyard. This caused our hens and rooster to scramble, leaving behind flying feathers and chicken squawks of protest. The driver raised his hand to a high-five position, looking for his comrades' approval as he sneered at the demolished fence. He then jumped off the truck and immediately cocked his rifle to enforce his authority to destroy our property.

In fearful anticipation, the four of us huddled together on the bench just outside our entrance door. The soldiers demanded to know if we had weapons, jewelry, money, or any other valuables and commanded their immediate surrender. Subsequent findings of concealed valuables would have consequences—perhaps death by firing squad, one of them declared. My *Oma* (grandmother) went inside and handed over all they asked for. Then they ran through the house, barn, and stable like wild animals on the loose, looking for hidden items. Despite the fury of their rampage, one Czech kept his rifle trained on us at all times.

The leader of this lawless mob, waving a piece of paper, quickly made his importance known. In convoluted German he read that we had one hour to pack our clothes, household goods, and food for one day; we were permitted forty kilos each, but no pets or animals. He continued reading that our house, our farm, and all real estate had become the exclusive property of the Czechoslovakian government. Furthermore, the entire village must evacuate, and a truck would take us to the city of Bischofteiniz. He ended his rambling speech with "Do not ask any questions!"

Since the end of the war in 1945, my grandparents and aunt had heard wild and gruesome rumors of expulsion in other parts of the Sudetenland. They feared that raising objections to these five rambunctious Czechs could be a deadly mistake.

We were about to step back into the house when Rex, our loyal German shepherd dog, came running into the courtyard. By nature gentle, obedient, and protective of his owners and territory, Rex now sensed danger on his turf. He barked and growled as he ran after the Czech soldiers. His behavior aggravated them; one soldier tried to kick him. Rex barked even louder and snarled threateningly.

A rifle shot shattered the air, and then silence.

Aunt Klara screamed in horror and ran to her dying dog, crying and bemoaning the lifeless body of her longtime family pet. "Murderers!" she shrieked hoarsely in her anguish. Two soldiers roughly pulled her from the animal, and a third aimed a gun at her. The message was clear: You will be next. Your German lives matter as little to us as this creature's. Sensing the danger, Opa stepped in: "Klara! Inside! Now!" Klara swept inside the house, rage and grief equally visible on her face.

My grandmother and my aunt could not stop sobbing over the killing of Rex and the reality of being forced off their beloved homestead just because we were Germans. In their grief, they hurriedly bundled up clothing, bedding, photographs, a few odds and ends, and all of their *Klöppel* materials for lace making.

My grandfather grabbed a big blanket and put his hand tools and some haphazard things in it. He, the normally silent optimist, thought aloud that we would be back soon and that the entire ruckus was a power play by the Czech government. After all, ethnic Germans had lived in these and other regions of Czechoslovakia since 1173 when Czech nobility had, in fact, invited in neighboring Germans, like Bavarians, Frankish, and Saxons—all known for their skills in the crafts, farming, and mining—as settlers. These Germans had assurance of specific rights: "Know that these Germans are free people; they have the right to live by their own laws," confirmed in the charter of the Bohemian duke Sobieslaus. The Germans chose to migrate to the uninhabited mountainous border regions of Bohemia, Moravia, and Silesia, bringing with them their language, culture, religion, and the legal systems of Nürnberg and Magdeburg. They built cities; they cultivated the land and developed industries and mines, not only in the colonized border areas but also in the interior of Bohemia. The city of Prague symbolized their creative spirit.

While Opa contemplated his heritage, he remembered an incident in early May when he was about to plow his fields. He tended a tract of land that extended to the border of Czechoslovakia and Germany. Only a slightly crooked, weather-beaten stone demarcated the border of the two countries. One side barely showed the C for Czechoslovakia, while the other side had a faint D for Deutschland. As Opa walked behind the plow and his animal that pulled it, two armed Czech soldiers appeared and interrupted him. They informed him with hand gestures and a few words in broken German to stop working and go home. They handed him a somewhat official-looking piece of paper, which showed a drawing of this parcel of land designated for *"Niemandsland"* ("no man's land"). Therefore, the Czechoslovakian state was confiscating his property.

Within the week, the farmers of Franzelhütte received instructions to suspend all fieldwork. By now, talk of ethnic cleansing, expulsion, and atrocities carried out by the Czech army in many parts of the Sudetenland had reached the villages and towns of the Böhmerwald. It was only a matter of time, it was whispered, before the people of Franzelhütte would meet the same sinister fate.

Since early 1946, there were obvious signs of Czech government activity directly affecting the villages of the Bohemian Forest. After the snowmelt, Franzelhütte experienced some unusual noise and traffic, foreign to this tranquil hamlet of 130 souls. The Czech army started to cut down trees, big majestic fir trees, the beauty and wealth of the Böhmerwald. Settlements in these regions were sparse, and for centuries, forests dominated over human dwellings. Gigantic army trucks, manned with boisterous soldiers, drove through the village leaving behind clouds of smelly burning fuel and deep ruts on the unpaved and narrow roads. Fear and uncertainty spread into the homes of this farming community and its surrounding villages. In neighboring Eisendorf, the Czechs took up post in the old customhouse—the same place where the Americans had located their temporary quarters some months earlier.

Now, in the Gerber kitchen, Oma and Aunt Klara were plunking sandwiches, leftovers, and whatever other edible goods they could find into a pack basket while I collected all my toys, my few books, and letters from my mother. Wotan, our old black tomcat, lay in his spot high up on the monstrous tile stove, watching the tumult below. He seemed rather uninterested until he saw Schnuri, my own playful gray kitten. Someone in our neighborhood had brought the little kitten to cheer me up when I cried for my mother, from whom I was separated, as she lived very far away.

My little suitcase had more things in it than when I first arrived in Franzelhütte one year ago and was hard to close. The colorful dollhouse with my name on it and the refurbished rocking horse sat next to my suitcase, ready to go. I could not understand why those strange men acted so mean to us. They had killed our good dog, Rex, and were making us leave Franzelhütte. I had many questions to ask.

However, most important, I needed to know how my mother would find me if everyone in the village had to leave. Who would tell her where I was?

The house was now in total disarray, and my aunt and grandmother had no time to address my concerns. They ran from room to room, crying, and in their distress could not agree on what should go and what should stay. Aunt Klara worked in Munich once and had brought back five hand-carved wall plates painted with colorful alpine scenes. Perhaps she had a sentimental attachment to those picturesque plates, because she insisted on packing them. Oma referred to it as *"Krempel"*—rubbish—and refused to waste valuable space and weight on them. Instead, she had her fine china cups and saucers in mind, the ones she had inherited from her grandmother. Opa settled the argument and recommended that only practical things must have consideration and that neither of these items qualified. My eyes drifted to my dollhouse and rocking horse. Seeing me, he bent down and gently said, "These are too awkward. They'll have to stay." He promised me a bigger dollhouse and an even larger rocking horse.

Our allotted time of one hour had expired, and the raging soldiers stormed into the house, screaming, "Hurry up," in their language and motioning with the shafts of their rifles for us to move toward the door, out of the house. Oma kept talking to herself, not quite able to cope with her emotional stress. Aunt Klara rebelliously walked from the house to the adjacent stable, where she heard the mooing of her pet cow, Pompern. A soldier followed her, watching. She whispered sad good-byes to all the cows, but Pompern she lingered over, hugging her and petting her head, tears rolling down her cheeks. As she was leaving the stable, the Czech soldier put two bullets in the animal and blocked her from returning. He grabbed her arm, but she defiantly pulled away from him and spit on the ground where he stood. He, drunk on power, seemed enraged, but another soldier interfered by telling him something in their language that prompted the soldier to disappear inside the house.

Oma, Opa, and I were sitting on the army truck with our thoroughly searched belongings, waiting for Aunt Klara, trembling in fear for her safety. I was still crying because a soldier had found Schnuri hidden in my backpack. He yelled at my grandparents and me for not obeying orders. He then grabbed the little kitten by its back fur and flung her with all his might toward the torn-down fence. Another soldier fired his pistol at the spot where the kitten had landed. Schnuri tried to escape into the bushes, but the bullet was faster. Oma pulled me toward her, shielding me from the ghastly sight. Terrified and scared, I quietly sobbed over my playful companion.

My grandmother let out a gasp of relief when she saw her daughter climbing up onto the truck. As the vehicle rolled away, the adults took one last glimpse at our sweet home; in agony, they stretched out their arms in a gesture of a last embrace.

Trapped in Limbo

Our truck screeched to a halt, and we slammed into each other. For a moment, Oma seemed confused; she had been deeply engrossed in her own thoughts. Even so, she immediately recognized our location. We had arrived at the Schaffer Farm in the hamlet of Eisendorf Hüttn. At the entrance stood a distraught Mr. and Mrs. Schaffer, their four toddler children, and Mr. Schaffer's parents. Three armed Czech soldiers were rummaging through their many bundles. My grandmother knew just about everybody in the entire county, including the Schaffers. Oma agonizingly called the name of the elderly woman, "Katl!" Immediately, an irate soldier screamed at Oma and told her to shut up, ordering that there be no more talking. Once the Schaffers and their belongings had been dumped on the truck, space became a problem. We kids had to sit on top of bundles, steadied by an adult hand. Some of the soldiers stood on the back bumper to guard against an escape. As the truck slowly rolled down the long driveway, leaving the farm behind, the Schaffers cried silently. Wistfulness marked the faces of all the adults in the truck. The bumpy ride to Bischofteinitz, the county seat, took over one hour, and we all sat dejectedly like lumps in that filthy truck.

Late that afternoon we arrived at the crowded train station in Bischofteinitz, a vital railroad junction, but no trains were in sight. An armed Czech soldier recorded our names and the village we came from. He also weighed our bundles, backpacks, and suitcases. Any weight over forty kilos per person was discarded on the spot. Opa had estimated the weight of our stuff, and he was close to being correct; we had no overage.

There were people everywhere, inside and outside the stationhouse, and many knew one another. Some were sitting on their possessions or lying on the bare ground; some were eating, others weeping or angry or simply waiting—waiting for the unknown—a picture of total chaos. No one knew the agenda of these rowdy Czech soldiers, and asking questions prompted a slap in the face or a hard kick in the groin.

More people arrived. Some came on trucks, others on foot pulling handcarts loaded with their meager possessions and escorted by armed soldiers. At dusk, the flow of newcomers stopped. Positioned in a circle, the soldiers looked to my young mind like fence posts, ready to fire at anyone who caused trouble, or worse, tried to escape. Everyone had to stay put in the same spot where one first settled down after arrival. Luckily for the people inside the overfilled stationhouse, they had a roof over their heads as night started to fall. We four were among the not-so-lucky ones who had to sleep in the open air, grateful that at least it was a warm summer night.

Opa had brought the two oil lamps that hung in his stable. It was now pitch black; only a few stars twinkled on the moonless sky. We huddled closer together, and someone wrapped a blanket around me. Opa lit one of the oil lamps, and it helped reduce the eerie stillness. Oma whispered to him what a smart man he was for bringing the little gadgets and matches. She reached in the pack basket and pulled out bread and *Speck* (bacon) for us to eat. Nobody was hungry except me. I did not like Speck but wanted a *Butterbrot* (bread with butter). She searched for a piece of well-buttered bread and handed it to me. Afterward, Aunt Klara picked up the lamp and took me to the bushes. I did not need to go, I told her, but she insisted. She also prepared a makeshift spot for all of us to rest for the night, and feeling her hand gave me the needed comfort to fall asleep.

July 16 dawned, and the sun promised another bright day. Some elderly people still sat in the same position as the day before. They probably never closed an eye during the night, staring in front of them or silently at each other. There were sick people who moaned and carried on, outdone only by the crying of small children. Mothers put babies to their breast, hoping to calm the infants. Other people chewed slowly and sparingly on the food they had brought with them. Opa ate Speck and bread while the three of us had apples and a cookie each. Thank God for the cool water from our two thermos bottles. We were not hungry, thirsty, or cold, but the valid question "What is next?" remained unanswered.

Several of the children knew each other. They organized games of hopscotch and jump rope. Aunt Klara encouraged me to join the group, but I felt a stranger with those kids, though I had mastered the Böhmerwald dialect and sounded just like them. As always, Oma arranged—or rather bribed with a cookie—for one of the little girls to come over and pull me into their games.

At noon, the Czech soldiers bellowed out everyone's name from a list and told us that a train would arrive in the afternoon to take us to our "new homeland—Bavaria, Germany." A murmur of disapproval went through the open-air camp: Our homeland was Sudetenland—Böhmerwald. Sensing the unrest, the soldiers quickly displayed their superiority, firing shots in the air and thus putting fear into a defenseless crowd.

The Herding of Human Cattle

Indeed, a train rolled in late that afternoon. This train looked different from the one my mother and I had traveled in when visiting my grandparents. It was a long freight train consisting only of boxcars and was pulled by a huge steaming locomotive.

First processed were the people camping outside the station house. Again, the soldiers called out our names and pushed and shoved belongings and people into the extremely hot boxcars. Without a doubt, these railcars had transported cattle recently; the hot summer heat accentuated the unpleasant stench. The guard packed thirty people to a car, and they decided with their lists and clubs in hand who went where. Many larger families had to deal with the anxiety of being split up, and that caused problems, even beatings, and delay.

The four of us secured a little spot in the back corner of our boxcar. I kept holding my nose trying to avoid the nauseating smell. Aunt Klara looked at me musingly and said that my grimace reminded her of my first few days after I came from the city to the farm, always holding my nose and complaining, "It stinks!" Oma rolled her eyes and wished Aunt Klara had not mentioned my coming to Franzelhütte; she knew it would get me thinking. Since the suspension of mail service and travel for Germans over a year ago, she had been troubled about my mother's fate and whereabouts. For my sake, she tried to avoid conversations about the subject. Now, in this damned *Viehwagen* (cattle car), she was in no mood to answer my endless questions and my need for my mother. Aunt Klara realized her carelessness and quickly volunteered to read my favorite story, *Rotkäppchen* (Little Red Riding Hood), for distraction.

The train station appeared vacant and deserted. Every boxcar seemed occupied to maximum capacity. The sun began to fall below the horizon, but no one cared to see the display of a beautiful sunset. The soldiers had completed the main part of their mission, and they were ready to close the slider door on the boxcars. Someone in our car kindly asked a guard to leave the door open by a gap, for some fresh air to flow in. He threateningly raised the club in his hand and yelled an immediate "No!" Nevertheless, we insisted. Finally, another guard grudgingly gave in to our request.

Our food supply had shrunk to a few apples and half a loaf of bread. The buttered sandwiches were long gone, and I was hungry, but not for dry bread. Oma had filled our thermos with more water from a fountain at the station house.

Bischofteinitz was less than twenty miles from the German border. Oma figured that we would not be very long on the train once it started moving. The people in our car came from other parts of the Böhmerwald, and we knew no one. Oma's natural generosity led her to share the rest of our food with some of the people who had nothing left to eat. Their journey had started a few days earlier. The soldiers were not responsible for meals but only for the quick removal of all *Němci* (Germans in Czech).

It was late evening and completely dark in the boxcar. Opa again lit our oil lamp. A sigh of relief: at least we could see one another. The adults exchanged personal data as well as shared hopes, fears, and remonstrations against the helplessness of destiny. Everyone was wide awake, waiting for the train to start moving, but nothing happened. The agitated guards outside the car mumbled something about a delay of the locomotive, which had disengaged after arrival in the afternoon.

The next day, July 17, began as a cloudy but warm morning, and the adults in our car were either standing or sitting up after a sleepless night, just waiting. Suddenly, we felt a big bump, and someone said that the locomotive had hooked to the train. Two soldiers with rifles hanging over their chests jumped into our car. The train set in motion, and our exodus from the *Heimat* (homeland) began. By this point, we were still not certain where this train would take us, and speculations ran wild. At one point the sun came out of the clouds, long enough for Opa to get a sense of direction and exclaim, "We are going west!" Tensions eased, as that was better news than going east.

After hours of stop and go, our train crossed the border at Taus, the last city on the Czechoslovakian side of the border. Ten more miles and the train entered the town of Furth im Wald in the Province of Bavaria, Germany. There, the soldiers jumped off the cars, leaving their weapons behind. They helped people off the train in a most courteous manner, putting on a show of human compassion in front of the approaching Red Cross representatives. Then the Czech guards picked up their weapons and disappeared in a hurry, on foot, back to Czechoslovakia.

2

They Became My Parents

❧❦ ❧❦ ❧❦ ❧❦

Mitzi

In 1914, five years before my mother was born, World War I broke out. Some historians deem that the war was sparked by the assassination of the Habsburg crown prince, Franz Ferdinand, in Sarajevo (the capital of Bosnia) by a Serbian student. Others suggest that the conflict had deeper roots in the escalated militarism, economic imperialism, and trade barriers of the day. Whatever the reason, the Habsburg Empire declared war on Serbia with a blank check of support by the powerful German Empire. Due to overlapping agreements of formal treaties and commitments of support in defense of a member state, many European countries came to be at war with each other within a matter of weeks. WWI, also called the Great War, developed into a global military conflict, left millions of people dead or wounded, disintegrated four empires, and created new states in Europe.

One such state was Czechoslovakia. Toward the end of WWI, the Czechs expressed their centuries-old opposition to Habsburg dominance by joining the Allied powers. After the war, the Czechs demanded a state of their own, together with the closely related Slovaks. The Allied powers—the United States, France, Great Britain, and Russia—granted their request. The ethnic Germans living in the border regions of Bohemia, Moravia, and Silesia opposed their integration into Czechoslovakia. They now proclaimed their homelands an entity unto itself, which they termed German-Bohemia, or Sudetenland, and demanded that they remain with the German-speaking states of Austria or Germany, thereby exercising the right of self-determination promised by US president Woodrow Wilson.

The newly created Czech government took quick action, sending in its military to invade and occupy the Sudeten territories. The Germans demonstrated against the occupation, and the Czech army retaliated by killing several dozen people and injuring hundreds more. Unfortunately, the Allies' 1919 peace settlement, the Treaty of St. Germaine, sanctioned the ruthless annexation of the Sudetenland by Czechoslovakia.

During those turbulent times, my mother Maria was born to Johann and Barbara (née Klarer) Gerber in Franzelhütte, a small village in the Böhmerwald, a mountainous region in the westernmost part of the Sudetenland bordering the Bavarian Forest of Germany. She was welcomed into house number thirteen, as the Gerber house was known, by her four older brothers. They called her Mitzi, an endearing name for a little kitten, but that name stuck like glue throughout her life. In 1921 the Gerbers had another baby girl. Her name was Klara, but the brothers called her Bua, a dialect word for boy.

Mitzi grew up on the family farm together with her brothers and sister. She attended the one-room schoolhouse in Franzelhütte, where she completed eight grades. From the beginning, the two sisters showed their distinct personalities. Mitzi, always prim and proper, with long beautiful hair, which she wore in braids, enjoyed playing inside the house. Klara, or Bua, had a name befitting someone who loved the outdoors.

When the girls reached school age, their mother taught them the handicraft of *"klöppeln"* ("tatting" in English), an intricate art of lace making. Most girls born in the Böhmerwald, and even some boys, learned the skill of *klöppeln*. The craft dates back over five hundred years and came about when silver mining in the Ore Mountains took a hard hit and breadwinners lost their jobs. These financial hardships made women creative, and lace making found its beginning. The skill very quickly spread throughout the mountainous regions of the Sudetenland and eventually became a successful home industry, orchestrated by women of all ages. Not only did women enjoy lace making, but it also afforded them the opportunity to earn income and, in some cases, a little independence. Those were good reasons to hand down the technique through the generations.

Mitzi was seven years old when her teenage brother, Franz, died from meningitis. In spite of Franz's tragic death, the other three brothers were determined to fulfill their family's expectations. Jule was the oldest Gerber child: a strong, tall lad who would take over the farm one day, as was customary for the oldest son in those days. He and the next oldest brother, Gustel, were the farmhands, while their youngest brother, Seph, a fragile boy, showed little interest in the farm. He was the studious type, and when he reached the age of ten, his mother decided to enroll him in the Gymnasium, a school of higher learning. She arranged for him to stay as a boarder with a family in Mies, a city about twenty-five miles from Franzelhütte. Seph spent eight years in Mies. After passing the *Abitur,* the final exam for Gymnasium completion and prerequisite for university studies, he entered Charles University in Prague. The Gerbers had the admiration of the people in Franzelhütte. They were proud that one of their own made it to university.

All the while, the Gerber girls and their mother earned a little money with lace making. Every extra penny went to Mies or later to Prague in support of Seph's studies. Besides klöppeln, Mitzi enjoyed sewing. Her mother had a Pfaff sewing machine, and from early on, Mitzi showed a vivid interest in sewing dresses for herself and her sister. She expressed her desire to learn more about dressmaking and begged her mother to let her live with an aunt in Weissensulz, where many tailor shops lined the streets. When Mitzi was fifteen, her mother finally gave in and let her follow her dream.

Weissensulz was a large village only fourteen miles from Franzelhütte and was known for its garment industry. Mitzi quickly secured an apprenticeship in a small dress shop. She liked her occupational choice and attended a trade school specializing in textile and apparel studies. Unfortunately, her ambitions of learning the dressmaker trade were put on hold when she was in the middle of her second training year.

In the mid-1930s, people in the Sudetenland experienced great hardships, partially due to an unhealthy political climate, compounded by the disastrous Great Depression in the United States, which quickly reached Europe. The government in Prague evinced its hostility toward the ethnic Germans by only assisting its Czech citizens. The relationship between Czechs and Germans deteriorated further after Dr. Edvard Benes succeeded Thomas Maseryk as president of Czechoslovakia in 1935. Families solicited the help of their children to survive the crisis. The Gerbers were no exception. Just accepted to postgraduate studies, Seph needed more financial support.

Tragically, Mitzi and Klara, who had herself just started as a trainee in a hair salon, had to take jobs—any job they could get—to help support the family. Barely seventeen, Mitzi took a position as a live-in housekeeper with a wealthy family in Komotau, a city of 34,000 people nestled in the foothills of the Ore Mountains. Her cousin Resl lived in Komotau and helped locate the job. Mitzi had never been two hundred miles away from home, nor had she ever visited a big city before. She was homesick for her family, Franzelhütte, and the tall, dark coniferous trees of the Böhmerwald. She missed the little dress shop, wondering whether other girls at the trade school had left the program and taken jobs. However, like a good daughter, she did not complain. Every month she faithfully sent most of her earnings to her parents.

Rudi

The Habsburg dynasty, which began around 1273, became the longest ruling dynasty in Europe. For seven centuries, they controlled many countries, autonomous kingdoms including the Kingdom of

Bohemia and the provinces of Moravia and Silesia, where ethnic Germans had settled centuries ago. However, the empire started to experience major problems in the latter part of the nineteenth century as people living in Central European territories expressed their desire to have their own nations more firmly. The Bohemian Czechs, the majority in Bohemia, revolted against Habsburg rule and demanded the return of an independent kingdom. The ethnic Germans also wanted their own German nation-state. Neither became a reality. By 1913, there were even greater unrest in the Balkan States, especially Serbia, and the empire seemed to weaken in popularity and economic standing.

In the midst of these dynastic difficulties, my father was born in Wteln, a hamlet in the periphery of Komotau, Bohemia, to Eduard and Anna (née Gerstenhofer) Veit. He was named after the Habsburg heir, Rudolf, crown prince of Austria, Hungary, and Bohemia.

Everyone called him Rudi, and he was the second oldest child of the Veits' four sons. When Rudi was five years old, his father died suddenly of pneumonia at the age of thirty. His mother, Anna, received only a small pension from her husband's railroad employment and the family struggled for years.

Joseph Veit, the older brother of Eduard and Rudi's uncle, was a master baker-confectioner and proud owner of an established bakery and pastry shop in the heart of Komotau. He and his wife Resi remained childless, and he proposed to Anna, his destitute, widowed sister-in-law to help her by taking in one of her boys. Together they decided that eleven-year-old Rudi, a tall, strong lad and the brightest of Anna's children, would live with Joseph and Resi.

Life in Komotau was rather lonely for Rudi, who missed his family and friends from the old neighborhood and school. He also missed the old circus fiddler who told great stories and taught him how to play the violin. One day, his mother came to visit and announced that she was soon to marry a Czech man by the name of Czerner. She and the boys were moving to Brüx, a small city not far from Komotau, where Czerner owned a butchery. Rudi was hoping he could join them. However, his mother made clear that Uncle Veit, as the family called Joseph, needed someone to take over the business one day, and Rudi had better be grateful for such an opportunity.

Anna did not want to hear that her son disliked Uncle Veit nor that he did not want to be a baker.

Aunt Resi, however, noticed the boy's unhappiness and tried to cheer him up by arranging private violin lessons. She realized Rudi's passion for the violin, much to her husband's chagrin. While Rudi went to school, dreaming of becoming a concert violinist, Uncle Veit had different plans for him. At the age of sixteen, Rudi had to quit his beloved *Bürgerschule* (a school of higher learning) and enter a vocational school twice a week, where he learned about the food industry as part of the baker's trade. During the rest of the week he was a baker's apprentice under his uncle's strict rules and demanding work hours. Although Rudi despised his uncle's decision, he defiantly completed the apprenticeship, took the exam, and earned a baker's certificate.

At nineteen, a resentful and sullen Rudi left the Veit Bakery. He enlisted in the Czech army, where his training as a baker proved to be useful, and he learned to cook. His main goal was to become proficient in the Czech language, hoping to gain some advantage in a tight job market. Two years later, he left the service to start a career with the railroad, like his father.

In the mid-1930s, unfair politics caused more tension between Czechs and Germans. Many ethnic Germans lost their civil service jobs to the ruling Czechs, and Rudi was no exception. Although he spoke the Czech language fluently, he could not get into a suitable career-training program with the Czech railroad but had to work as a stoker. Soon he lost that job and with no prospects for another, he had little choice but to return to work for his tenacious uncle in the Veit bakery for slave wages. There was no love lost between the two men.

3

Sudetenland—My Origin

~~~~~~~~~~~~

They Met in Komotau

Every morning at precisely 7:00 a.m., Mitzi strode into the Veit Bakery to buy freshly baked *Brötchen* (crusty buns) for her employer's family breakfast. The young baker, Rudi, waited anxiously for her arrival. She was always in a hurry, but that did not dissuade the new hire in the bakery. Smiling at her and cheerfully holding the door open when she left the store, he wasted no time in approaching Mitzi for a date. She was a young, innocent country girl who had no experience in such matters. She had never dated before but agreed to meet him on Sunday, her day off. He had a compelling effect on her, and she was smitten by the charm of this tall, handsome man. She felt herself blushing every time when she stepped inside the bakery, and her heart pounded a little harder.

Continued economic depression and loss of jobs and freedom in the Sudeten territories did not go unnoticed by the charismatic leader of Germany, Adolf Hitler, even in the early 1930s. For several years he cleverly plotted his campaign toward the plight of the Sudeten Germans. Hitler informed the major powers of Europe, Great Britain, and France about the Sudetenland crisis and his plan to annex these German-speaking territories within Czechoslovakia into the German Reich.

Just as in the days before WWI, there were alliances of nonaggression, and the countries of Europe were not ready for—nor did they want—another war. To appease Hitler, Great Britain and France put the pressure on Czechoslovakia to cede the Sudetenland to Germany. The "Agreement of Munich" made it official, and on October 1, 1938, Hitler's army triumphantly marched unopposed into the Sudetenland. To the elated Sudeten Germans it was the final vindication of their demands made in 1919 and a reversal of the unfair Treaty of St. Germaine. Stripped from power, the Czech government stepped back. Its president, Edvard Benes, resigned and fled into exile to Great Britain.

While these political changes affected everyone's life, Mitzi and Rudi were in love. They met every Sunday at Komotau's city park by the famous flower clock. There they sat for hours and forged plans for a future together. Rudi confided in her of his unhappiness at his uncle's bakery and his desire to leave there for good. He decided to apply for a job once more with the railroad, now under German management and called *Reichsbahn*. Rudi could not wait until Sunday to tell Mitzi the good news of getting the job at the railroad. He stopped by the stately house where she worked and told her to quit her job, because they were getting married. She was confused and needed more time to think about her commitments to Rudi and her parents, but he was impatient.

Shortly after the annexation of the Sudetenland, Hitler occupied all of Czechoslovakia. Rumors of war created a frenzy, and many young couples, uncertain of the future, hurried to marry. That made the waiting period at Komotau's civil registry office rather lengthy. Still more delays stemmed from the multitudes of applications for proof of Aryan purity, a new law imposed by the Nazi Party. Finally, in the spring of 1939, Mitzi and Rudi stood in front of a judge who pronounced them husband and wife. The couple moved to a small apartment near the Veit bakery where Mitzi helped behind the busy sales counter. All this time, she had kept Rudi a secret from her family, due to his mistake of a brief marriage at the age of nineteen.

Over two years had passed since Mitzi saw her parents or siblings. Mitzi sent a telegram and informed her parents of her impending arrival. She did not mention Rudi. The newlyweds boarded the train in Komotau and traveled to Eisendorf in the Bohemian Forest. Mitzi's brother Jule was waiting at the station with their cow, Pompern, harnessed to a wagon to take them to Franzelhütte. Delighted as he was to see his sister, Jule could hardly conceal his surprise that the man with her was her husband. The rest of the family shared a similar view, and the news of Mitzi's visit and her marriage ran through Franzelhütte like a wildfire.

My Arrival

The unusually cold winter of 1939/1940 kept Komotau wrapped in a white blanket of snow and ice. France and Great Britain had declared war on Germany after Hitler's army had invaded Poland the previous September. Mitzi was eight months pregnant. And so the story goes: One morning, on her way to the Veit bakery, she stepped on a snow-covered patch of ice, lost her balance, and fell to the ground in the worst way. That evening, January 16, 1940, a midwife was on hand to help with the birth of a five-pound baby girl—me.

It had been decided while my parents were still expecting that, if a girl, my name would be Erika. My mother's brother, Seph, had fallen in love with a girl named Erika, a fellow student at the university. Neither my mother nor anyone in the Gerber family would deny Seph any request, including a name he liked for his sister's baby.

Both of my parents came from a Catholic upbringing, my mother more so than my father, and at one month old, it was my turn to be inducted into the same faith. My mother's sister, Klara, still living and working in Munich, was on her way to Komotau to be part of my first milestone. Just eighteen years old, she was delighted to become my godmother. It was the custom for a child to take the godmother or godfather's name as a middle name, and thus I acquired my middle name, Klara.

The baptism took place in Komotau's *Stadt Kirche* (city church), also known as Dekanal Church, completed in 1539 and a central element of the city's picturesque skyline. Once the church tower belonged to the city government. Its spire was the tallest of all the city churches and housed the biggest bell. In those days, the tower had an occupant, the tower keeper. His job was to ring the bell on the hour, morning to evening, make public announcements, and call out the names of citizens who had died. In 1825 the city extinguished the tower keeper's job.

Soon after my arrival, my parents moved to a big house on Leimberg hill. Surrounded by meadows and a bounty of fruit trees, the large fenced property was a horse farm. Adjacent to the main house were long rows of stables housing various breeds of boarding horses. My parents never met the owner but heard that he was a wealthy man and had moved to Switzerland. The hired estate manager and his wife, Mr. and Mrs. Bruskowitz, a childless middle-aged couple, lived on the first floor of the house. The vacant second floor became our quarters, and my father paid the rent to Mr. Bruskowitz.

Duty Calls

In the summer of 1940, my mother took me on my first major train ride to Franzelhütte in the Böhmerwald to meet my grandparents. According to my mother, I was small at six months old, showed barely a tooth, and was bald as a coot. In my grandmother's eyes, I was beautiful. She would make sure that Franzelhütte caught a glimpse of her cute and already bright granddaughter.

My uncles had their own agenda that summer and were away from home. Every year during the summer months, Jule earned his money in the world-renowned spa city of Marienbad, where he worked as a bellhop and porter in the famous Hotel Rübezahl. The tips were superb, and there was Maria, a maidservant whom he really had an eye for. Seph had completed his dissertation that July. Besides trying to earn some money in a band, playing the zither and violin in a Prague nightclub, he was preparing for his doctoral verbal exams. Gustel had been drafted into the military for Hitler's invasion of Poland. Aunt Klara was in Tyrol, Austria, completing her mandatory duty in the "Hitler Jugend: (HJ) Bund Deutscher Mädels" (BDM)

("Hitler Youth: Federation of German Girls"). Before 1938 the BDM was an organization of voluntary members, but with the onset of war, it had become a six-month compulsory service for all single German females ages seventeen to twenty-five. Besides daily fitness, their primary function was in agriculture and domestic services. Klara's nonpolitical upbringing and a dislike for the Nazi regime made her cautious in her association with the other females. However, she met some like-minded girls her age, and their forged camaraderie and friendship lasted a lifetime.

My mother, realizing the shortage of helping hands on the farm, decided to extend our stay. It was the time of the year when a huge threshing machine came to Franzelhütte to process the grain crops for all the farmers in the area. My grandmother, busy in the kitchen, as she had to feed several mouths who helped with the harvest, still found time to visit neighbors just to show me off. One day, she mentioned to my mother that I seemed to reach with my left hand rather than my right, and God forbid if I should be left-handed. No one in the family had been left-handed, and she cited some of the myths surrounding such "unfortunate people." My mother dismissed her concerns, feeling that I was too little for the family to need to worry about such things.

Seph

In the spring of 1941, my mother's brother Seph graduated with a PhD in European Literature from Prague's Karl's University. His proud mother looked on as he stood in the middle of the auditorium surrounded by professors who ceremonially administered the orals to each PhD candidate. It was customary for the audience to throw flowers from the galleries for each correct answer. My grandmother witnessed her son receive sixty-eight bouquets, and everyone in Franzelhütte and beyond heard about that event and number. Indeed, Seph's family could not have been more elated and proud of his accomplishment. Finally he would earn his keep, but first, a deferred military obligation needed to be satisfied.

Reluctantly, for he strongly disapproved of war, he reported for basic training. After six weeks, he wrote home that his new assignment was an armor unit and he would be deployed to the Eastern Front. He became part of the June 1941 operation code named "Barbarossa," an invasion of the Soviet Union. It was to become the largest military invasion in history in both manpower and casualties. The German army encountered immense resistance from the Russians, known as the "Red Army." In a forest near the Ukrainian town of Velikye Luki, Seph's platoon came under a surprise attack, and he was killed. He was buried there in one of the many mass graves. It was August 1941, and he was twenty-five years old.

Tragedy Strikes

A black-rimmed telegram arrived in Komotau. It came from Klara. She wanted to inform her sister of their brother's tragic death. My mother, inconsolable from the news, got the suitcase ready at once. The next day, she and I were on a train to the Böhmerwald. This time, Gustel picked us up from the train station. He was wearing a black armband on his sleeve, indicating a death in the family. On the way to Franzelhütte, he told my mother that Jule had been drafted. According to his letters, he, too, was preparing for the Eastern Front. Ironically, Seph met his fate while his brother Jule was on his way to the Caucasus in Russia.

Jule had also had a military deferral, since he was the oldest of the three boys. With Seph in school and Gustel in the army, he qualified for hardship deferment. When Gustel returned from Poland, Jule despairingly reported for duty. The Gerber boys grew up in a nonpolitical environment and had no tolerance for the Hitler hype and even less for the war-mongering attitudes in the Sudetenland after annexation.

My grief-stricken mother was glad to be home with her family in the security of Franzelhütte. My presence at nineteen months old eased some of the sadness that had befallen the Gerber house. The Gerber women wore black for one solid year to mourn their son and brother's ill-fated death. My mother and her sister found solace recalling the many wonderful memories they had of their brother, but there were many tears. Both women tried to reconcile this tragedy, the loss of the beloved brother, with their long efforts to help him achieve his dreams at the price of their own. All seemed crazy and in vain.

Three weeks after Seph's death, two NSDAP (acronym for the Nazi Party) officials came to the Gerber home to present posthumously to Dr. Joseph Gerber a bravery medal, the "Iron Cross Second Class." My grandmother, ignoring their "Heil Hitler," took the medal with a gesture of disgust and, without a word, slammed the door shut. After that incident, the family worried about repercussion by party officials. Fortunately, nothing came of it. Those were dangerous times; the slightest hint of anti-Hitler sentiments could have serious consequences. She later buried the piece of "bloodstained metal," as she called it, by a rosebush in her garden.

The Girl from Poland

Aunt Klara tells of the time, in the fall of 1941, when she and her father were hard at work with the potato harvest. Gustel helped out sporadically, but he was rather busy with Linde, a girl he met in Poland. He barely had returned home from Poland when Linde showed up in Franzelhütte at house number thirteen, the Gerber home. The Gerbers had never heard of Linde. Obviously, it was a surprise when this young woman, who hardly spoke German, suddenly appeared at their doorstep carrying all of her belongings in one suitcase and looking for Gustel. Acting dumbfounded, Gustel concocted some doubtful story, which he later retracted to admit that he had simply fallen in love with this indigent Polish girl. Of course, Oma wished her son would have chosen a local girl and not someone from a foreign country. For her it was bad enough when Mitzi brought home a husband from a faraway city.

What a Circus

In early spring of 1942, the circus came to Komotau. It was an exciting event for all ages. Older Komotauers liked to remember how the city prided itself on the fact that in 1903 the famous American circus Barnum & Bailey rolled into Komotau. They came on a hired private train to perform for one day only, quartered overnight at the elegant station house, and then went on to Prague.

My parents met with my father's brother, Joseph, his wife, Friedl, and their two children, three-year-old Horst and baby Uschi, not quite one. They, too, lived in Komotau, but we never had visited with them until that day. We all walked toward the huge circus tent supported by massive iron posts. According to my mother, I let go of her hand and ran as fast as I could straight ahead into an iron post. I was screaming and a bloody mess in a matter of a few seconds, and my parents noticed the gash between my lower lip and chin. Instead of going to the circus show, the three of us rushed to the Komotau hospital. The doctor stopped the bleeding but decided against stitches. He assured my dithery parents that given the location of the wound it was best left to the natural healing process to avoid scarring.

By the time summer arrived my wound had disappeared in the fold of the chin. Our family planned a trip to Franzelhütte. Komotau was usually hot and humid during the summer months in comparison to the pleasant, moderate climate of the Böhmerwald. My father could only stay two days. His work schedule at the railroad had become very demanding, since the war claimed more personnel for the military.

My mother, Aunt Klara, and my grandfather worked the farm, and my grandmother, still in mourning, was visibly more cheerful entertaining her little granddaughter with the *"Hoppi Hoppi Reiter"* ("hop hop rider") routine. Oma told this story many times. I could not get enough of the Reiter game, and when her legs got tired, my grandmother would frantically call for Rex, the German shepherd dog, and command him to sit down next to me. She knew how much I enjoyed playing with him, and it got her off the hook swinging her legs up and down while I sat on them to get the sensation of floating in the air. Rex was a gentle dog and loved licking my face but could only endure so much of my shaking his front paws or pulling his tail and ears. Soon he would retreat to the corner bench, which encircled the large kitchen table, and crawl underneath or leave the room.

All the while, Wotan, the big, black cat, was watching from his warm spot on the giant white tiled kitchen stove. He felt protected up there and came down only to eat or to go outside. Wotan was old and no longer played or hunted mice in the barn, as he used to. On several occasions, when I tried to catch him by the tail, he bit and scratched me. It was the setting of a short drama when it happened. I would cry and carry on, showing my *"Wehweh"* ("booboo")—a scratch, a nip, or both—to anyone in the house for a little sympathy. My mother would get upset with my already distressed grandmother for letting the cat near me. Aunt Klara, a fanatical animal lover, in turn shouted out her feelings about the poor mistreated animals. My grandfather, a very quiet man now agitated with everyone, abruptly opened the front door; Wotan and Rex willingly leaped over the threshold and left the house. Finally there was silence by all and I stopped my whining with a contorted facial expression. A short time later, I remembered the *Hoppi Reiter* game and somebody sacrificed their legs just to make me laugh and happy again.

A Draft Notice

Back in Komotau, my father was eagerly waiting for our return from Franzelhütte. He had received an official-looking letter from Berlin—a draft notice. Four years earlier, when Adolf Hitler victoriously marched into the Sudetenland to bring it home to the "German Reich," my father, unlike my mother and her family, actually voted for Hitler in that sham election. In fact, 90 percent of Sudeten Germans embraced the event. They believed in his promises and rhetoric. They became a receptive audience. He cleverly manipulated the Sudeten Germans into war—his war.

My teary-eyed mother thought of her fallen brother, Seph, as she was reading the orders. It had to be a mistake. Her husband was nearly thirty years old, past the usual draft age. But it was no mistake! The war had claimed many lives everywhere, especially the Eastern Front. The *Wehrmacht* (armed forces) needed the service of every capable, healthy male, regardless of age. Besides, *"Jedermann hat eine Pflicht zum Vaterland."* ("Everyone has a duty to the Fatherland.") That was one of Hitler's propaganda themes. It was also the strong belief of Uncle Veit, also a Hitler admirer who had served for the Austro-Hungarian Empire in the Balkans during WWI. When he mentioned this, Aunt Resi usually mumbled something under her breath, sounding anti-war and anti-Hitler. A gesture of her hand made clear that she did not approve of her husband's political ideology.

Shortly before my father's departure for duty, we had an unusual visitor. Grandmother Czerner, my father's mother, had come to Komotau for a brief visit. My mother had met her once, but Grandmother Czerner had never seen me, nor did she show great interest in her grandchild during that visit. It would be the first and only time that I met her. She never contacted us again. My father did not attempt to keep up a relationship with his mother. He could not forgive her for sending him away from the family when he was barely eleven years old. He felt unloved by her. I have no recollection of ever seeing any pictures of her in our house.

On Christmas Eve 1942, my mother and I were by ourselves. My father had left two months earlier to report for military training in Rakonitz. I missed my "Papa" as I called him and could not understand his absence. *Christkindl* had brought a small tree along with a stuffed animal, a gray and white shaggy dog. My mother read me the letter Papa wrote where he promised to be home for my birthday.

It was January 16, 1943, and I spent a good part of the day waiting by the window looking at a wintry Komotau below, hoping for my father to appear. Finally, in the distance, a man in a uniformed coat made his way through the snow coming closer to the house. It was Papa; he kept his promise, and we celebrated my third birthday.

The following day, my parents took me to a studio for my first professional photo shoot. My father wanted a picture of me to take with him to his new assignment in France an infantry unit stationed in Cherbourg, Normandy. His furlough was rather brief, and on a snowy morning, we accompanied him to the bustling Komotau train station. My mother was holding me in one arm, crying, while her other arm waved after the moving train that took the man we both loved far away.

Jule Missing

In midspring, a letter arrived from my grandmother urging my mother to come home to Franzelhütte. She had received some news from the army of the Eastern Front. Labeled as "unofficial," they informed her that Julius Gerber, stationed in Stalingrad, was "missing in action." Immediately, my mother prepared the luggage. Two days later, we boarded a train to the Böhmerwald.

As we reached our destination, the train slowly drove into the small *Bahnhof* (railroad station) of Eisendorf. Just a few people got off the train, and Aunt Klara was easy to spot waiting on the platform. She leaned on a handcart in which sat the steadfast Rex. The two sisters fell into each other's arms. Tears ran down their cheeks—sadness; happy smiles; hugs galore. Rex's wagging tail and licking tongue revealed how pleased he, too, was to see us again. I sat on top of the luggage and held onto the rails. The two women pulled the handcart, walking and talking all the way to Franzelhütte, with Rex leading the way.

When we arrived at the house, my grandmother, dressed in black and looking frail, could hardly talk while sobbing and hugging us. For her, Jule's missing status in Stalingrad had the feel of a death sentence. She was convinced that, even if he had not been killed by a bullet, he had starved or frozen to death during the bitter, cold Russian winter. She never heard from Jule again. Her life was filled with grief and hatred against war and an unconscionable Nazi system, which demanded the ultimate sacrifice of her two sons.

Years later, many more details unfolded about the horrific Battle of Stalingrad, one of the bloodiest in the history of warfare. Oma always cried silently when she heard the name Stalingrad mentioned.

Finding Paradise

The summer of 1943 turned out to be a mixture of sad times and good times. Our visit seemed to have a therapeutic effect on the Gerber family. My toddler personality soon brought laughter and some joy back to the old farm kitchen, the favorite place for the family to congregate.

Something new sat in one corner of the kitchen. Over the winter, Opa had built a fine-looking rocking horse for me. He was immensely pleased that his idea generated such happiness for his little granddaughter. I loved rocking on that horse and showing off my daredevil side. "Not so wild; the horse could tip," I was forewarned. Fortunately, my heedful mother always had one eye on my rompish rocking. One day, the horse did tip. She was right there and prevented an accident.

My mother and I stayed in Franzelhütte for four months. I started to speak the local dialect. My curiosity was insatiable, and my family made sure I was included in all aspects of farm life. Adjacent to the farmhouse, Oma had a garden and a big berry patch. When the berries were ripe for harvest, I helped pick all sorts of berries: gooseberries, raspberries, and red and black currants. By the middle of August, the wild blueberry season started. Most of Franzelhütte's women and children hurried to the woods and picked gallons of them. Oftentimes, my empty little bucket but blue-stained mouth revealed where my pickings went. As a result, I experienced episodes of severe colic from eating too many berries.

My aunt was utterly delighted when I showed a vivid interest in the farm's animals. She had names for all of their four-legged creatures, and she happily taught them to me. Each day, the nameless ducks and geese needed to be driven down to the pond. After making a few trips with an adult, I was ready to take on the noisy flock with a big stick in my hand. Nevertheless, someone always came along, just in case I could use a little assistance. Occasionally, the gander came chasing after me. I ran for my life, screaming for help. I stayed away from the pigs; they just smelled too awful. The goats did not like my petting their offspring and, forewarned, I left them alone. I liked the cows and watched the milking process. However, a few times I had my face whacked by their busy, filthy tails, and I left the stable in a hurry.

One day, while chasing the little yellow chicks, I discovered an egg nest in the chicken coop. All excited, I rushed to Oma and reported my finding. Though somewhat apprehensive, she showed me how to remove the eggs and place them carefully in the small basket. I became the official egg collector. When the egg basket was still empty passing the three-day mark, an unhappy Oma stopped my overeager visits to the coop. Apparently I had created a disturbance in the chicken coop; the hens no longer had a chance to lay eggs due to my continuous checking. I was devastated. After promising to make only one trip a day to gather up the eggs, I got the job back.

As time went on, I met children my age at the pond, and with few restrictions from any adult, I could play to my heart's content. Hunger was the least of my worries, as long as I had playmates.

However, when hunger pains became too intense and to avoid going home, I knocked on anyone's door and bashfully begged for a piece of bread, *"auch ohne Butter bitte"* ("even without butter please"). My silly conduct embarrassed my family when they heard of my rather adorable begging routine, and they scolded me severely. Eventually, all of Franzelhütte got to know the Gerbers' little beggar granddaughter. They accepted me as a child of the "Franzelhütte." Even my mother could find forgiveness for marrying outside the Böhmerwald.

My happy little world knew nothing of real hunger, war, or sadness. Franzelhütte, the farm, was my paradise, and I did not want to hear of ever leaving this place. However, a letter from my father arrived informing my mother that he might come home for a short military leave. She was elated and anxious to return to Komotau. Unfortunately, once back home she got word that something had changed in his unit; his furlough was canceled. She tried to hide her profound disappointment but fervently wished we had remained in Franzelhütte.

Winter Fun and Frost Bites

During Christmas 1943, nasty chicken pox covered my body, but Christkindl did bring a tree and a brand new sled. We had plenty to eat due to my grandmother's generosity when we left Franzelhütte in the fall. Additionally, Uncle Veit and Aunt Resi made certain that we had an ample bread supply and some tasty sweets for the little sick person. Uncle Veit, by now in his late sixties, had to work the bakery by himself. The draft had summoned his two assistants and the other help into military service. He felt disillusioned indeed about the war. Only in the safe company of Resi and my mother did he verbalize his anger toward "Hitler and his bandits," as he called them now.

The postman delivered a letter from my father to wish me a happy fourth birthday. He mentioned how much he missed us and that the war would be over soon. He encouraged my mother to visit Franzelhütte in the spring, for he should be back from France by the start of summer. She liked reading the letter many times over. Her passionate mind secretly prepared for a trip home and the return of her husband. However, it was just the middle of January 1944, and many cold winter days lay ahead still.

Komotau's north side was bordered by the foothills of the Ore Mountains. We lived on a hill called Leimberg. During wintertime, this was a favorite place for children and adults to come for sledding or beginner skiing. In the summer months, people took leisurely walks to the hilltop, where the zoo and nearby Alaun Lake waited for their enjoyment. Before the war started, the *Kastanien* (chestnut) gardens, with its live entertainment, dancing, fancy restaurants, and cafés, provided fun and pleasures for young and old.

Nothing could tame my enthusiasm for sledding. I had found my winter playground. With every descent, I became less fearful and kept going until dusk set in. Everyone left for home, and I had the hill all to myself. Although I heard my mother call my name, I ignored it. After a short while, my mother would appear and remind me that giant *Rübezahl* might be on the prowl. I knew that story well and did not want to end up in the bewitched forest. Rübezahl, an ugly ogre, snatched the children who did not listen to their parents and locked them up in a tree cave, never to be seen again. Antsy and looking worriedly over my shoulder, I wanted to go home quickly. According to my mother, that tale worked every time.

Clumps of snow and ice stuck everywhere on my clothing. My high-top leather boots were drenched, my fingers and toes frozen stiff. Once inside the house, I could not stop crying; it hurt terribly. Immediately, my mother prepared a warm bath, and then she wrapped my body in wool blankets. All was forgotten the next day, and I was back on the slope again. There were a few more episodes with frostbite that winter.

D-day and a POW

The boarding horses were gone. Mr. Bruskowitz, at age forty-seven, was drafted and put on a supply train to Russia. The radio transmitted Hitler's speeches about the German Wehrmacht winning battles on all fronts even more than usual. My mother, skeptical of anything that came out of Hitler's mouth or his propaganda machine, asked Mrs. Bruskowitz if they could listen to her husband's radio with the special antennas. It allowed them to listen to an Allied radio station speaking in German. If caught, such action was punishable with jail, hard labor, or even death in repeat cases. The two women trusted each other. After I was asleep, they would listen and hear of the advancing Allied troops and devastating defeats of the German army. This is how they found out about D-day, June 6, 1944, when American and British forces landed on the beaches of Normandy.

One day a letter arrived from the war ministry. They informed my mother of her husband's possible capture by enemy forces during the invasion of Normandy. The sinister news confirmed her sneaking suspicion. Overcome, she made plans for us to leave Komotau immediately and go to Franzelhütte. Hurriedly, we went to the train station for ticket reservations and found the station besieged with German soldiers. After a long wait to reach an agent, we were told that no seats were currently available for pleasure travel; the German military needed the trains for troop and supply transportation. Her mind already troubled over the news of my father and her plans smashed to pieces, my mother felt abandoned and miserable. We walked home to a desolate house. Mrs. Bruskowitz had left some weeks earlier, and my mother sobbed all the way.

Menace in the Sky

By August 1944, the war had reached Komotau. Loud, distressing sirens could hardly keep up, warning the population of the persistent air bombardments of the city by Allied forces. Komotau was one of the larger industrial cities in the Sudetenland with an important railroad network, a prime target for air attacks.

The city government distributed flyers indicating the locations of air-raid shelters. It was about a half-mile from our house to the shelter to which my mother and I ran for our lives. A nearby brick manufacturing company had built the shelter into a hillside and concealed it with a working clay pit. The interior had a long, narrow passageway dimly lit by flickering oil lamps. Alongside the damp wall stood benches and several bunk beds. The people seeking refuge were mostly women, children, and seniors. Some children screamed in fear when the loud noise of nearby bomb explosions seemed to rock the entire mountain. I sat on my mother's lap, my head buried in her chest. Everyone looked worried and scared, anxiously waiting for the madness on the outside to end. Afterward, wailing sirens signaled that the air raid was over. Panic-stricken people ran back to their homes, not knowing what destruction they might have to face.

We were lucky. Our house never had a direct hit, although the property had a few craters caused by shell explosions. But on several occasions, we returned from the air-raid shelter and had no windows or door intact. One Sunday, my mother had prepared a rare beef goulash for our noon meal. We were about to sit down when the sirens sounded. We raced for the shelter. After our return, we found the glass of our kitchen window splintered in the bowl of a good-looking goulash. The plates with noodles, still sitting on the dining room table, were coated with debris. My favorite meal was no longer edible. I just cried. In the simple thinking of a four-and-a-half-year-old child, I questioned my mother about the lunacy of sirens, bombs, and our running to the place on the mountainside.

Sometimes the alarms went off simultaneously with the low-flying bomber planes approaching the city. There was not enough time to reach the shelter. In such instances, we went down to our basement, hoping the menace in the sky would spare the house. On a few occasions, we spent the entire night down there. Through the one small window we saw red, glowing flares. They looked like luminous Christmas trees hanging from the dark sky over the city. I remember the stunning scene. In my innocent mind, I just knew that Christkindl was flying through the night, guided by the luster of radiant Christmas trees. My mother let it pass as that. She knew these flares were markers for the planes carrying incendiary bombs to hit their targets more accurately.

One day, the *Vollalarm* (severe warnings) went off, and though there was enough time for us to reach the shelter, my mother, as if by premonition, decided that we should wait it out in our basement. How fortuitous for us! A firebomb hit the clay pit and destroyed the shelter. Seventeen people paid with their lives. A few days after the incident, the local newspaper reported the tragedy as an act of sabotage.

By the end of September, the air raids stopped. Living without the different sound levels of the warning devices was a welcome relief. Our lives returned to some kind of normalcy, and we felt lucky to be alive. Many people had lost their homes and businesses. Some paid the ultimate price with their lives. Reduced to rubble and ashes were most of the thriving industries. The inner city had lost its once majestic skyline.

Family Trivia

The Veit Bakery, unscathed by destruction from the bombs, was still the place where women customers exchanged their bits of gossip. Rumors had it that the Gestapo (Secret Police) was in pursuit of my father's brother, Joseph—Horst and Uschi's dad. He apparently had gone around town dressed in an officer's uniform with an Iron Cross hanging from his neck. Those honors he did not achieve through commendation or bravery. Most likely he obtained them by fraudulent means, and that was a punishable crime in the Nazi system. Joseph was the only card-carrying member of the Nazi Party in the Veit or Gerber families that we had knowledge of. My parents often wondered about his active military status and nondeployment into a war zone. His wife, Friedl, the daughter of a Komotau merchant, married the naughty but sharp-looking Joseph in 1938. She seemed rather uninterested in her husband's activities or financial matters as long as she could maintain the social butterfly status that her affluent family provided. Later, Friedl admitted that Joseph had deserted his family and went into hiding in Austria. She divorced him in absentia and never married again. After the war, she and her two children were expelled to Jena in East Germany, where she died in 2009 at the age of ninety-one.

After the annexation of the Sudetenland to the German Reich in 1938, my father, a civil service employee of the Reichsbahn, had to endure tremendous pressures by his superiors to join the NSDAP. He never joined. However, he wore a commemorative Sudetenland annexation pin with a small swastika in the middle on his suit lapel and working uniform. Display of the swastika did not mean membership in the Nazi Party. It was the symbol of the regime and was used on badges, money, and all official documents throughout Germany.

A Birthday Surprise

My mother turned twenty-five on September 28, 1944. It was a rather somber day for her. She had not heard from my father, and her concerns for him grew daily. After the bombings had stopped, we were able to walk to the inner city again and visit with Uncle Veit and Aunt Resi at the bakery. At least there my mother could meet people who knew her from the time before she became Rudi's wife. Usually, the dominant subject was the misery of the war, the many lives lost, and speculations of when would it end. She would lament about her husband's POW situation in France. Then her tears had free rein while Aunt Resi sympathetically joined her in a good cry.

On the evening of my mother's birthday, the downstairs doorbell rang. Somewhat startled my mother looked out from the big picture window in her bedroom to see who was at the door. She let out a scream of joy—"Rudi!" She grabbed my hand and shouted, "Erikale, your Papa is home." We ran down the stairs to open the door. There my father stood smiling and reaching out his arms to both of us.

My father had escaped from a British POW camp in Caen, France, as he was about to be shipped across the English Channel to Great Britain. In the days before his capture, he first fought the Americans during the battle of Cherbourg. Later, a command decision transferred him to nearby Caen, where the British fought a hard battle for that city. Eventually the Germans surrendered, and my father was taken prisoner in July of 1944. The Allied landings on D-day made a good story for him.

The Secret

Winter came early, and heating fuel, like food, was a scarce commodity. The war demanded first consideration for everything. Sacrifice for the *Vaterland* (fatherland) was a constant reminder over the radio. People became scavengers. Forests and bombed-out houses alike were raided for firewood. They stole anything that would burn just to cook a meager meal and stay warm. By contrast, my father was back on the job with the railroad. He had access to coal, and we always had a good supply in our house. He never talked about whether he had permission for those sacks of coal he occasionally brought home.

On Christmas Eve 1944, my thoughtful grandmother had sent a care package with food and goodies considered a rarity in those days. To my dismay, I had missed Christkindl again. However, there in one corner of our large kitchen was a tree decorated with tinsel, candles, and real cookies hanging from the branches, the kind Oma sent. Next to it was a *Kubusbaukasten*, a wooden cube puzzle with six different motifs. Our little family was happy and grateful to be together again. We huddled around the tree and feasted on my generous grandmother's delectables.

Early morning on Christmas Day, my father found a wild rabbit entrapped in his homemade snare. What luck—the rabbit provided the meat for our Christmas meal! Most uncommonly, Uncle Veit and Aunt Resi showed up for dinner on Christmas Day. An unusually cheery Uncle Veit handed my father a small, black leather-bound book. The imprint in gold letters read *Sparkasse* (savings bank); it was a bankbook. Inside, it listed the account holder as Rudi Veit, showing a balance of 32,000 Reichsmark. My father took it as a practical joke and started laughing. However, the older man, serious and somewhat agitated, conveyed to my father that he had saved the money for him. He had a new house in mind, perhaps after the war was over. My father, speechless and profoundly touched by this gesture, embraced his uncle for the first time in his life.

Soon the calendar showed that January 16, my long-awaited birthday, had finally arrived. I was five years old. Ever since Christmas, I was convinced that we were rich. After all, I was unable to pronounce the amount of the bankbook balance—*Zweiunddreissigtausend* Reichsmark! I kept talking about it and wanted to share our new wealth with the rest of the world. My father tried to discourage my enthusiasm by telling me a little story. He spoke of a gnome transforming into a rich prince who could not keep a secret. As a result, he lost his fortune and became a poor gnome again. That story definitely made an impression on me. I avoided talking about "our secret" when visiting the Veit Bakery. Instead, I showed off my birthday present, a small wooden framed blackboard with my name on it and a writing *Griffel* (slate pencil) hanging on a string from the frame.

In the spring of 1945, the situation in Germany became more precarious by the day. Even the Nazi's propaganda machine could no longer stop the broadcasts describing Allied forces crossing the Rhein River into Germany moving east. In the east, the Russian army pushed its way toward the west. My parents, as well as the people around them, hoped for US troops to reach the Sudetenland before the Red Army would.

By the end of April, Komotau had a surprise air attack, seeking out the train station only and destroying this major hub. During that raid many people were killed or injured. My father was not on duty that evening. In horror, the three of us watched the raging inferno from our big bedroom window. The next day, my father reported for duty. The trains were not running; the entire rail system was inoperative. He assisted in the clean-up operations and witnessed the removal of human remains from still-smoldering trains and the wreckage of the once-elegant station house.

4

Aftermath of War

The Russians Were Coming

In early May of 1945, Russian tanks and hundreds of soldiers rolled into Komotau and occupied the city. They set up tents in various locations around Komotau, including on the property where we lived. Our house was now their domain. Only officers had permission to enter the premises. For unknown reasons, they allowed us to stay in our quarters upstairs after searching every room for weapons and Nazi paraphernalia. They found nothing. The officer in charge, a captain, spoke some broken German. He asked my father if he was SS in the Wehrmacht and made him take off his shirt to inspect for the insignia tattoo of SS soldiers. My father was not a member of the SS or any other elite military group, and it saved his life more than once. The Russian kept telling my father, "Hitler kaput," referring to Hitler's suicide in Berlin on April 30. Germany's population, except Hitler's inner circle, was unaware of these events that took place in the Berlin bunker, the impenetrable underground Nazi command headquarter.

On May 7, 1945, Germany signed the unconditional surrender document, and the war officially ended on May 8. The Russian army liberated parts of the Sudetenland, Prague, and the rest of Czechoslovakia while the American army penetrated into the western regions of the Sudetenland. Edvard Benes, the former Czech president, returned from his London exile and quickly reestablished a makeshift government.

Scarlet Fever

While all these political events took place, I was lying in bed with a very high fever. My father fetched the old doctor. With a worried look, he told my parents that he suspected scarlet fever, a streptococcus bacterial infection. I needed to be in the hospital. My father carried me, wrapped in a blanket, to the Komotau hospital. At the entrance, we were refused entry and told that the hospital administration was now in Czech control and admitted Czech citizens only. My father kept talking and pleading in their language, but the answer was the same: no Němci allowed.

The Russian captain had knowledge of my illness. When he found out that the hospital refused to treat me, he hinted to my father, *"Czech nix gut"* ("Czechs are no good"). Being their liberators, he could not interfere. Dr. Senger had no medication to give, but he came daily to check on me. He informed my parents what to expect in the next few days. Penicillin had just started to be mass-produced in America but was not available in Europe, though it was the Scottish doctor Sir Alexander Fleming who discovered the wonder drug.

In a most miraculous way, the Russian officers occupying our house showered us with food and praised my mother's cooking. Every morning, someone slipped a little bag of Russian candy under my pillow. They genuinely took an interest in my getting better. When that awful rash covered my face and body, a side effect of scarlet fever, a Russian field doctor had just the remedy—a green, cool ointment. At first, Dr. Senger was skeptical. He tried a little dab in my groin area. The next day, the rash there showed less redness and felt less itchy, and he gave the okay to use it on my whole body.

The high fever slowly subsided. My throat felt almost normal, and I started to develop an appetite. The scaly rash faded with every day; I had survived the very serious and oftentimes deadly illness of scarlet fever.

A Rescuing Angel

While the Russians camped on our property, my young mother had to disguise herself as a raggedy, smelly, and limping woman. She used such trickery when she absolutely had to leave the house for an errand and walk by the soldiers' tents. First she would stop at the adjacent horse stables and roll on the ground to pick up some Eau de Cologne fragrance: "*fumier de cheval*" (horse manure). The soldiers never bothered her but held their noses when she walked by. The captain knew of her ploy and thought it quite clever.

However, one day there was an incident. My memory still flashes back to the horrible scene I witnessed at age five. I was still recuperating from my illness, and Dr. Senger prescribed lots of fresh air. Dusk had just set in when my mother and I came back from a short stroll on that warm spring day. As we were going up the stairwell and reaching the landing, a Russian soldier jumped down from the upper stairs. He grabbed my mother and commanded her to lie down on the steps. Totally caught off guard, she refused his demands. He became impatient, his face flushed with anger. He bellowed his orders, and his actions were rough and forceful. He pulled out his pistol and placed it on my mother's temple. All the while, she held my hand tightly. Sensing danger, I cried and begged him not hurt my *Mutti* (mother). He paid no attention to my petition, engrossed as he was in unbuckling his belt and unbuttoning his trousers with the other hand. Ripping my frightened mother's blouse, he motioned for her to get down on the floor. With the weapon held to her head, she pled for her life: "Please don't; please, please no, no!" Suddenly, out of nowhere, but heaven-sent, the captain appeared, grabbed the pistol from the soldier, and kicked him off the landing, where he tumbled down the flight of stairs. The captain apologized to my obviously shaken mother. He concluded that the soldier seemed drunk and she needed to conceal her youth and looks at all times when stepping out of the house.

Rumors of atrocities by the occupying forces circulated throughout the community. The fear of rape kept women, young and old, off the streets and hidden away. These unrestrained Russian soldiers entered houses, smashed them up, and took whatever they thought had value. A slight resistance by a protective owner could trigger a severe beating or even death. Transfixed by wristwatches, they ripped them off people, dead or alive. They proudly showed their loot hanging on their arms. Stalin's unruly and somewhat uncivilized army was most notorious for leaving behind a path of destruction and brutal assaults on woman.

Two weeks had passed since the Russians surrounded our lives, and now they were ready to move on—"West"—the captain said. Their presence had kept revengeful Czechs from invading our home. Yet my mother was relieved when she heard about their decampment. My father, truly appalled by my mother's ordeal, anticipated even greater dangers ahead. He still had a job with the railroad, now under Czech control. Most of his German colleagues had been dismissed the day Germany signed the surrender papers. Speaking the Czech language gave him an advantage, and for now, he worked as a trainer for the newly hired Czech personnel.

Plotted Revenge

While in voluntary exile, the president of Czechoslovakia, Edvard Benes, had ample time to prepare the laws of his land, better known as the Benes Decrees. He signed these rather shaky ordinances into law throughout 1945 with the blessings of a provisional Czech parliament. Fifteen of these decrees singled out Sudeten Germans and other minority groups, and it became their living hell.

These radical changes imposed on Germans by the Czech leaders made life an intolerable misery. An ordinance proclaimed that all Germans, when outside their houses, must wear a white armband with a big black N, identifying them as *Němec*. Failure to comply was punished by beatings and imprisonment. Alarming food shortages had people waiting in line for hours. Disbursed rations had an equivalent of 1,200 calories per day and consisted mainly of starch and vegetable products. Butter, milk, meat, and sugar were not available for the Němci, not even the children. There was a curfew. No Germans in the parks, streets, or any public places after 7:00 pm. Leaving the city was prohibited, as was the use of car, bus, train, or trolley. The German language could not be spoken in public, nor could Germans use the sidewalks. Komotau's population was over 90 percent German, and these proclamations gave the city the appearance of a ghost town. Restaurants and entertainment places closed. Public transportation came to a halt due to mostly empty seats. Only the railroad showed signs of life. The new government had decided to resettle Czech citizens from the interior of Czechoslovakia. Peasants and gypsies from Slovakia came by the trainloads to the German cities and districts of the Sudetenland.

Over the course of a week, the Czech militia confiscated most of Komotau's German-owned business district. The Veit Bakery was no exception. Although disowned, the old Veits were required to use their skills and keep the bakery going. Uncle Veit had to do all the baking, while Aunt Resi helped him the best she could and did the cleaning. The new proprietor, not a baker, moved into the upstairs living quarters. An old storeroom became the Veits' new place to stay. They did not receive any monetary compensation for their fourteen-hour days, only a measly and grudgingly furnished evening meal.

The Notorious Death March

The posters read in big, bold letters: **NARIZENI** (order) **"All German Males of Komotau Ages 16–65 Must Report June 9, 1945, by 10:00 a.m. at Jahnsplatz. Women, Children, Seniors Must Stay in their Homes—Failure to Comply will be Punished with Death."** These posters were mounted throughout Komotau and the vicinity. In the early morning hours of June 9, the Czech militia drove through neighborhoods, using mobile loudspeakers to announce the message once again. My self-assured father tried to console my worried mother as he embraced her. He reminded her that, less than a year ago, he had survived the bloody battles of Normandy and escaped from a POW camp. Surely, he declared, he would overcome whatever it was that would face him on this Saturday morning. He left the house determined and confident to be back before evening, when he was scheduled to work his shift. Little did he know that he would never see his residence again.

History has a name for the ordeal of six thousand men—young, old, and sick—who showed up at Komotau's Jahnplatz: it became the infamous "Komotau Death March." After an inspection of military tattoos, men whose Nazi association was thus discovered were pulled out of the lines; they were savagely beaten and kicked. Some were shot instantly. Others had their names called out. They were loaded into trucks and driven away. The heavily armed Czech military divided the men into groups, and they were now prisoners. The soldiers piled onto machine-gun-equipped trucks and escorted the men without food or water for two days up the mountains. Under constant threat of violence, they had to march to the crest of the rugged Ore Mountains, where the border of Germany (Saxony, under Soviet control) and Czechoslovakia divided the two countries.

The Czech commanders approached the German mayor in the small border town of Deutschneudorf and told him that they were delivering several convoys of Sudeten German men designated for labor in Siberia, Russia. The mayor knew nothing of any political ramification and told the Czech commanders to wait until he had authorization from the Soviet High Command in a nearby town. The mayor equipped his small police force and private citizens with weapons and ammunition to prevent further entry by the Czech soldiers while he was seeking help. During that waiting period, some prisoners succeeded in escaping. Others, who failed in their attempt, received a bullet to the head by the Czech soldiers. Hours later, armed Russian soldiers, their commander, and the mayor drove up in Soviet trucks and started negotiating with the Czechs. The Russians were not interested in these men or their entry into East Germany.

A Concentration Camp Named Maltheuern

Rejected was the Czechs' evil plan to dump human commodities into the Soviet sector of Germany. They felt scorned and enraged. The prisoners, hungry, thirsty, and some quite ill, trekked down the mountains. Whoever could not keep the pace, complained, or grew too sick to continue received a beating or a shot to the head and was left on the side of the road like an animal. Along the way, curious villagers had to stay in their houses and have the curtains drawn while the columns of fatigued men passed through their streets, or else they, too, met a bullet.

After two days of marching, the exhausted men reached their new destination—the Czech concentration camp Maltheuern. The facility could only accommodate one-third of the men. Others ended in similar horror camps of Glashütte and Theresienstadt, all near Komotau.

Maltheuern had a reputation of notoriety. Many inmates did not survive the treatment and tortures of this camp. After the inhumane experience of the rightfully labeled "Death March," my father became a detainee in Maltheuern. While most prisoners marched daily to a severely bombed hydraulic factory and worked there as slave laborers, my father, with his abilities to speaking fluent Czech, baking, and cooking, was chosen to become a prison canteen cook. His Czech military time counted for additional privileges. He had access to leftovers of the meager meals. Unlike many of his fellow prisoners, he never had to endure torturous beatings. And above all, he was able to communicate with my mother, through a mutual friend who was married to a Czech man.

Her name was Liselotte. People who knew her called her Lisel. She and my mother were well acquainted. Lisel came from Weissensulz, and the Gerber name had no foreign ring to her. She knew my mother from the days of her apprenticeship in Weissensulz, and she was married about the same time as my mother. Her husband was a Komotau Czech who spoke German better than his native Czech language because he had attended German schools while growing up. He, too, chose a career with the railroad, and after the Czech takeover, he was quickly up for a promotion. The couple helped facilitate my father's letters from the concentration camp to my mother, and vice versa. Mail service for Germans was suspended, and without their friends' address, my parents could not have communicated with each other.

At the end of June, Lisel came by our house and delivered a letter from my father. My mother had not heard from him since he kissed us good-bye on that Saturday morning. She had cried copiously in the previous weeks, especially upon hearing the horror stories about these men and their disappearance. My father's letter made her smile again; he was alive and able to contact her. She affectionately hugged Lisel for the good news.

Days of Uncertainty

With my father imprisoned, my mother and I felt dangerously isolated and alone in the big house. On a daily basis, we stood in line for some sort of *Eintopf* (stew) without meat and a piece of bread. We had very little to eat, and she worried about leaving the house for fear of being beaten or killed. Paramilitary groups of criminals and thugs, endorsed by the Czech leaders, roamed the streets of Komotau. They had free rein to terrorize the women, children, and seniors of Komotau's German population while the husbands, fathers, and sons were locked away in Czech concentration camps or were POWs in some foreign country. The rest of 1945 was a time of wild retributions and constant waves of violence by the Czechs against the defenseless Germans.

One day, two Czech soldiers came to our house and informed my mother of her new Czech name. While there, they demanded our radio, weapons (if any), bank savings books, cash, watches, and jewelry—even the gold wedding band from my mother's finger. They ransacked the whole house. On their way out, they spotted my father's bicycle, sat on it, and peddled away. A week later, two different Czech officials rang the doorbell looking for "Marie Veitova." They handed my mother a piece of paper. In German, it stated that she must report for work at the listed address immediately. Failure to comply would be punishable with jail.

Early the next morning, we were on our way to my mother's new work place. She knew the neighborhood well. It was Komotau's *"Villenviertel,"* an exclusive residential area formerly occupied by wealthy local businesspeople. Impressive homes lined the lifeless avenues, and the once perfectly manicured gardens seemed neglected and overgrown. When we arrived at the given address, a woman came to the door, seemingly half-asleep and not very friendly. She did not speak German. Obviously she knew of my mother's coming and motioned for us to follow her. However, she kept pointing the finger at me while talking and shaking her head. When we reached the messy kitchen, we met a raucous family, including Babischka, the grandmother. The five children ranged from eight months to twelve years of age, and to my dislike, they were all boys.

Every day, except on Sunday, we walked to the house of the newly resettled family from Slovakia. My mother worked from 7:00 a.m. to 6:00 p.m., and for now, I was able to stay with her. Anna, the mistress of the house, had objections to my playing with her boys. They all called my mother *Sluzka*, meaning maid, and my name was *maly Sluzka*, little maid. Anna and Janosch, her husband, spent most of the day lounging in their big bedroom while Babischka, Anna's mother, tended to the baby. The four rowdy boys, unsupervised, roamed the streets and got into fights with the Czechoslovakian kids whose families were new settlers as well. Soon it became evident that the Czechoslovakian families felt superior to the Slovakian families, who came from the very poor regions of Slovakia's Carpathian Mountains. Despite minor slang differences, they all spoke the same Slavic language but denounced their kinship otherwise. However, all these transferees had one thing in common: they seemed awkward and lost in their new environment.

Anna did most of the cooking for the main meal at noon. Though a peasant, she was the woman of the house, and in her culture, she had the obligation of cooking the meal. Now she had a servant who would serve it. Her limited menu consisted of soup, dumplings, sauerkraut, and more kraut with potatoes. Meat was served on Sunday when the Sluzkas were not there. I hated her cooking, except for the dumplings filled with marmalade. My mother kept reminding me not to make a fuss or else we would get no food at all. There was no food waiting for us at home, and we went to bed early to overcome the feeling of being hungry. Since my mother had a job, though forced on her, that provided meals for her and her child, we no longer received those valueless ration cards.

Most Sundays, we visited the old Veits in the city. Oftentimes they had a little surprise waiting for me—pastries. Uncle Veit swiped them from the bakery when nobody was watching. In my little world, I lived for those Sundays when I could revel in rare delights. My mother derived comfort from seeing me happy and smiling, devouring every sweet in front of me. She, too, needed the familiarity of family to talk about Rudi, forced labor, and entrapment by a vengeful Czech regime. They had heard of horror stories in connection with the started expulsion of the German population. When will it became their fate? They were scared.

Burn, Němec, Burn

In the far corner of the villa's courtyard, four boys, ages seven to twelve, busied themselves piling up wood for a fire. Their plan was to burn a five-year-old *Němec* girl. I stood there unsuspectingly watching the boys. Suddenly they grabbed me. I tried to scream. Their hands covered my mouth and muffled my screams. I struggled to free myself, but they were too many, too strong. They dragged me toward the fire. I was frightened out of my mind. Would I burn to death?

One final push and I lost my balance and the flames engulfed my hand. The boys laughed triumphantly while I cried out in piercing shrieks of pain, which caught the attention of my mother. She came running out of the house and shuddered at the sight of the horror scene in front of her eyes: her child in danger, letting out screams of agony, and the boys chanting, "Burn, Němec, burn." She picked me up and ran back to the house where she put my injured hand in cold water and tried to console my wailing and pain.

Mistress Anna stormed into the kitchen. Highly agitated by my loud moans, she ordered my mother with hand gestures to make me stop. Anna took one look at me and left the room to fetch her Czech neighbor, who spoke some German. Through him, she informed my mother to arrange for me to stay somewhere else. She would no longer provide food for me—I was nothing but a nuisance in her house. Besides, her boys did not like Němci, especially girls, and that could lead to more problems. She gave my mother one week to find a solution.

Later that evening, we snuck our way to old Dr. Senger's house so he could look at my burned hand.. I cried even before the doctor examined my hand. He put some salve on the wound, wrapped a gauze bandage around my hand, and assured my mother that at my age the healing would go fast; my hand would probably be unscarred. In later years, my own children would point to the side of my palm and ask about the scar. After I told them the true story about some evil little boys, they always kissed the area on my hand to make it feel better. Eventually, the scar disappeared completely.

Silent on the Train

Once again, my mother had to impose on Lisel, who had all the privileges of a Czech citizen. This time she needed a great favor from her friend. She asked Lisel to take me to my grandparents in Franzelhütte. It was a heart-wrenching decision for my mother to separate from her only child. However, no other plan would better ensure her child's safety and survival. In her mind, only the familiarity of Franzelhütte, the farm, her parents, and her sister could provide security and well-being for her Erikale. Holding back her tears, she discussed our separation with me. I seemed excited and receptive to this temporary arrangement. She told me she would soon come for me and pick me up. In the meantime, I could play with my little friends in Franzelhütte, go berry picking, and enjoy good eats. I could help tend to Rex and Wotan, the chicken coop, and all the animals at Opa and Oma's farm. She packed my clothes and some toys in a small suitcase and pointed out that a letter for Oma was in an inside pocket.

Embedded in the cradles of the children of the Böhmerwald are the virtues of responsibility and a spirit of charity. It is the tool of survival and happiness in a semimountainous region. Industries and resources, other than timber, are nonexistent, and the people live off the penurious land. Lisel, a woman born into those values and temporarily my surrogate mother, gently held my hand as we walked toward a waiting train at Komotau's demolished train station. Lisel's husband waved us farewell. In order not to jeopardize the plan, my saddened mother stayed behind at home that Sunday. Days before our departure, Lisel and my mother coached me not speak a word to anyone while on the train—not even if someone asked about the bandage on my burned hand. They impressed upon me that no one must know that I was a German child, or else Lisel may get into real trouble for taking me on the train. At five years old, that concept had to be hard to grasp. However, I sat in my seat the entire trip and kept my mouth zipped. After an almost five-hour train ride, interrupted by stops and changes in cities along the way, Lisel and I arrived safely in Eisendorf. From there, we walked the two kilometers to Franzelhütte to the house of my shocked but delighted grandparents and aunt.

My memory does not allow me to recall the trip very clearly, but years later I found out that during that train ride, passengers commented on my quietness. Lisel, speaking Czech in a subdued voice, told them that I was her "special child, born with a handicap—deafness." To my family she recounted that I would pull on my lips but not make a sound until she gave the okay to talk. This was still true after reaching Eisendorf and leaving its usually sleepy train station, then swarming with American soldiers.

A few days later, all of Franzelhütte and beyond knew of my arrival and the circumstances associated with the trip. In some sense, Lisel and I achieved a bit of hero status. *The Gerbers' little Erika*, went the story, *just five years old, and so brave, deluded Czech authorities by playing deaf on a long train ride.* Lisel, on the other hand, captured the respect and admiration of every adult in the area for her courageous deed and vivid example of friendship. Knowingly, she put herself and her family at great risk by aiding Germans. Czech authorities harshly punished such acts. She could have ended in a concentration camp, regardless of her husband's citizenship or any clout he may have had. My family was forever grateful to Lisel and her husband.

Separation Anxiety

I was asking daily when my Mutti was coming to take me back to Komotau. Although I had plenty of good foods to eat and played to my heart's content, I missed my mother. Sometimes I received a letter from her in which she assured me of her coming to Franzelhütte very soon. In the meantime, I needed to be patient, well-behaved, and helpful to Oma. Aunt Klara read the letters to me, and unbeknownst to a five-year-old, she was the actual writer of them. I kept on talking about my parents, the Veit bakery, and the kindergarten in Komotau. Cousin Horst and I would go to school there when the leaves on the trees turn a different color.

Answering my incessant questioning was no easy task for my grandparents and aunt. They tried all sorts of things and solicited advice from the close-knit community. Someone brought me a little gray kitten, which I named Schnuri. Opa put a dab of red paint on a young chick and told me that one was mine alone. Aunt Klara introduced me to the exciting *Grimms' Fairy Tales* as well as other stimulating stories, and as we read, she taught me the alphabet. I had brought along my birthday gift, the small blackboard with Griffel, where I started practicing writing my name in cursive.

Twice a month on Friday, Oma had a bake day. She called it her *Backtag*. The night before, she took the saved sourdough starter and prepared the basic dough. Early the next morning, her kitchen was transformed into a bakery. Opa did his part and lit the fire in the specialty oven, located in the small, white building next to the main house. It was a clay structure resembling a beehive with a tall chimney and a big, black iron door. After several hours fueling the wood fire, the ashes were pushed to the side. Raised to double its size, the dough was removed from the round baskets and placed on the hot stones inside the oven. There the loaves baked until crispy brown, and a pleasant aroma let the neighbors know that Wonger Waberl, as she was known, was baking bread again.

Besides baking delicious bread, churning butter was another constant on the Gerber farm. Opa's cows had multiple purposes. They pulled loaded wagons of hay and grain, a plow, or a harrow in the fields, but mainly they were dairy cows that had to be milked twice daily. Usually, Oma and Aunt Klara performed the job sitting on a footstool, holding a bucket between their legs, using two hands to extract the milk from the cows' udders. My aunt always talked to the brown-and-white-colored cow Pompern while milking her as if she were a person.

The monstrous dairy machine designed for butter making looked rather complex and required long hours of manual labor. However, the results of this tedious process were tasty butter and buttermilk for our use and skim milk for the pigs. Oma's finger marked a small cross on each bar of butter. She also believed in carving three tiny crosses on the floury backside of a new loaf of bread before cutting it. My grandmother grew up in the home of her grandparents, where religion and rampant superstition were paired together and played an intricate part in their lives.

The Magical Season

Almost five months had passed since I had left Komotau and come to stay with my grandparents and aunt in Franzelhütte. Profound new impressions and fun experiences preoccupied my mind, and the longing for my mother had subsided considerably but not entirely.

By the end of November, frost and dancing snowflakes competed with each other and dropped a white sheet on the brown soil. Mr. Winter was on his way. The two conifer trees behind the barn provided the fir branches for an advent wreath, which was placed on the little table below a kitchen window. Four used candles, representing the four Sundays until Christmas, were a welcome leftover from the previous year. In 1945, a candle became somewhat of a luxury item, nor was the Advent calendar available this year. Even without opening little calendar doors, I still counted down the days until Christmas.

December 6 is the birthday of "*Sankt Nikolaus*"—Saint Nicholas. Aunt Klara had told me spellbinding stories about good Sankt Nikolaus and Knecht Ruprecht, his servant and helper. She told me that they both live in a magical fir forest, somewhere in the Böhmerwald. The night before the good saint's birthday, I placed my clean and shiny boot outside by the front door. Early the next morning, I checked whether my boot had sweets or switches left by Ruprecht for the little troublemakers. I considered myself good, but one could never be sure. Indeed, St. Nikolaus rewarded my good behavior with *Lebkuchen* (gingerbread) and candied apples. I felt very special and happy.

"*Alle Jahre wieder* ..." ("Every year again ...") was my favorite Christmas carol, and I knew the lyrics of all three verses. Finally, the long-awaited Christmas Eve had arrived. The snow came down relentlessly all day. Old Rex and even older Wotan never moved from their warm spots near and above the humongous *Kachelofen* (tiled kitchen stove). The kitten Schnuri chased after a small wool ball, which she playfully moved back and forth with her little sharp-clawed paws. Oma had been laboring in the kitchen since dawn, baking, cooking, and lastly plucking the remaining feathers from the lifeless body of a goose intended for the Christmas Day roast. Aunt Klara, the perpetual animal lover, refused to take part in the preparations involving any animal for feast consumption. She kept busy with cleaning and other chores. Opa took care of the stable occupants, and then he disappeared for a short time. When he returned, his handlebar moustache glistened from tiny clumps of frozen snow and he had a faint, impish smile on his face.

Oma, as always dressed in black, had changed her apron for a clean one, thereby signaling time to sit down for the traditional Christmas Eve dinner. There was Schnitzel with sauerkraut, potato salad, and summer's preserved green beans. First she would light a candle by Jule's photograph and plead, "If he is still alive in Stalingrad, please someone, give him something to eat and keep him warm." After a moment of silence, tears rolling down on her and Aunt Klara's cheeks, she would look up and whisper, *"Selige Weihnachten"* ("Blessed Christmas").

After dessert, the customary stewed fruits and home-baked *Weihnachtsstollen*, the time for superstitions and old wives' tales had arrived. Oma reminded Aunt Klara that the laundry was not to be left hanging in the attic on Christmas Eve or someone in the family would surely die. Opa started cracking nuts harvested in the fall from the mighty walnut tree behind the barn. Oma warned him to be careful, not to choose a rotten one, or else … She told tales, one in particular about an apple seed, and all had the same gloomy outcome of sickness and death. Only Aunt Klara was telling of something uplifting. She had heard that animals speak during the magical night of Christmas Eve.

"Enough witchery for one evening" Opa said. He was anxious to share what he saw in the parlor when he brought in wood to make a fire—"a glimpse of Christkindl leaving the house!" I immediately ran to the *gute Stube* (parlor). There in the cozy, warm room stood a tall tree, decorated with lustrous tinsels, cookies, sparkly glass ornaments, and blazing candles. "Just like the one in Komotau," I exclaimed. "How did Christkindl know that I was in Franzelhütte?" I asked. Consumed by this magic, I nearly overlooked a dollhouse almost as tall as me, with real curtains and miniature wood furniture and my name painted in small red letters on the front door. All eyes were on me. "But, Christkindl forgot to bring my Mutti," I said, "and that's what I truly wished for." I started to cry and left the room. A short time later, I returned with my boots and coat on, my suitcase in hand. Through heartbreaking sobs, I expressed my need to go to Komotau and see my Mutti. "Perhaps Christkindl could fly me there on her wings?" Oma gently sat me on her lap, wiped off the tears, and tried to console me.

A new year arrived. It was 1946, and I anxiously waited for my birthday. For some time, Opa had been working on an old decrepit sled used by my uncles when they were my age. One day, a freshly painted sled stood upright and ready by the front door. Oma baked my favorite cakes, a *Quarkkuchen* (cheesecake) and a *Mohnkuchen* (poppy seed cake) while Aunt Klara gathered my three little playmates and brought them to the house. We sat in the parlor, where Opa had made a glowing fire in the black cast iron stove. Only for special occasions did they use the room, and my sixth birthday certainly qualified for the cause. The delectable-looking cakes had cooled off and were ready to be served. Afterward, my aunt helped build a big snowman. Then it was time for our first attempts on the refurbished sled, which was long enough to accommodate all four of us. The slope past the Gerber house gave us the fastest speed. We usually ended on the frozen pond. The snow lingered on into March, and the renovated sled definitely saw lots of action during that winter.

A Minor Smuggling Operation

Eslarn is a tiny border town on the Bavarian side of Germany. The Gerber family had friends there, and until 1945, people from Franzelhütte or Eisendorf walked back and forth without ever seeing a border patrol. Taking the back roads from Franzelhütte, Eslarn could easily be reached in less than an hour by foot. Based on all those rumors of expulsion, my grandmother and aunt decided that some valuables, considered family heirlooms, needed to be taken to Eslarn for safekeeping. One day, each of the women strapped a pack basket on her back filled with documents, klöppel lace, and ornate figurines of fine china from the Habsburg era. I wanted to come along, and my little *Rucksack* (backpack) contained a bit of jewelry—Uncle Seph's watch and ring. The three of us took a narrow path through familiar woods, always watchful for Czech soldiers or unusual noises. The path led to the hamlet of Tillyschanze, an active border crossing less than a mile from Eslarn, where Czech guards patrolled the small checkpoint. Before reaching there, we abandoned the trail and disappeared in the thicket, quietly, almost tiptoeing toward our destination.

When we reached the farm of Heiner and Emmerl Pokorny in Eslarn, Oma's good friends and distant relations, we gratefully accepted their hospitality. Our fragile and valuable freight got stored away, and Aunt Klara and Oma seemed pleased with their accomplishments.

During the social part of our visit, the Pokornys urged the Gerber women to leave Franzelhütte and move in with them, perhaps temporarily, until the situation in the *Tschechei*, as they called Czechoslovakia, had settled down. Aunt Klara welcomed the proposal instantly. Oma, not easily swayed on anything, promised to mention it to Opa. I do not know if she ever discussed that option with my grandfather, but nobody moved to Eslarn. With time, our smuggling excursions became more daring. We transported all of Seph's big, heavy books, including his dissertation, as well as a sewing machine and the beginnings of Aunt Klara's dowry. No one expressed any concerns about being caught until one day when we bumped into a patrol before reaching the border. My quick-witted grandmother made up a story of being severely lost. That close encounter ended our smuggling operation.

Matchmaker

Aunt Klara had a pretty face and a slender body with feminine charm. Her twenty-fifth birthday was coming up in July. Hidden under her mattress she kept a small photograph of a young man whom she had met while working as a housekeeper in Munich. She did not talk about him, but Oma caught her several times looking at the photo. Such incidents usually ended in a shouting match between the two women.

One day, when again patronized by her mother, Aunt Klara expressed her unhappiness on the farm and her desire to move to Bavaria. She mentioned Neunburg vorm Wald, where her brother Gustel lived and where she would like to continue learning the *Friseuse* trade. Oma would not hear of such talk. She reminded her daughter of an obligation to Stampfel Toni, a young man who was a POW in Russia. His father, Stampfel Toni Sr., operated the "Gasthaus Beim Stampfel," the only tavern in Franzelhütte. (In Böhmerwald and Bavaria, it was customary to refer to a person by his or her last name first, followed by their given name.)

Klara and Toni were close in age and grew up together. Prior to Stampfle Toni's military draft in 1943, he and Klara had some flirtatious encounters. They exchanged friendly, chummy letters while he served at the Eastern Front. There were no promises or commitments made by either, and Klara viewed their relationship as solely a friendship. However, Oma liked Stampfel Toni, a first-rate zither player, as well as his entire family. She would have gladly used any love potion to enchant Toni to become her son-in-law, had he been available.

5

Ancestral Anecdotes

An Unusual Name Change

On that crisp, sunny July morning in 1946, Barbara, alias Wonger Waberl, sat quietly in the back of that stinking truck struggling to decide if she should be angry or sad about her cruel eviction from her homestead. She was in a state of disbelief. At the age of sixty, her life had abruptly ceased to exist in the familiarity of Franzelhütte, her village and that of her ancestors. Where would it continue? She did not know.

Just a week earlier, she had visited the little cemetery at the edge of the village to bring some early blooming dahlias from her garden to the grave of her beloved grandparents. She liked coming to this peaceful place on the hill. There she could sit in the shade of a weeping willow and pour her heart out when tragedy struck or simply have a conversation with her grandfather, who was like a father and mentor to her. She waited for a sign from him by looking up to the tree where the gentle breeze made soft rustling sounds like a whisper in the leaves. Indeed, he had heard her. Before leaving, she always made a quick stop for a prayer in the old grave section. One could hardly make out the name on the weather-beaten, moss-covered stone, but she knew it was the resting place of her great-grandparents, Ferdinand and Rettel Klaner.

Like in a trance, Barbara had time to reflect back over her life and that of her mother. She vividly remembered her grandfather telling her many stories, starting with the mix-up in his last name. No one discovered the mistake until little Karl started school and the teacher checked names for attendance. He called for Karl Klarer, but no hand was raised. The teacher looked straight at Karl and waited, but Karl corrected his teacher, telling him that his name was Klaner, like his father. The frustrated teacher insisted that he was right, because the data came from the parish priest who personally had logged it in the parish register. When Karl's parents checked into the name confusion, the priest pointed to the birth certificate and exclaimed, "Look, look, it reads Klarer, and what's the difference anyway?!" Unfortunately, the old German writing of the letters "n" and "r" are very similar, but the priest's atrocious handwriting caused the error. Back in those days, nobody argued with a man of the cloth, especially a transplant like Ferdinand Klaner, who came from Austria.

Coincidently, when the Klaner brothers came to Franzelhütte, the nobleman Baron von Zucker had just been put to rest. They quickly found out that the glass industry in Bohemia was a lucrative, in-demand business, and it had made the baron, who had come from ordinary means, into a very wealthy man. His real name was Anton Lenk, a son of the Lenk family in neighboring Eisendorf. One day, and not by chance, Anton met the Baron von Zucker, who had lost his wealth to gambling and irrational investments gone sour. His debtors were relentless in the collection of their extended credit. The baron saw no way out but to sell his cherished aristocratic title to the highest bidder. Anton Lenk was the man with the money, and he bought the nobleman's title and prestige. The new Baron von Zucker, alias Anton Lenk, and a handful of crafty glassblowers founded Franzelhütte in 1750. He was the proprietor of a well-established *Glashütte* (glass hut, also known as glass works), and named it after his daughter, Franzel. This is how Franzelhütte got its name.

Wheelwright Wonger

From early on, Karl showed a vivid interest in working with wood, unlike his father, Ferdinand, who was a successful glass blower. Karl liked playing with the tools in his father's shed, and everyone predicted that with such natural talent he would become a carpenter. As he grew older, he expressed his admiration for the craft of wheelwright. He pursued his dream and became an apprentice in one of the shops in Eisendorf. Franzelhütte had none, and Karl, smart cookie that he was, saw a real need for such a business. Every family had at least one wagon and a cart, which at one time or another needed a new wheel or a repair.

Just as predicted, the wheelwright business was flourishing in Franzelhütte. But Karl, who everyone referred to as Wonger, had inherited the *Wanderlust* from his father. Not married or tied down by family, he had heard that good wheelwrights were sought after by the royal court in Vienna. His father and uncle came from that imperial city, and they often talked about their beautiful birthplace.

Wonger decided to visit Vienna and meet some of the relatives his father had mentioned over the years. He liked the people he met and was truly fascinated by the size of the city and its vibrancy. In addition, luck was on his side. He applied for a position as a wheelwright at the Schönbrunn castle, the summer residence of the emperor, Franz Joseph I, and was hired. Wonger impressed his superiors with his strength and precision in producing wheels, which required talents of both a carpenter and a blacksmith.

On a visit back to Franzelhütte, Wonger married the girl he had been in love with since his apprenticeship days. She was from Eisendorf, and her name was Nannerl. In his younger years, he never made any promises to her, but she had inkling that one day she would become his wife. After the marriage, she declined moving to Vienna with her husband but decided to live with his parents, the old Klaners, and tend to their needs until they passed away. Once a year, for an extended period, Wonger made the grueling trip home to Franzelhütte. By the time he left again, so it seemed, Nannerl was usually pregnant. By 1866, their sixth child, Katharina was born. Wonger saw it necessary to enlarge the house of his parents, which he inherited, and had two more rooms added to house number thirteen.

While the family in Franzelhütte was growing, Wonger earned a promotion to an elite team of *Kutschenmachers* (carriage makers) at the royal carriage maker's workshop. He learned the craft under the watchful eyes of highly experienced and renowned carriage makers.

A Three K

Around 1850, after a series of upheavals throughout Europe, the powerful Habsburg monarchy had experienced tumultuous political challenges, including the loss of lands. In 1854, the young emperor Franz Joseph I had fallen in love with a free-spirited young woman of sixteen, his stunningly beautiful cousin, Duchess Elisabeth (Sissi) of Bavaria, and married her. She became empress of Austria. In 1867, her husband, the *Kaiser* (emperor) Franz Joseph I, was also crowned *König* (king) of Hungary while Sissi was crowned queen in a grand coronation ceremony at St. Matthew Church in Budapest. The Habsburg Empire became a dual monarchy, officially called the Austro-Hungarian Monarchy.

These major changes within the monarchy prompted a more appropriate title for Wonger. He was now a Three K, *"Kaiserlicher, Königlicher, Kutschenmacher,"* and his earnings reflected the new position. He now could afford to buy a ticket on a *diligence* (stagecoach), which took him three-fourths of the way to Franzelhütte and shortened his travel time considerably. In later years when the Royal Railway replaced other long-distance transportation means, he boarded a train in Vienna and traveled in style to Prague. From there he completed his journey by stagecoach. During these travels, he sometimes met interesting and accomplished people like Andreas Hartauer, the songwriter of the world-famous folksong *"Dort Tief im Böhmerwald."*

Hartauer was a successful glassblower and came from near Winterberg, a small town about thirty miles from Franzelhütte. He, like many glassblowers, moved from *Hütte* to *Hütte*, and his wanderlust took him all over Bohemia and Austria. Finally, he settled down in St. Pölten, not far from Vienna. He had everything a man could want—a beautiful wife, the big house with a garden, and money in the bank—but his heart was plagued by homesickness. During one of these bouts of nostalgia, he confessed his feelings on paper in three verses of sentimental memories offering an eternal farewell to his Böhmerwald boyhood home. Besides writing the lyrics, Hartauer, a self-taught musician, also composed music to the song. Brass bands throughout Europe played the waltz-style music, and people just loved it. During his lifetime, Hartauer never realized the impact and fame of his composition.

As the years passed, Wonger, too, became an affluent man, and his prosperity was reflected in his six children. They all attended school and learned various trades of their choosing. When his youngest daughter, tall and pretty Katharina, turned seventeen, he took her to Vienna with him and enrolled her in a finishing school for girls. There she would learn about culture and etiquette, and hopefully, one day, meet an eligible match for her future. She stayed in the house of a great-aunt, where she enjoyed comfort and good companionship. In younger years, the aunt worked as milliner. In those days, the profession was fairly common as women, regardless of their class, had to wear hats. The aunt was clever and talented and did well for herself. Katharina listened to her many stories, including some about her "big loves" gone sour and the reason why she never married.

Katharina

Some days, when Wonger had plenty of time, he and his daughter would take a leisurely stroll through the Schönbrunn castle grounds. Bustling gardeners were always hard at work keeping up with the beautification of the gardens on the royal property. Katharina reported to her father of her happiness in his choice of schooling and in her accommodations at her great-aunt's home. Wonger was immensely pleased. At times, he had some silent concerns that she might like life in Vienna too much and, God forbid, settle down instead of returning to the Böhmerwald. He would quickly wipe these thoughts from his mind when thinking of his wife Nannerl, who did not approve of her daughter's educational ventures in faraway Vienna.

It was time for Wonger to take his annual leave and arrange for a trip home. Katharina was not ready to return to Franzelhütte with her father, although she had completed the one-year program at her school. The great-aunt, who was in her late seventies, begged Wonger to let Katharina stay on with her. She enjoyed the teenager's gaiety and that of her girlfriends, who came to visit often. They all seemed very interested in the aunt's vintage hat creations, which were on display all over the house, and her entertaining stories from the old millinery days.

Katharina kissed her father good-bye, handed him a letter for her mother, and wished him a safe journey to Franzelhütte. At times—and now was one of these agonizing moments—she missed her mother and siblings terribly, but her father did not need to know her present feelings.

In the absence of Wonger, Katharina felt freer to join her girlfriends for outings in the meadows of the Schönbrunn castle, where royal cavalry members held training exercises nearby. Oftentimes, soldiers would ride by to get a closer look at the young women, playing and giggling, or stop when they caught the glances of some pretty girl.

Summer had ended, but a beautiful, warm fall day prompted Katharina to attend what was likely to be the last picnic of the year. As usual, some soldiers mingled with the women, and Katharina met a dashing, young *Hussar* (Hungarian cavalry member, renowned for their elegant dress uniform). That evening, she told her aunt about a young man whose name was Andreje. The old woman recognized a passion in Katharina when she talked about this man and suggested that Andreje should come to the house for a visit. She was thinking more in the lines of scrutinizing this intrusive male than extending a social visit, but she kept that thought to herself.

Wonger had returned to his job at the court. Most peculiarly, Katharina came to see her father several times a week. She did not tell him about Andreje or the reason why she visited her somewhat surprised father so often. Being at the castle gave her a chance, perhaps, to spend some moments in the arms of the man with whom she had fallen in love. Only her great-aunt was in on the secret, and the sweet old lady really liked this attractive twenty-two-year-old Hungarian soldier.

Andreje was born in Budapest. He came from a large family, and his father operated a struggling blacksmith business shoeing horses. After military school, Andreje, an ardent lover of fast horses, chose to enlist in a Hussar regiment. Transferred to Vienna, he became a member of the Royal Cavalry Hussar Regiment, an elite group of a few hundred men specifically assigned to functions at the royal court.

A few days before Christmas, Katharina not only told her father about Andreje but also of their forthcoming engagement on New Year's Eve. This doubly surprising news left Wonger almost speechless. He felt disappointed and even betrayed but conceded that his eighteen-year-old daughter had the right to make decisions without his input. He was anxious to meet Andreje.

The New Year's Eve of 1885 would be the beginning of a fairy tale for the young couple. Surrounded by a few friends, distant relatives, and the father of the bride-to-be, Katharina and Andreje celebrated their engagement. It was a small group of people, and the party was not elaborate.

The happy pair made plans for a summer wedding in Vienna. They both wanted their families to be present. Katharina asked Wonger if he could send for her mother and siblings instead of him going to Franzelhütte. Andreje wrote a long letter to his parents in Budapest and invited his entire clan to the wedding. He was hoping that their presence would result in the celebration of some of the old Hungarian wedding customs, particularly the spicy paprika-flavored foods that he missed so dearly.

The wedding date was set for early July. That spring, Katharina kept busy with preparations for her big day. Andreje had spent every free moment with her, as he was about to leave for the Hussars' spring training exercises outside of Vienna.

One day in late May, Wonger, who lived at the court in quarters befitting his title of Three K, was the first to hear about the appalling misfortune of his future son-in-law. Wonger went to see his daughter quite early that morning to bear the grim news of Andreje's fatal accident. During a drill maneuver of Andreje's cavalry unit, his horse unexpectedly reared in terror and threw him. The impact of the bizarre fall caused a broken neck. Field medics transported him to a hospital, but he succumbed to the injury several hours later.

The grieving young woman and her father boarded a train in Vienna. They were en route to Franzelhütte. Katharina had just experienced an unspeakable tragedy in her young life: the heartbreaking loss of her beloved fiancé and the father of her unborn child. Earlier, still in Vienna, she confided to Wonger of her pregnancy and the desire to have the baby in Franzelhütte. Though she had taken into consideration the gossip of an illegitimate child spreading like a wildfire in a community of respectable citizens, she was hoping her family would not judge but support her. On January 31, 1886, Katharina gave birth to a baby girl in house number thirteen and named her Barbara.

Life after Tragedy

It was Wonger's last trip to serve his royal employer in Vienna. He had reached the age of sixty-six, and his accumulated wealth secured a very comfortable living for him and his Nannerl. His children, all grown and accomplished, some more than others, had left home and were scattered between Germany and Austria. The oldest son, Gustel, stepped into his father's footsteps and operated his own business as a wheelwright in Eisendorf. He had married a woman born in Linz, Austria, with a bourgeois mentality and a keen business sense. She demanded to live in a villa, not just a house. A devoted Gustel did not waste much time and contracted with a builder of fine reputation. Regarded as the most grandiose homestead in the region, the Klarer villa stood between Eisendorf and Franzelhütte When Gustel's mother, Nannerl, visited there, she always brought little Barbara along so she could play with her cousins.

Three years had passed since that fateful day in Vienna. Katharina, ready to begin living again, wanted to accompany her father on his final trip to Vienna and pursue her acquired talents as a milliner. Her great-aunt had passed away, and Katharina needed to find a place to stay. Most of her former girlfriends, married and with families, had little or no time for their single friend. Life as she knew it once had changed drastically, but she had confidence in herself. She was grateful to her mother Nannerl, who happily agreed to take care of little Barbara until she was established and was able to deal with the demands of raising the child.

In less than a year, a radiant Katharina attracted the attention of brewery master Fritz Meier, ten years her senior. She married him just six months after their first date. He had been an indulgent bachelor with lots of friends and money to burn. She could not modify his old habits, and the marriage was no match made in heaven. A complacent Katharina accepted her husband's amorous escapades. After their daughter, Luise, was born, Katharina quite often came to visit Franzelhütte. Was her motive to see her "love child," still in the care of her parents, or to find refuge from the unhappy life she had naïvely chosen? Her husband never accompanied her on these visits, and she made artfully attempted but lame excuses for him.

Shortly before Wonger retired, he met the brewery master and was unimpressed by the highfalutin' fellow. He could hardly conceal the disappointment in his daughter's choice of a husband. But then, even Andreje had not met his full approval. Hussars had a reputation for heavy drinking and womanizing, and they were generally not ideal husband material. He never conveyed his skepticism to his daughter since Andreje was young, idealistic, and very attentive toward his daughter. However, Wonger's disdain for Fritz was no easy task for him to keep secret.

Barbara

It was Barbara's fifth birthday. Her mother came from Vienna and brought along her new baby sister, Luise. Barbara knew that Katharina was her mother and referred to her as such. However, her grandparents, Wonger and Nannerl, in whose custody she had grown up so far, were the center of her happy and carefree world. On this visit to Franzelhütte, Katharina hoped to convince her parents, and more so her daughter, to live in Vienna with her. An anxious Barbara clung to her grandparents, and they, too, were of the opinion that the child was better off in Franzelhütte than in a large city like Vienna. Wonger did not mention his dislike for Fritz Meier but implied Katharina's need to provide attention to the new baby, Luise. Over the years, Katharina had two more children, and on every visit to

Franzelhütte it became harder to make her case and take Barbara to Vienna.

Barbara had completed her schooling when she expressed a desire to get to know her half-sister, Luise, and live with her mother in Vienna. From the beginning, she had a dislike for her mother's husband, Fritz Meier. Luise, only nine, and Barbara, a fourteen-year-old teenager, could never quite develop a loving sisterhood nor ignore the fact that they had different fathers. Louise's other two siblings were boys, much younger, and neither girl enjoyed their brothers.

At the advice of Meier, Barbara reluctantly enrolled in a vocational school for secretaries, although her love belonged to klöppel and embroidery, crafts that Nannerl had taught her. She completed one year, but by then she no longer could pretend contentment in the Meier household or her unacquainted ways in the mammoth city. She was homesick for the familiarity and simplicity of Franzelhütte and of her beloved grandparents, Wonger and Nannerl. An unhappy Barbara left Vienna never to return. Shortly after her arrival back home, Wonger died in his sleep; he was eighty-one. Nannerl followed him two years later. Both lay next to each other, buried in the obscure little cemetery nearby Franzelhütte.

After Nannerl's death, Barbara unsuspectingly inherited house number thirteen. Her grandparents willed the house exclusively to her. What a blessing! She had always loved the roomy, well-constructed house with the white stucco façade and red tile roof. Franzelhütte was her home, her security, and she had friends here. Every so often, money arrived from Vienna, and the sale of her lace creations provided enough income to keep her comfortable.

She knew that she had caught the eye of one of the Gerber boys, Joseph, two years older than her. Their romance started at the village well. Barbara, called Wonger Waberl since she was about ten years old, came every morning to draw water for her own consumption and for the small domestic animals that Nannerl had raised. Joseph usually sat waiting on the narrow stone wall surrounding the well, twirling the leftovers of what once looked like a daisy. Passing time, he grabbed another daisy and played a game of *"sie liebt mich—sie liebt mich nicht?"* ("she loves me—she loves me not?") The last petal put his mind at ease, and he patiently awaited her. As she approached, he quickly removed the wooden shoulder carrier from her and mounted it on himself. She didn't mind and attached the filled buckets to the hooks, now dangling on each side of his shoulder. Loaded down, they walked slowly toward her house. He unloaded, and she rewarded him with a dialectal *"Dank Schön"* (thank you) and a bright smile. Eventually, he let her know of his intentions to marry her and his plans for their future. By trade, Joseph was a carpenter, and three of his five brothers made a living as musicians. Like his father, he had a fondness for farming, especially dairy farming.

Joseph Gerber and Barbara Klarer married quietly in 1908. Their combined savings allowed for a notable down payment on some parcels of land and livestock and actualized Joseph's ambition of farming. In 1911, their first child, Julius, called Jule, was born in house number thirteen. One year later another boy, August, or Gustel entered the world in house number thirteen. Franz came along in 1914, the same year WWI started. In 1916, Joseph, named after his father but shortened to Seph, opened his eyes in house number thirteen. Shortly after Seph's birth, Joseph decided to enlist in the Austro-Hungarian military service, a sure source of income for his now struggling family. The monarchy needed soldiers, especially since Italy had declared war on the Habsburgs in 1915. After training in alpine warfare, he joined a mountaineer troop at the border of Austria and Italy in the Tyrolean Alps. The Italian army had provoked several battles in the area to regain the land that once belonged to Italy but had since been under Habsburg control. During a reconnaissance patrol, Joseph and his group walked into a waiting ambush. He tried to escape, but a bullet in the back killed him instantly. The news of her husband's fate in the Dolomite Alps of Tyrol devastated Barbara. She never imagined being a widow at age thirty.

Johann Gerber, the four-years-younger brother of Joseph, had just become engaged to a girl in Schönsee, a larger village close to Franzelhütte, on the German side. Besides helping on his father's farm, he found employment as a forest worker in Baron von Kotz's private forest holdings. Johann, the good brother that he was, had made a pledge to the worried Joseph before he departed for his military enlistment. In the event that something should befall Joseph, Johann would see to and take care of Wonger Waberl and the four boys. Johann Gerber's plans for his future changed in an instant when the sad news of his brother reached Franzelhütte. Time had come for him to put his own life on hold and make good on his promise.

After an appropriate mourning period, Johann approached Barbara and told her of his solemn promise to his deceased brother. She had known Johann all her life and liked all the Gerber boys, but she had married the one she loved. Yet she needed help with the farm and the children, and so she gratefully accepted his offer. In time, she became quite fond of Johann, a quiet, unselfish man and married him. They had two children, the girls Maria and Klara, born like their brothers in house number thirteen. Johann was a loving father to the girls and to "his boys," as he called them. For many years, the boys did not know that Johann was not their biological father; only Jule had faint memories of his real father. It came out when Seph entered the university in Prague and had to present a birth certificate on which his father was listed as Joseph Gerber. Seph told the registrar that there was an error with his father's name. The correct name, he confidently announced, was Johann Gerber. He could not understand such an error, but his mother finally revealed the true story to him and his siblings. The boys loved and respected Johann and were proud to have a man like him as their father.

6

Expellees and Refugees

❧❧❧❧

Welcome to the American Zone

Our train had the look of an ordinary long freight train, except its cargo was hundreds of expellees from the Sudetenland. The steaming and hissing locomotive pulled into the train station of Furth im Wald, a small town in Bavaria less than seven miles from the Czech border. We had arrived in one of many transit camps in the American zone. Red Cross and Caritas (a Catholic help organization) representatives approached the long train and tried in vain to organize the short walk to the camp.

Motivating hundreds of distraught people who were torn just two days earlier from their homes and their land proved to be no easy task. When we reached a fenced area with many wooden barracks, we assumed that it was a transit camp. A line formed quickly to the barrack with toilets and decent wash facilities. Finally, hot meals were distributed. After embracing those basic needs, the US military personnel took charge. "Denazification" was their first order. Adults had to give sworn statements by filling out a form detailing his or her past, specifically pertaining to the Nazi era. Untruthful, misleading, or withheld pertinent information was punishable with jail time, the form indicated in bold print. My grandparents and aunt, who had simplicity and honesty written all over them, obtained exoneration on the spot. Some people expressed verbal dissatisfaction about their transfer to a detainment center. Others received a notice to show up in civilian court later. After we had completed many forms and were fingerprinted for some sort of ID card, a medical team took over. Everyone, including children and babies, had to undergo delousing with DDT powder as well as a physical examination.

A camp hospital took in the sick and injured people. Our assigned barrack housed processed refugees only, and we would stay for one night. The wood barracks seemed clean and at least had cots with a thin mattress to sleep on instead of a hard floor. These plain accommodations were surely an improvement, considering the pitiable conditions of the last two days.

The next morning, after a plentiful breakfast, we heard our names called; we were kindly ordered to take our belongings and board the same smelly train again. Still being, as they were, in a state of limbo, people followed orders without raising questions as to where this train will take us. Several Red Cross workers accompanied the train, bringing along food and water. The train traveled faster now, and after a few hours, a large sign announced Nürnberg *Hauptbahnhof* (central train station). We passed heaps and heaps of rubble and found out later that Allied bombardments had destroyed the entire inner city of Nürnberg. Everyone had to get off the train, use the restrooms, and make their way inside the mainly demolished station hall where some food was distributed.

When we got back to our boxcar, the train had shortened considerably. For the first time an official informed us that one-half of the train was routed to Augsburg and the other half to Hockenheim. We belonged to the Hockenheim group. Aunt Klara mentioned that she had been in Augsburg once, during her working days in Munich, and she liked the city. People there spoke the same dialect as ours. She wished we were on the train to Augsburg.

But where was Hockenheim? The people in our car, now a different group, had never heard of that place either. What was awaiting us there? A million questions rushed through the air, with only speculations for answers. After leaving Nürnberg, the train did not stop until the sign read Heilbronn–Hauptbahnhof. We did not know it, but we had entered our last phase of the trip that had started in Furth im Wald early that day. The train traveled very quickly through the countryside, and the further west we went, the more destruction caused by the war became visible.

Someone standing near the slider door yelled that he had seen a sign that said Hockenheim. The train started to reduce its speed, driving slowly into the small Bahnhof with a one-room station office. There was not a soul in sight, not even a signalman. Perhaps ours was the last train of the day, we mused; it was evening, after all. We unloaded our possessions. The escorts, in an almost whispering tone, encouraged us to make a formation as we walked away from the station. Dreary streetlights provided some sense of life; otherwise, the town appeared rather inanimate. Finally, we stopped at a granite rock structure, an old, unused school building that had served as a collecting point for Poles during the war. After the war, it became a center for refugees, expellees, or displaced persons, as we thousands were. Inside, large whitewashed halls with lots of windows and long rows of iron bunk beds gave the impression of a hospital ward. An attendant announced that we had two options: two to a bed or one of us on the hard floor. We knew that Hockenheim was a temporary shelter for all of us.

A new day, July 19, 1946, dawned. Three days had passed since Czech soldiers forced us to leave Franzelhütte. Traveling west three hundred miles, we had arrived in the *Bundesland* (province) Baden-Württemberg, Germany, and, by extension, the American zone of occupation. Hockenheim, a small town of nine thousand people near the Rhein River, also served as a transit camp. The US military oversaw camp operations administratively and provided most of the food rations for the refugees. The powdered eggs and milk, the cans of potato and tomato soups, and the sweet potatoes left a lasting and disgusting taste in my mouth. (To this day, I have a dislike for canned foods, especially soups.)

Aunt Klara temporarily landed a part-time job in the camp kindergarten, where she was paid in cookies instead of money. I no longer ate the awful camp food but waited for her by the gate to be first to get my hands on those cookies. Yes, I was hungry. One day, freshly baked German bread and *Schwartenmagen* (headcheese) arrived—and plenty of it. It was the happiest event during our dismal stay in Hockenheim. We had been discouraged from leaving the school grounds for fear of angry townspeople. They were unhappy with this constant influx of refugees into their quiet little town. Like all refugees, my grandparents had no money, and sightseeing was the furthest thought in their minds. After three weeks in Hockenheim, a few families, us included, were loaded into army trucks with our bundles and suitcases. We were on our way to our final destination: a village called Neibsheim, in the county of Bruchsal, in the Bundesland Baden-Württemberg.

A Reception to Remember

When our two trucks rolled into Neibsheim, people came out of their houses and lined the cobblestoned main street. At first we took their gesture as a sign of welcome. A closer study revealed grim, angry faces with "unwanted, unwelcome" written all over them. The trucks stopped in the middle of the village by the small square, where the schoolhouse and the *Rathaus* (town hall) stood next to each other. As we unloaded our belongings for the umpteenth time, the good citizens of Neibsheim formed a circle around us. From the top of their lungs, they hollered insults like *"Gesindel, Zigeuner"* ("riffraff, gypsies") and "Go back where you came from, you thieves." We were the bad Nazis who caused the demise of their Germany. Eventually, the *Bürgermeister* (mayor), *Herr* (Mr.) Göpfrich appeared and interrupted the mob-like behavior. He told them to go home and make room in their homes, for these newcomers will be placed there—like it or not. He continued, "These people are just the first batch; there are more to follow." In a soft-spoken voice, he explained to us that for the next few days, we were to stay in the temporarily vacant school building, and he apologized for the inadequate arrangement. With the help of men in our group, he set up a tent. He and his wife brought several large pots of hot, milky soup and bread from across the street, where they lived.

After one week of camping inside the schoolhouse during the night and waiting, languishing and hungry, under the tent during the day, some of the refugees—my grandmother included—had enough of this humiliation. They walked next door to the Rathaus, where the Bürgermeister worked a few hours in his office in the morning. They demanded a change in living conditions and adequate food. They insisted on milk, butter, and eggs, at least for the children. Herr Göpfrich knew, as the Bürgermeister, that he had a duty to comply with the Commission for Refugees in Bruchsal, an agency under the direction of the American military command of Baden-Württemberg. He personally had the best of intentions and a great deal of compassion, but the citizens of his community did not share in them. The refugees and the Bürgermeister, a farmer himself, came to the agreement that they would work for the farmers to bring in the harvest in exchange for food and shelter. That suggestion found some appeal, particularly with the Neibsheim farmers whose sons or husbands did not return from the war or were still POWs.

Lucky for us Gerbers, the Bürgermeister took us in and provided a clean room on the second floor of his house for the four of us. The room had two beds with bulky straw mattresses, a table and four chairs, and a *Schrank* (wardrobe). In one corner stood a wash basin, and nearby sat a small stove with a long black stovepipe. The windows, adorned by white tulle curtains, gave an inviting appearance to the space, and we were most appreciative to have landed in the house of very decent people.

Coping with Refugees

When we arrived in Neibsheim in early August of 1946, the village, surrounded by lush green hills, had a population of less than nine hundred people. It was a farm community where most houses connected to each other. Behind big wooden doors were the stables and a courtyard, where a smelly *Misthaufen* (dunghill) or a liquid manure pit could certainly provoke the olfactory nerves on warm summer days. Otherwise, the village appeared clean and tidy. Its citizenry had been spared from air attacks during the war. A small creek, Talbach, wiggled its way through the village past both mills—the upper and the lower mill. The Catholic church of

St. Mauritius, a tall baroque structure built in 1791–92 and the only church in the village, played an important part in the daily life of Neibsheimers. Besides two grocery stores—one was a combination of general store and post office—the village had two bakeries and one butcher shop.

Neibsheim also hailed its four *Gasthäuser* (taverns). There the locals met for an evening *Schoppen* (half pint), dancing on weekends and to celebrate the win or mourn the loss of the F.C. Neibsheim Fussball Verein (soccer club), the pride and joy of this tight-knit community. They were devout Catholics, good Samaritans to each other, and preferred to marry within the village boundaries, as was evident in the dominance of the surnames Hauck, Frank, Gerweck, Strobel, and Martin. An outsider had little chance of becoming "one of them" unless he or she brought along a respectable dowry and, of course, the right religion. Therefore, when the refugees interrupted their perfect Eden, the Neibsheimers retaliated with hostility to the invaders, the *Flüchtlingesindel* (refugee riffraff).

Aunt Klara and my grandfather worked with Herr Göpfrich and his daughter, Maria, to bring in the harvest from his wheat fields. Herr Göpfrich had reason to be late this year. There was the problem of uncooperative weather and the mental anguish over the death of his only son, killed in action at the end of the war in 1945. *Frau* (Mrs.) Göpfrich, like my grandmother, wore only black, and her sad eyes always looked red and puffy in her otherwise pretty face. She was a quiet and very religious woman who attended mass every morning at 6:30 a.m.

Oma helped Frau Göpfrich with all household chores and in the preparation of the daily midday meal. At noon, the two women, with me tagging along, delivered a hot meal with loaves of bread and the common drink *Most* (fermented cider) to the workers in the field. After a moment of prayer, we all sat in a circle and silently tucked into the hearty meal. By now, I ate any food handed to me and no longer made a fuss.

New Beginnings

On September 2, 1946, for the first time since the end of the war in May 1945, schools all over Germany went into session. It was my first day of school, and I was unexcited. Oma fixed my hair and braided it into the usual two short tails with a ribbon on each end. All summer long I had walked barefoot, but the school required shoes when coming to class. My only pair, the old, shabby black boots, a size too small and hurting, had to do for now. I had outgrown most of the clothing from the little suitcase; nonetheless, I wore one of my old dresses, too short and too snug on me. Oma said, "You look pretty." She reminded me to take along my small blackboard with the Griffel. She also emphasized holding the Griffel in my right hand only, as we had practiced, and to forget that I even had a left hand. To her, lefties were weird, peculiar people; they didn't exist in her family.

Oma and I walked across the street to the yellow schoolhouse. Less than a month before, we had spent a week sleeping on the floor of these classrooms, sharing one sink and one toilet with twenty people. Now the walls had a coat of fresh white paint and the wood floors were newly oiled. Mr. Ruf, the principal, introduced himself and asked for my name. I overheard the conversation my grandmother and Mr. Ruf had about my situation. It stirred my memory, and I started to cry. Suddenly, someone took my hand and said, "I am Mr. Osang, your first-grade teacher, and I have been waiting for you." I have only a vague recollection of that first school day, but I told Oma, "I did not like it."

More refugees arrived in Neibsheim, much to the chagrin of the locals. There was a group of Sudeten Germans from Moravia, but the majority came from the southeastern parts of Europe, countries like Hungary and Yugoslavia. For months, they had been in German refugee camps in an overcrowded British zone. Through humanitarian relief efforts, the American zone granted them acceptance.

My first-grade class kept on increasing, and I started to make friends with other refugee girls. The children of locals followed their parents' lead and stayed within their own group. They referred to us as "filthy *Flüchtling*." Mr. Osang, our teacher, had lost his home during the destructive air bombardment of Bruchsal and could better sympathize with the plight of refugees. He did not tolerate the word "Flüchtling" in his class. He seated us alphabetically by last name, regardless of gender or ethnic roots. That arrangement assured me a seat in the back of the classroom, since my last name started with a V.

First grade had no appeal to me, and I did rather poorly. I had a mental block, or perhaps I simply did not care to deal with numbers. Most of my answers in arithmetic, when questioned by Mr. Osang or my family, were reliably incorrect. This frustrated my grandmother to no avail. She would lament, "How can that be? This child, half a Gerber, cannot solve simple problems. It must be the Veit side that has impaired her learning ability." If my father could have heard such aspersions, it would have led to a huge family conflict. Those comments reminded me of my parents' absence. I kept on needling Oma and Aunt Klara about their whereabouts, my mother's in particular. Realizing that I was getting older, they spoke more freely on the subject and what to do.

Aunt Klara had an idea. She wrote a letter to her brother Gustel in Neunburg vorm Wald, Bavaria, where he and Linde had lived since their marriage in 1942. She informed him of our expulsion from Franzelhütte and our present location and family situation. She indicated that the whereabouts of Mitzi and Rudi were unknown and was hoping that Gustel might have heard from them. In the fall of 1946, the postal system was still in a state of havoc. Under the censorship of the Allied occupiers, it was extremely difficult to send mail from one occupied zone to another. However, Gustel, like us, lived in the American zone, and the letter, Klara felt, should get there—it was just a question of when. Mail service had low priority within all zones.

In early December, Irma Hauck, the postmistress, delivered a letter from Gustel and Linde. The opened letter invoked hopeful excitement. Unfortunately, Gustel had no news about my parents. He was aware of the Sudetengerman expulsion and assumed that all Böhmerwald people were deported to Bavaria; thus he was surprised to hear that we ended up near the Rhein River, so far west. Oma was glad to read of her son's well-being but saddened not to hear a sign of life from Mitzi.

Black-Market Days

Food was perpetually in short supply. Meanwhile, the official currency, the Reichsmark, gradually became worthless. An underground economy began to flourish. Neibsheim farmers bartered away flour, butter, eggs, cured meats, and sausages. In exchange, they requested cigarettes (preferably American-made), coffee beans, chocolate bars, silk stockings, and even fur coats. Many peddlers came on bicycles from the surrounding cities of Bruchsal, Karlsruhe, and Heidelberg. Impatient farm wives proudly wore those fur coats to church on Sunday, long before the weather justified such attire. Some parishioners frowned on the ostentatious acquisitions, and in hushed whispers they guessed how many sacks of flour the husband had to trade for the furry critter skins.

After the harvest was in, the Allied Control Council (governors of the four zones) required farmers to render a certain portion of their gathered crops. In exchange for grains, potatoes, and sugar beets, they received seed, coal, or light farm machinery. Farmers in Baden-Württemberg experienced a bad crop in 1946 due to unusual weather conditions. Nevertheless, the two mills in Neibsheim had plenty of business grinding grains into many sacks of flour, and the illegal black market flourished.

Every so often, a US military truck came to the little village square. The two drivers unloaded boxes of food for refugees initiated by the CARE program of the United States. The Bürgermeister took charge of dispensing these parcels in a fair and prompt manner. We children excitedly hung around the truck, just waiting for the *"Amis,"* as we called them, to hand out chewing gum. They were always nice to us kids, even though we could not understand a word they were saying, except "okay."

On one occasion, the Amis delivered boxes of clothing and shoes. Everyone, including the locals, had clothing allowance cards and could make a written request for these items. I finally got a pair of new shoes, brown oxfords with insoles as filler. They were one size larger than I needed, but shoes had to last for two years; that was the rule. Besides the oxfords, I received a winter coat and a dress not quite my size yet; but I would eventually grow into it, I was told.

The Göpfrich farm had horses and only a few dairy cows. Aunt Klara milked them in the morning and evening and kept the stables and animals clean. She worked for another farmer doing the same job, and he paid her sparingly with flour, lard, and molasses. The Bürgermeister quickly realized how handy and hardworking my family was in the fields and around the farm. He was favorably impressed by my grandfather's knowledge in the forestry branch. He mentioned to Opa a possible job as a forest caretaker, if the authorities in Bruchsal would approve his request. My otherwise quiet Opa could hardly contain his excitement at such an offer. Meanwhile, he replenished the Göpfrichs' firewood supply. For several weeks, he was cutting timber, splitting it, and stacking it in their woodshed. Mr. Göpfrich allowed him to take some for his own use. Winter having arrived early, we were happy to enjoy the warmth of a glowing fire in our stove.

A Flüchtling Christmas

It was our first Christmas in Neibsheim. The ground had a thick cover of snow—perfect for sledding, I thought. School was out for the holidays, and I brought home my first report card. Nobody exclaimed with oohs or aahs, but Oma seemed surprised and pleased about the two *Einser* (As) I had earned.

Farmer Hauck wished Aunt Klara a merry Christmas and handed her five homemade sausages for diligently milking his cows in the last five months. Oma boiled some shriveled potatoes salvaged from the potato fields after the harvest was in, the farmer having given his permission. Without thinking of traditions, we silently feasted on sausage and fried potatoes for our Christmas Eve dinner. For dessert, Oma took the most rotten apples and pears, removed the bad parts, added water and molasses—sugar was not available—and boiled them to a mash. Those fruits we had picked up from the ground back in September, with the permission of the owner of the trees.

We had neither a Christmas tree nor presents. I just knew that Christkindl could not find us due to all the commotion of moving and being Flüchtling. Oma could not hide her melancholy this Christmas Eve in 1946 and kept repeating the question: "What have we done to be chased from our Heimat? What have we done to deserve this misery?" Aunt Klara, teary-eyed, chimed in, bemoaning the loss of Pompern and Rex and contemplating the fate of the animals left behind. I mentioned Schnuri as well as my chick with the red dot and the old tomcat, Wotan, while Opa wondered where the rest of his family might be. He found it odd that another Gerber family from Franzelhütte, not related to him, ended up in Neibsheim.

Everybody in the room was so lost in thought that we almost missed the knock at the door. Frau Göpfrich and Maria stood there holding a big basket decorated with fir branches. Its contents consisted of dairy and meat products, including a piece of pork meat for a Christmas roast and a little bag of hard candy for me. Maria handed my aunt a coat, a knitted hat, and gloves, apologizing that these items were not new, having been worn by her. My appreciative aunt cried and laughed all at the same time. Oma, touched by this generosity, called my name, and said, "Erikale, Christkindl did find us."

Maria Göpfrich, the nineteen-year-old daughter of the Bürgermeister, was a fine catch for any respectable Neibsheim lad. She possessed beauty and poise and would eventually inherit a good-sized farm. Her family had influence, and her father's brother was the longtime priest of Neibsheim's Catholic Church, St. Mauritius. That alone carried status in a community as devout as this village.

A year and a half had passed since Maria's own brother had met his fate on a battlefield. In those days, the typical mourning period lasted one year. Mourning involved wearing black and avoiding participation in public events. Maria invited Aunt Klara to join her for a big New Year's Eve dance at the Gasthaus Zur Rose. Reluctantly Aunt Klara accepted, and an excited Maria pulled her by the arm out the door and assured her safety and fun. They had a blast ringing in the New Year of 1947. Both women happily danced the night away. When it was time to go home, the two young men who were always nearby to ask for the next dance when the music started accompanied them home to the Göpfrich house. The clock showed 3:00 a.m. Oma had waited up for her twenty-five-year-old daughter and chided her for the late hour.

Rendezvous in the Courtyard

After two weeks of Christmas holidays, school started again the second week in January. My first-grade class had now forty-six students, a few more than before Christmas vacation. The principal added more school benches. The room was wall-to-wall with desks, and Mr. Osang had to squeeze sideways to get through the rows.

Each desk accommodated two students, with one inkpot holder to share. Underneath the slanted desktop there was a storage shelf for books and personal items.

The calendar in our classroom had a circle around January 16 with my name written underneath the date. Our teacher marked the birthdays of all the kids in class. I turned seven on that January day. Apparently it was an uneventful day, since I have no recollection of it. In later years, Oma would reflect back on those years and reiterate how destitute we really were. At the same time, she assured me that she and my aunt did bake a meager *Streuselkuchen* (crumb cake) for my seventh birthday, using lard and leftover molasses.

One day, Maria excitedly told Aunt Klara that her father had arranged for a small room in the Westermanns' house where Klara and I could stay and sleep in our own bed. Oma and Opa would have their own bed as well, since those beds were single-size only. Aunt Klara liked the idea a lot, but it did not appeal to me. It meant I had to sleep by myself … but my opinion did not count.

We moved our few belongings to the house around the corner from the Göpfrich home, across from the Talbach creek. The Westermanns, also farmers, lived in a big old farmhouse with a huge rounded door, wide enough for wagons and horses to come through into the sprawling courtyard. They already provided quarters for a Flüchtling family of six from Yugoslavia. However, as a personal favor to the Bürgermeister, they could do without the room once used for storage. The room was long and narrow, and a small wood stove sat in the corner next to the door. Two cots stood along the wall, and a small round table with one chair barely fit underneath the curtain-less window facing Main Street.

Sometimes a young man by the name of Yani came visiting on a Saturday evening. He and Aunt Klara sat on her cot talking and laughing together. She had taught me some silhouette clip art, and it was one of my favorite pastimes. I entertained myself while she had a visitor. Aunt Klara made sure I had plenty of paper, the brown-paper-bag type, and a borrowed pair of scissors. After Yani left, she always seemed very happy. She asked me not to mention Yani's name to Oma, nor that he come to visit here. I loved my aunt and my Oma but promised Aunt Klara that I would not tell Oma, or anyone, and it was to be our secret. However, I wanted to know why. She explained in simple terms that Yani was her friend and, like us, a Flüchtling from Hungary. Oma did not like Hungarians, and she did not know the reason.

I was too young to understand the meaning of romance, but I was curious and kept my ears perked when the adults quietly talked or whispered to each other. Yani came to visit more frequently. Sometimes late in the evenings, Maria and Yani's friend, Alexe, showed up as well. The four of them would leave the room and sit on the bench in the dark courtyard. Aunt Klara knew I was perpetually scared of the dark and of being alone. She left the dim room light on, did not close the door all the way, and assured me that she was just outside the door. These secretive gatherings in the secluded courtyard lasted for several weeks.

One evening, Maria stopped by and told Klara that she would not meet Alexe anymore. Her parents had found out about her and Alexe's *tête-à-tête*, most likely through the ever-nosy Mrs. Westerman, our landlady. Besides, Erich Strobel, a twenty-four-year-old bank clerk and only son of the Strobel farm, had returned from a POW camp in France. Maria confided in Klara that she had had a crush on Erich since she was fifteen. Recently he had stopped by her house and invited her for the upcoming First of May celebration picnic. It would please her parents immensely if she and Erich could build a future together. After all, he would inherit a respectable-sized farm, was nice looking, and was a local. Maria left before Aunt Klara had a chance to even congratulate her.

Easter Service and a Venerable Procession

In 1947, signs of spring, after a long harsh winter, brought a welcome change. Farmers once again tended to their fields, and the still impoverished refugees willingly provided cheap labor. It was hard physical work from early in the morning until dusk, hoeing and operating manual farm machinery pulled by horses, oxen, or cows. Opa and Aunt Klara worked for the Göpfrichs or whoever requested their help, and they earned enough food to feed the four of us. Oma had turned sixty-one the past January. The varicose veins in her legs gave her major problems, and she needed to be off her feet. She was glad to have brought the yarns and her Klöppelsack, adorned with hundreds of colored pinheads, all the way from Franzelhütte. Oma was ready to return to lace making. When Mrs. Göpfrich saw Oma klöppel for the first time, she kept staring at her hands in fascination. She had never seen this type of handicraft and praised Oma for her skill of a most remarkable lace creation.

Another important holiday was before us—*Ostern* (Easter). Christmas, Easter, and Pentecost are two-day holidays. In addition, school closed for two weeks, and I could have not been happier. Oma made some alterations to my dresses by lengthening or widening a seam, whenever she found enough inseam. Between her and *Tante* (Aunt), they unraveled the wool of my outgrown sweaters and knitted a larger one.

Easter Sunday, Tante rose early and encouraged me to get up. For the first time since our arrival in Neibsheim, we would attend a high mass at St. Mauritius church. I put on the remodeled outfit and my freshly cleaned oxford shoes. Tante braided ribbons into my hair and readied herself putting on the one dress she always wore for special occasions. We walked to my grandparents, and I was curious whether the Easter bunny had left something for me. Indeed he had. To my delight, I found three faintly colored eggs on a plate lined with fresh-smelling grass and a small bar of chocolate. Years later, I found out from Oma that she acquired the chocolate from a black marketeer in exchange for a klöppel lace doily.

The bells of St. Mauritius chimed for worship on this Easter Sunday, and the three of us slowly made our way toward the church. Opa decided not to join but took a walk in the forest instead. When we stepped into the big ornate but rather cool church with beautiful stained glass windows, a bland-smiling church elder decisively pointed us to a pew in the back. It was the darkest part of the church, where the overhang to the choir balcony obstructed the influx of light. We joined other Flüchtling families already sitting there.

The service started with a grand entrance of Father Göpfrich. Following him came two additional priests, all in ceremonial white robes, and eight altar boys, each holding a tall, flaming candle. The Mass was read in Latin. A pipe organ created rich sounds, vibrantly resounding in the large church, and an impressive choir complemented the festive Easter worship service. After mass, the congregation gathered in the park-like garden adjacent to the church, and the priests wished everyone *"Frohe Ostern"* (Happy Easter) and shook hands. Oma did not want to mingle with the crowd. As we were leaving, Father Göpfrich, who knew me from catechism class in school, called my name and said, "I am glad you came to church today with your family, and I hope to see all of you again." Oma took this opportunity and expressed her displeasure in having to sit in the back of the church. She told him that she felt like a leper and that where she came from, the church accepted all people equally, and seating was a matter of individual choice. The priest listened and assured her that he was of the same belief and would speak with the overzealous elder. Future attendance revealed the priest's sincerity, and we could choose where to sit.

Fronleichnam (Feast of Corpus Christi) is one of the Catholic holidays honoring the Eucharist. It is always on a Thursday, some sixty days after Easter. In Neibsheim, this feast enjoyed a popular tradition. Every house participated by decorating its front façade with flower garlands and its windows with statues of saints flanked by greenery and burning candles. A procession started at the church. Girls in white dresses carried baskets filled with roses. They cast petals in front of the priest who walked ceremoniously under an embroidered canopy, holding up a monstrance with the consecrated Host showing through the glass. Acolytes swinging censers with incense, nuns in their habits, seminarians, and important locals made up the rest of the formal parade. It proceeded down on Main Street, where beautiful fresh flower carpets with clever designs of religious motifs lay on the cobblestone. Only the Holy Host carrier could step on them. Bystanders crossed themselves and knelt as the Host passed by them. The procession stopped at all three for-the-occasion-built altars, and the priest read intercession prayers and administered blessings. Before reaching the village square, the parade turned into a side street for a final stop. There, by the tall sandstone cross with a beautiful Pieta, Father Göpfrich read mass. He thanked the villagers for their tremendous efforts, enthusiasm, and creation of such ingenious flower arrangements. Memories of this religious event in Neibsheim have stayed with me throughout the years.

Lice and Good News

July came in a hurry, and school let out for summer vacation. I had completed first grade. My report card showed improvement, and I was quite proud to get a promotion to second grade. Oma laughed and said, "I did not expect any less than for you to advance; after all, you inherited the Gerber smarts." But I had also brought home something less welcome than my sudden braininess: lice, most likely from school. Everyone was aghast and had different ideas of how to get rid of the parasites infested on my head. Mr. Osang, my teacher, who was quite familiar with the pest, gave Oma a repellant powder to strew in my hair. It eliminated the lice quickly, but the nits (the eggs of lice) hung on, and their yellow-brown color blended perfectly with my hair color. Oma washed my hair, applied the powder, and searched my scalp for two weeks daily. Finally I was rid of the vermin. That summer, while being deloused, I developed a real interest in reading and wore out the one storybook I possessed.

Someone from the Hauck's makeshift post office delivered a letter addressed to my grandparents. Oma recognized the writing and knew instantly that it was from my parents. She read the letter for the second time, and tears of happiness rolled down her face. I was happy, too, but had to digest what she was reading. The letter said that my parents lived in a city called Oschersleben in the Russian-occupied zone of Germany. *Onkel* (Uncle) Veit and Tante Resi were there as well. My father was trying to find a way to visit Neibsheim, but it was difficult to receive permission from the Russian authorities to visit another zone in Germany. My mother wrote that she missed me endlessly and could not wait to see how tall I had grown. For once, I was wishing for school to be in session. I wanted to tell Mr. Osang and my classmates that my parents found me through my Uncle Gustel and that they would come soon and get me. I was excited and could hardly wait for Aunt Klara and Opa to come home from the fields. I had waited for this moment for a long time.

Every day I was asking someone in my family about my parents' coming, and I always received the same answer: "Be patient." Since the letter arrived, I thought of them all the time and tried to picture the three of us together. Although I could not quite recall my father's demeanor, I had a vivid remembrance of my mother. Two years had passed since I had last seen my parents. The photograph that I had brought with me from Komotau confirmed a better memory of my mother. With my lack of understanding of all these zones, I asked if they were the reason for the delay of my parents' coming.

In 1947, relentless hot July temperatures of 40 C (104 F) broke all records. The Talbach creek, a favorite hangout for kids to wade in or jump in from rock to rock, had dried and shriveled up from the heat. The only place to get some relief from the heat was the forest. Oma's swollen legs could not walk that far. It was too hot to play outside, and the sweltering heat kept the streets deserted. I stayed with her in the one room, shaded by the wooden shutters. She usually loosened her braid, and I combed her gray, thick hair that almost reached to her buttocks. She liked my fingers working in her hair, and I was pleased to try out my newly learned braiding techniques on her. During those sultry afternoons, she told me many stories about the Franzelhütte, her mother, and her grandparents who raised her. Here with me, she could give vent to her homesickness.

An Unexpected Visitor

One evening in early August, Maria brought a visitor upstairs. Oma, stunned and staring at the man in the doorway, shouted, "Jesus, Maria, und Joseph, it's you!" It was my father, and, for a moment, it seemed as if a ghost had appeared and struck us motionless. He walked toward me, extended his hands, and said, "Erika, I am your Papa." He did not resemble much the man in my mind, who had a mustache and a face without hollow cheeks. Not sure what to do, I gave him my hand, curtseyed, and smiled. I felt a distance between this stranger and my imagination. Aunt Klara hugged him, invited him to sit down, and inquired if he wanted something to eat. Indeed, he was hungry, and Oma served what little food she had available. He had been traveling all day and was visibly tired. That did not stop Oma from bombarding him with questions covering the more than two-year period of our separation. I interjected and needed to know why my Mutti did not come. He realized my disappointment and reassured me that my mother very much wanted to come but emphasized the complications and dangers of this trip. It was their plan to leave Oschersleben and for us to be together. First he had to find us in Neibsheim and secure permission to move here. All that talk made some sense, even to my naïve thinking, and his simple explanations broke the ice between us.

My father stayed for two days. Aunt Klara and I walked him to the Gondelsheim train station, a two-mile walk. Neibsheim had no rail connection. He and I had made up for lost time, and I was sad to see him leave. I knew in my heart that he, my mother, and I would soon be together. Our good relationship with the Göpfrichs, their compassion for people, and the Bürgermeister's willingness to bypass inconsequential regulations made it possible for my father to obtain the much-needed authorization for my parents to relocate to Neibsheim. My entire family never forgot the many good deeds the Göpfrichs facilitated in a time of exigency.

In 2007, my husband and I visited seventy-eight-year-old Maria in Neibsheim. She still lived in her parents' house upstairs, now remodeled and nicely updated. During this nostalgic visit, she brought out a small "Poesy Album," where my parents, Aunt Klara, and I had all made an entry and dedicated a poem to her. The date of my inscription showed December 1947, and I was amazed at the neat cursive script written in blue ink. I did not remember Maria asking me to write a dedication, but she certainly had the proof and was proud to share it with me, exactly sixty years later.

> *ROSEN, TULPEN, NELKEN*
> *ALLE BLUMEN WELKEN*
> *NUR DIE EINE NICHT*
> *UND SIE HEISST*
> *VERGISSMEINNICHT*

The poem's verse about roses, tulips, and carnations ended rhyming with the little flower *"Vergissmeinnicht"*—"forget-me-not"— how congruous.

Red Tape

During my father's short stay, I heard him tell of the complexity in traveling to Neibsheim. Living in the province of Saxony-Anhalt in the Russian-occupied zone was like an internment in one big gulag.

After the war, with Germany divided into four zones, the Russians in charge of the Russian zone encouraged the German expellees to leave and find residence in other Allied zones. Over two million people did just that. The Russian dictator, Stalin, schemed to convert his assigned part of Germany into an extension of Russia and relocate Russian citizens to Germany. When that plan failed, due to strong Allied rejection and disagreement, the Russians decided to isolate their zone in 1947. They installed armed guards at the shared borders with the British and American zones. People could no longer move freely, even within their zone, and had to endure a system that took control over their lives, provided little food, and imposed communist ideologies.

After the expulsion from the Sudetenland, my parents ended up in Oschersleben, a city very close to the British zone. My father found a less-staffed zone crossing where he was able to slide in and out of the two zones. He applied for permission to enter the overburdened British zone but was denied. However, luck was on his side when he coincidentally ran into an old army buddy who had also served in Normandy. He lived in Braunschweig, the largest city in the British zone, and held an important position with the Flüchtling commission. He helped my father obtain a permit to the British zone and offered his personal address for correspondence purposes to Gustel and us in the American zone. Once my father had legal access to the British zone, he could travel to the American zone without restrictions. The Americans and Brits came to an agreement on January 1, 1947, to merge their zones (bizones), eliminating unnecessary red tape and making it easier for people to travel.

Free School Meal

With the new school year beginning September 1947, the Americans launched a new program, called *Schulspeisung* (school meal). A doctor from Bruchsal came to Neibsheim and examined all school children. Based on his findings, he decided who was a candidate for the free meal. All the Flüchtling children qualified, me included, since malnutrition was a common problem among refugees. The Schulspeisung provided an additional 350 calories per day in form of semolina pudding, porridge, succotash, or minestrone soups and milk.

Every school day, at 10:30 a.m., when the big break began, two women from the church rectory pulled a handcart with containers of steaming food into our schoolyard. We kids had to bring a tin and a spoon. Most days there was ample food, and the local kids helped devour the leftovers. On special occasions, we received a biscuit, peanuts, and chocolate. Mr. Osang divided the three bars of chocolate among all students in the class, and each got a tiny piece, the size of a Domino tile. Peanuts were most foreign to us, but we all seemed to like the six peanuts counted out to each child. Our teacher auctioned off the empty peanut can based on good behavior. For quite a few children, the Schulspeisung was their only decent meal a day.

Best Friends

Also in September 1947, I started second grade, and Mr. Osang was my teacher once more. Writing paper was as scarce as food and fuel. We used our slate blackboards again. However, each student received one very thin exercise booklet for learning to write with ink and a pen. Certain textbooks were not available. The American command did not authorize schoolbooks used before the end of the war, and new ones were readied for print. My attitude toward school had improved considerably, and I had good reasons to be happy. We received a letter from my parents indicating an estimated arrival date of early November, provided they did not encounter unforeseen obstacles leaving the Russian zone. Filled with excitement to see my mother, I imagined ways to welcome her properly.

Kati Selthofer, a Flüchtling girl from Yugoslavia, was my best friend and desk partner in school. One day, her large extended family left Neibsheim for a new country—Australia. The truck loaded with the Selthofers slowly drove down Main Street out of Neibsheim. Kati vigorously waved her hand and called my name. I ran behind the truck to the end of the village, and so did other kids. Then the vehicle accelerated and took off. Kati's hand waved for another moment, and then she disappeared into the distance. Her moving away made me very sad. I went home and cried. I never heard from her again, but that doleful scene on a September afternoon left a lasting impression on my shattered mind.

I looked for another best friend and quickly found one in Gretel Pechtl. Gretel was born in Franzelhütte. Her mother was born a Gerber before she married Mr. Pechtel, but there was no relationship between those Gerbers and our Gerbers. Mrs. Pechtl, her siblings, and their families, including their widowed mother, the old Mrs. Gerber, were the other families from Franzelhütte besides us. Before the expulsion, the two Gerber families had little contact with each other. I knew of them only because the Gerbers' big house was also the schoolhouse in Franzelhütte. My mother took me there once, when she showed me where she went to school.

The old Mrs. Gerber, a tall, skinny woman, always wore black. Her skirts reached down to her ankles, and the black scarf tied under her chin covered her head and half of her face. She reminded me of the witch in the Grimms' tale of "Hansel und Gretel." Sometimes, my grandmother and the old Mrs. Gerber visited each other. From a distance, I observed Mrs. Gerber's hands with the long bony fingers. Her partially hidden face did reveal a long, pronounced nose, which appeared slightly hooked. My imagination left no doubt: she was "the witch." I kept that secret discovery to myself, as I was convinced that my family would have severely scolded me for such comparisons.

A Kindly Woman

Aunt Klara and I still slept in the little room at the Westermanns'. One evening, Yani and my aunt had a big argument in the courtyard. As usual, the door was left open by a gap, and I could hear their quarreling. I pretended not to be overly nosy, but I kept hanging out near the door to hear well. Whatever their discord, it cooled their relationship, and Yani no longer came to visit. When Oma found out a Hungarian male was sweet on her daughter, she was horrorstruck. She confronted Aunt Klara, and they had a spirited discussion about Yani. It reached the point where the two women stopped speaking to each other for over a week. In the midst of all these silly conflicts, Maria Göpfrich announced her engagement to Erich Strobel and their plans for a summer wedding in the following year.

The Göpfrichs approached my grandparents and gently explained to them their need for room after Maria's wedding. Mr. Göpfrich assured Oma and Opa comparable housing and mentioned the name of a widow whose lawyer nephew had landed a job in Stuttgart and was moving out of her house. Her name was Anna Martin, and one day she stopped by and introduced herself to us. She and Oma meshed instantly, and they agreed that we would move to her house after Christmas. In her strong Neibsheim dialect, Anna Martin offered most of her second floor to our disposal.

7

A Family Again

ର୍ଷ ର୍ଷ ର୍ଷ ର୍ଷ

Reunited at Last

Indeed, my parents had escaped the Russian zone and made it to Neibsheim just as planned. Exhausted but enormously happy, they stood in the doorway of my grandparents' kitchen, each with a suitcase in one hand and a tightly wrapped bundle hanging over the shoulder. My mother dropped whatever she held in her hands and ran toward me, crying and calling my name—"Erikale!"—repeatedly. She squeezed me lovingly, caressing and kissing me, as if she had to make up for the two and a half years we were apart. Her amazement over my gain in height, my hair being long enough for braids, and other developing changes kept her in awe. I sat in her lap, feeling content, and stared at her secretly. She had not changed. I was pleased that her looks were the same, just as the photograph showed her. My father felt a little neglected but understood my emotional behavior. For the next two days I did not go to school but stayed at my mother's side. For several days I was on cloud nine, exulting with happiness.

Aunt Klara, my grandparents—everyone—felt overjoyed to have my mother back in their midst again. For them, too, it was a tremendous relief to transfer the responsibility and well-being of a little girl back to her parents, where she belonged. Although happily reunited with my parents, my grandparents and aunt continued to be an important part in my growing-up years and beyond.

Aunt Klara abandoned the room at the Westermanns. Soon, she and my grandparents would move to Mrs. Martin's, where she would have her own room at last. She gave my parents the two cots that she and I slept on and solicited one more from her friend, Yani, with whom she was on speaking terms again (unbeknownst to Oma).

The Landlords from Hell

My parents and I walked to the Strobels (no relation to Erich Strobel) to introduce ourselves and perhaps take a look at our room assigned to us by the mayor. Barstel Strobel informed us immediately that he had not volunteered to provide a room to "Flüchtling Gesindel." His baleful looks and menacing tone made us uncomfortable and frightened. Gertrud, his sister—another sinister-looking face—dashed by us and, without saying a word, opened the door to the upstairs and led us to a room full of clutter cobwebbed by years of spider activity. "There, that's your room," she bellowed and proceeded to go downstairs. My father asked her if they or we could move the stuff out of the room to some other space. She nodded her head and pointed to another room. After taking a peek in that room, we realized that the whole upstairs was one pile of junk and that time had stood still in that house.

The next day, we cleared the room somewhat and set up the cots. My mother changed the duvet covers on the down quilts and pillows, which she had dragged from Komotau via Oschersleben to Neibsheim. The Bürgermeister gave us a two-burner spirit stove for cooking, a table, and a bench. Oma shared her limited supply of pots, pans, and flatware. The room had no running water and no washbasin nor any source of heating. It was the beginning of December and freezing cold. The first few days, we slept with our clothes on. My father commended my mother's foresight in lugging these down comforters over half of Europe. Frau Martin heard of our dilemma at the Strobels' and gave us a small wood stove, which Opa and my father installed.

The Haucks, who lived two houses down from the Strobels, brought us a small tub and two water buckets. Their son Peter and I were in the same grade. He told his parents of a girl in his class whose parents fled from the Russians in East Germany to be reunited with his classmate. The Haucks, longtime neighbors who had seen the same dark side of the Strobels as we had come to know, felt most empathetic toward us.

School let out for Christmas vacation, and I was happy to have more time with my parents. We relied mainly on my grandparents, Aunt Klara, and good Samaritans like Frau Martin for food and winter clothes for my parents. Their ration cards had not made it through the system, and they had few opportunities for work, as farmers did not need much help during the winter months.

The Strobels kept insulting us every time we came down the stairs. We ignored their contemptuous looks and verbal rudeness as we had to pass them in the hallway. Their house had to be the most primitive structure in all of Neibsheim. Most villagers had electricity, running water, and partial indoor plumbing; the Strobels house had none. Opa gave us one of his oil lamps, for daylight hours were much shorter during winter. We had to pump the water from a well in the small courtyard, and my mother always worried about poisoning. When Barstel felt very wicked, he put a padlock on the dilapidated outhouse. My mother and I disliked using the place because some of the boards had rotted and left big gaps for anyone to peek inside. Regardless of the weather, we would walk to my grandparents' and use the toilet there. Eventually we got a bedpan; during the winter months, it was a convenient gadget to have.

Our small room at the Strobels' looked neat and clean, but nothing gave even the slightest hint that it was Christmas. There was no tree, presents, or good smells, yet I was the happiest little girl on that wintry Christmas Eve in 1947. Reunited with my parents, I snuggled up to my mother, telling her how thankful I was to Christkindl for making my wish come true. Later, the three of us walked down the street to the house of the Bürgermeister where my grandparents still lived. They shared with us the food my aunt and Opa had received from the farmers as Christmas gifts, for their diligent work throughout the year. (I think Oma had a connection to a black marketeer.) On her kitchen table sat a vase with fir branches releasing a pleasant pine scent, and hidden in there, she pulled out a bar of chocolate, and handed it to me, "From Christkindl," she said.

Another Story of Expulsion

The new year of 1948 arrived quietly. My grandparents and Aunt Klara had moved to Frau Martin's, where they now had a spacious kitchen and two bedrooms completely furnished. School was in session again, and my class recognized me on the day of my eighth birthday. After school, I hurried to Oma. I knew she was clever and somehow would find a way to produce a cake, for the occasion. I guessed right. Oma had a cake with a big number eight on top waiting for me.

Like every year, it was a snowy birthday, and I sat with the adults listening to the stories of their momentous events experienced over the last three years. My mother talked about her forced labor at the Slovakian family and their children's coarse treatment of her. They kicked her, and she showed the permanent bruises on her legs. I chimed in and reminded her of Anna, the mistress, not liking me and those awful boys who threw me into the fire. I still had the scar on my hand to prove it. She had no recourse but to stay with that dreadful family until a day in July 1946.

Czech soldiers came to her house early in the morning and told her that she had ten minutes to gather her things and vacate the home. She grabbed two suitcases and threw in family documents, photographs, Rudi's violin, and some of their summer clothes and underwear. At the end of the allotted time, she tossed the down quilts, sheets, and curtains out the window. She then tied the bedding together and hurled it on the truck. The soldiers took the two suitcases downstairs and inspected them for valuables. Disappointed at not finding any loot, they catapulted the suitcases into the vehicle. They then hauled her off to Glashütte, a former Czech concentration camp presently used for a collection point. There she met up with Uncle

Veit and Aunt Resi and several families with the same surname of Veit. Aunt Frieda and her children were not among them.

My father liked to continue the story by telling how he and my mother met up with each other. He had been a prison cook and prisoner in the Czech concentration camp Maltheuern for over a year. The Czechs needed to dissolve the camp and expel the remaining few hundred men who were lucky enough to have survived the epitome of hell. He conversed in Czech with the prison commander and took the liberty of asking to be reunited with his wife before being expelled. A few days later, the commander handed him a release from detention and a transfer to camp Glashütte. He walked away from Maltheuern, a place where he had witnessed death and human suffering of the worst kind, and, in the end, saw a glimpse of humanity.

A truck took him to Glashütte. He approached a uniformed Czech who seemed important enough to ask for occupant Maria Veit. Looking over the endless lists of names, the guard found her name and directed him to her barrack number. He saw her sitting on her suitcases, forlorn and emaciated. Overcome by emotions, he screamed her name: "Mitzi!" She heard the call, recognized the voice, and almost fainted as she saw him running toward her. Onkel Veit and Tante Resi, too, cried and carried on when he could finally be persuaded to let go of Mitzi.

A Train to the Russian Zone

Two days later, the camp started to vacate, and everyone climbed into boxcars covered with soot and the smell of tar. Their destination was unknown. My father, a railroad man, recognized the route leading to Eger, a quaint town close to the border of Bavaria. Once across the border, the train stopped in Wiesau, Germany, and everyone expressed relief to have reached Bavaria, the American zone.

Wiesau was a refugee transit camp one hundred km north of Furth im Wald, where we were processed, and my parents went through the identical procedures. The following day, they boarded the train again, except several boxcars shorter, but still had no clue to where this train was taking them. The next stop was Hof, Germany. There, the devastating news reinforced their sneaking suspicions: the train would take them to Halberstadt, in the Russian-occupied zone.

Unfortunately, refugees had no alternative; they were only processed, not accommodated. The Allies had their plans of dealing with the influx of 12.5 million refugees coming from the eastern parts of Europe into a war-torn Germany.

Traveling for hours in the direction of northeastern Germany, the train finally arrived in Halberstadt. Russian-made trucks took everyone to a temporary camp where they stayed for three weeks. My parents watched out for the old Veits and shared with them little extras my father received for working in the camp kitchen scraping, scouring kettles, and cleaning floors. Ultimately, they ended up in Oschersleben, a small, bleak coal-mining town of seven thousand people in the province of Sachsen Anhalt. The locals did not have to absorb newcomers in their homes; as a result, indifference rather than outright hostility met the refugees.

The Russians had tirelessly built housing complexes and refurbished empty barracks since the end of the war. In 1947, they realized that their plan to rule Germany, and eventually all of Europe, would not materialize. My parents and the old Veits each received a room in a housing complex with no indoor plumbing. My father and Uncle Veit had no choice but to work in a coal mine and pay rent for their room. Ration cards provided food for one thousand calories per day per person, and coal for heating was also rationed. My mother worked in the fields, which were under collective ownership, a communistic doctrine imposed by the Russians.

East Germany, once the Russian-occupied zone, became an independent state, better known as the DDR. For over forty years, fifteen million Germans lived under Communist rule, until its collapse in October of 1989 when East and West Germany were reunited into the Bundesrepublik Deutschland and the Cold War ended.

Escape from the Russian Sector

From the time my parents got word that their train was traveling to the Russian zone, they made plans to leave the area as soon as possible. After having established contact with Uncle Gustel and my father's visit in Neibsheim, they carefully designed their escape from Oschersleben. They did not reveal the plan to the old Veits until the last minute for fear that they might innocently tell a neighbor of "their Rudi's" intention.

By November of 1947, the Russians had increased their border guard presence to the adjacent Allied zones. For weeks, my father observed guards on several crossings and made notes of regular habits and procedures. He decided to risk the escape on a Friday when the Russian guards liked to drink their vodka, especially on cold November nights. My mother was fidgety, but she had the suitcases packed and the bedding tightly bundled. First my father and then my mother left the dark apartment complex, hoping no one would see them at 2:30 a.m. They had established a meeting point near the border. Back in those days, neither bright streetlights nor sophisticated searchlights existed, and the foggy November night was surely in their favor. They chose to cross through a pine grove and hid behind the tree trunks until the voices of the guards faded into the distance. Swiftly, they moved from one tree to another. When the somewhat dim floodlights from a nearby watchtower searched the area, they halted their movement and my mother whispered Hail Marys. At last, a big sign read, "You Are Entering the British Zone." Embracing each other, they knew that their freedom to the West was no longer in jeopardy.

My father always had some melancholy in his voice when he spoke of Oschersleben where the old Veits stayed behind. Eventually, he established mail correspondence with them, and in 1954, they received permission for a visit to the West. By then, both Veits had well exceeded the retirement age of sixty-five, and the East German government preferred to see these seniors leave and not have to pay a Social Security–type pension.

Uncle Veit and Aunt Resi did come for a visit, and my father encouraged his aunt and uncle to relocate to the West and stay with us. However, their zest for life seemed sucked out of them, and they were too tired to make another change. By 1956, both had died, and only my father took the risk and attended their funerals in Oschersleben. During the Cold War, the DDR was notorious for keeping lists of people for numerous reasons; therefore, my parents decided not to chance a visit to East Germany together.

Toughing It Out

In the spring of 1948, three years had passed since the war ended. For the millions of people who had lost everything when cruelly chased out of their homelands, life was still a tremendous struggle. My parents literally begged farmers for any type of work in exchange for food. The ration cards provided for a bare minimum, "a starvation diet." The free meal in school for me was a true blessing. We had no money, and, even if we did, it had lost all purchasing power. The stores were empty, and while the barter business drove a very active black market, we had nothing of value to barter with. Rumors of a currency reform started to circulate.

Once a week a big truck came to the Rathaus, and we stood in line to receive our meager weekly allowance of groceries in exchange for ration coupons. Mrs. Martin generously helped my grandparents, and in turn, they shared with us. Anna Martin attended Mass every day but also lived her life in the true sense of a Christian. Our family thought of her as an angel on earth, a saint.

The loathsome Strobels thought of ways to make our lives fearful and miserable, though Gertrud Strobel, a "holier-than-thou Christian woman," attended Mass every morning. One day, Barstel pursued my mother with a pitchfork while she pumped water from the well in the courtyard. She tried to run inside the house as Barstel chased after her, and Gertrud, watching from the window, quickly locked the door. My mother, screaming for help, was able to reach the gate to the outside, where she ran down the street to her mother. Trying to catch her breath, she reported what had happened. Aunt Klara listened, said very little, and left the room. A short while later, a flushed Klara returned and announced, "I just beat the crap out of Gertrud Strobel. I warned her that if she or her brother ever tries to harm my sister Mitzi again, they both will not see next day's daylight." Sweet, gentle Aunt Klara apparently put fear in both of them; there were no other incidents of this sort. Nonetheless, my mother and I avoided staying in that one room by ourselves.

8

Humble Beginnings

❧ ❧ ❧ ❧

A Marriage Proposal

Georg Gerber, better known as "Schorsch" and a son of the other Gerbers in Neibsheim, had returned from a POW camp on the Crimean peninsula. He had survived five years of confinement in a Russian labor camp. After his release in 1948, he just started walking. He walked for three months from the Black Sea to a transit camp in Austria, where he received help and information about his family. His fifteen-hundred-mile trek made quite a story, and he became somewhat of a hero among the Flüchtling community in Neibsheim.

My grandmother had known Schorsch since childhood, and this tall, slender man was thirty-two years old and still unmarried. She wished her daughter, Klara, would exhibit an interest in Schorsch: after all, he was from Franzelhütte, came from a decent family, and, since his trudging over half of Europe, had achieved status and some fame. Oma had several discussions with Aunt Klara on the subject, but Cupid's arrows had not struck her heart, and she resented her mother's (once again) audacious matchmaking. She reminded her of past interferences in her friendship with men, and, at almost twenty-seven years old, she felt quite capable of choosing a mate. Opa agreed, and my mother relented.

Every year, Germans celebrate *Ersten Mai*—the First of May, a national Labor Day. In 1946, the Allies gave permission to honor the tradition again as a holiday. The younger people celebrate the night before with bonfires and erect a tall *"Maibaum"* (Maypole) that held a wreath on the top decorated with flowing streamers, sausages, and home-baked pretzels. Young males climb up the pole to fetch one of the decorations and present it to their sweetheart as a sign of love and masculinity. Many families spent the day hiking, bicycling, or having a picnic with friends. In the evening, almost every Gasthaus had live music with the motto *"Tanz in den Mai"* (Dance into May).

Aunt Klara had an invitation to a *Mai* dance from Schorsch Gerber on that First of May in 1948. She accepted, and to Oma's delight, they continued seeing each other. After a short courtship, Schorsch asked Aunt Klara to marry him. She felt worn out to resist her mother's matchmaking powers, and, she told herself, why not marry a decent, unassuming fellow like Georg Gerber?

A New Currency

Finally, the rumors about the Reichsmark growing obsolete and being replaced by a new currency, the Deutsche Mark (DM), became reality on June 20, 1948. The Western Allies—USA, Great Britain, and France—enacted the currency reform in their occupied zones to facilitate the introduction of the Marshall Plan and simultaneously to eliminate the out-of-control black market. Each person received start-up money in the amount of forty DM and a second installment of twenty DM a month later. This new money seemed to work magic. Overnight, shop windows displayed an array of merchandise. Nobody could figure out where this abundance of goods came from.

Two days later, the Russians announced their own currency reform, the new Ostmark, but it was only to apply in their occupation zone and all of Berlin, the four-zone city. The Western Allies opposed the inclusion of the four-zone city and introduced the DM in the three

Western sectors of Berlin but not in the Russian sector. The Soviets responded with a blockade of the Western sectors' railway and road access to Berlin. This situation, the infamous Berlin Blockade, lasted for eleven months. During that time, the Western Allies organized the Berlin Airlift and supplied the residents of Berlin by air with four to five thousand tons of food and heating fuel daily. The Berlin Airlift has marked its place in history as the greatest humanitarian event ever.

Several Neibsheim farmers pulled together and opened a cooperative creamery. We called it the *Milchhäusle* (milkhouse), where fresh milk, butter, and *quark* was sold on weekday evenings from 6–7:00 p.m. Someone gave us a beat-up, one-liter aluminum milk can, and twice a week my mother sent me to fetch one liter (one quart) of milk, for which I paid thirty-eight Pfennig (1 DM=100 Pfennig). I looked forward to the errand. While waiting for the store to open, I tried my acrobatic skills on the iron bars serving as a guardrail on both sides of the narrow bridge over the Talbach creek. Other kids had the same idea, and those bars were in high demand and the bridge a favorite hangout. One day, a kid fell off the bars onto the rocks that lined the Talbach creek bed. The boy had a serious concussion and needed many stitches on his face and head. That incident ended the monkey bar business for good.

A Big Event

The marriage of Maria Göpfrich and Erich Strobel took place during the latter part of July. It was the wedding event of the year in Neibsheim. Maria looked gorgeous in her mother's wedding dress, changed by minor alterations to incorporate a more modern look. The two little flower girls spread rose petals in front of the beaming bride and groom as they walked into the church toward the altar together. Both witnesses—by custom, a female attending to the bride and a male to the groom, carrying the wedding rings—were standing near the presiding priest, Father Göpfrich, Maria's uncle. St. Mauritius Church was decorated with fragrant summer flowers and packed with people, mainly spectators wanting to catch a glimpse of the attractive couple. After the nuptials, the newlyweds walked from the church to the bride's home, where friends and acquaintances had prepared every detail for a *"Hochzeitsschmaus"* (wedding reception). Oma helped in the kitchen, and Aunt Klara busied herself as a server.

Although these were tough times economically, Maria's parents put on a show to remember. A month before the wedding, the Göpfrichs butchered a pig for the occasion. There was no shortage of meats and sausages accompanied by a variety of homegrown vegetables, potatoes, and cured sauerkraut. The Göpfrichs and the Strobels and all of their relatives baked delectable-looking torts and cakes days in advance, and plenty of them. One of the local bakeries felt honored to provide the two-tier wedding cake as a gift to the Bürgermeister's daughter. The lengthy guest list consisted of a rather large family crowd, some out-of-towners, and the couple's close friends.

Keeping with tradition, after the festivities, the newlyweds distributed leftover food and sweets to their neighbors and acquaintances who were not part of the wedding but knew the couple well.

A Dose of Family Life

Once a week, Dr. Stofer came to Neibsheim in his black Opel P4, a vehicle straight out of the 1930s, to make house calls. He checked on chronically ill patients and visited the sick who called for his service. He was a short, skinny man with round, black-rimmed glasses and a tiny mustache and was not very friendly. However, he seemed to know his business. When I complained how badly my throat hurt, he would wave his hand and say, "Don't be so sensitive; weeds don't wither." I did not think it funny, since I was not a weed. Once I overheard him tell my mother that I seemed to have a vitamin deficiency, based on my thin, limp hair and brittle fingernails, and I needed to gain some weight. He prescribed a daily dose of cod-liver oil. That was awful stuff, and, after the daily gagging, I disliked Dr. Stofer even more.

School was out, and I had finished second grade. I still used my left hand for most everything, except writing. I was a lefty. My parents, Oma, and my teacher kept admonishing me to use my right hand. All my rebellion to their "correct way" enabled a triumph of sorts as I became ambidextrous.

Both my parents tried to earn some money working in the fields when farmers needed help with the harvest or with splitting wood. One evening, my father returned all excited from a hard day in the field. Someone had told him that the faraway country of Canada had opened its border to war refugees who had lost their homeland and wanted to emigrate. Convinced that he would never see his Sudetenland again, he was ready to chance such a move. By nature, he was somewhat of an intrepid adventurer, and Canada seemed like a golden opportunity. My mother, horrified by the notion of leaving her parents and sister again, said "no" immediately. All she could remember was her fear and loneliness in Komotau during my father's absence and the politically imposed separation from her family. She and my father had a few powwows on that issue. When my grandmother got wind of it, he knew that this was a no-win situation, and he dismissed the idea.

That summer, I learned all about mushrooms, edible and poisonous ones, especially the beautiful-to-look-at *Fliegenpilz* (toadstool), the most poisonous in the world of mushrooms. I liked going mushroom hunting with my parents on weekends. We started early in the morning, before the worm had a chance to attack the fungi. My father had an eye for spotting mushrooms, even when they were well hidden under blankets of leaves covering the forest floor. He used a knife to remove the whole mushroom, as they will grow again the following year if the root is not disturbed. We discovered several edible types in the woods around Neibsheim. Before we could place a mushroom in the basket, my father checked for authenticity and wormholes. Discarded were the mushrooms with even one wormhole showing in the stem. That was my father's rule. All summer long, we consumed fresh mushrooms galore, prepared in a wide variety of delicious meals. During winter, we ate dried ones, always reflecting back to the good season we had. For years to come, we found such delight in the art of "mushrooming."

Gerber Married Gerber

For two weeks, every evening Aunt Klara sat at Frau Martin's treadle sewing machine, working feverishly on her wedding gown. She had saved a little money and purchased the material at the

Hauck's general store in Neibsheim. They only offered one kind of white, silky fabric, which had a tendency to fringe easily and was hard to handle. However, Tante finished her creation, a simple long dress that fit to perfection. Maria gave her some leftover tulle used in her wedding, and after Tante pieced it all together, the result was a rather pretty veil. Since I was her flower girl, I, too, needed a white dress, but we had no means of buying one. I don't recall who, but somebody gave me an awful-looking dress made of white cotton twill, and I had no choice but to wear it. The other flower girl, Schorsch Gerber's niece, Gretel Pechtl, my new friend and classmate, wore a white organza dress, and I was jealous.

The moment had arrived for Gretel and me to scatter rose petals in front of the bride and groom as they walked down the aisle at St. Mauritius Church, with Father Göpfrich once again officiating. My mother was her sister's witness. Schorsch chose his brother, who had lost a leg in the war, and he, too, had just returned from a POW camp. It was a small wedding, mainly family, but I do remember seeing Yani in the back of the church.

Suddenly related through the marriage of her uncle and my aunt, Gretel and I counted our lucky stars at having our friendship sealed forever. In reality, we never were very good friends but were competitors. We both were the best students in our class, and we each wanted to be number one.

The newlyweds used Tante's room as their bedroom and shared the kitchen with my grandparents. Some weekend after their wedding, they took a train to Eslarn to pick up most of the items we had smuggled from Franzelhütte and stored at the Pokornys. Aunt Klara was glad to recover her started dowry and Oma's Pfaff sewing machine. To my grandmother's great disappointment, not all of Uncle Seph's books and trinkets could be brought back on this trip. In her at times unreasonable demands, she blamed her son-in-law Schorsch for being insensitive toward Seph's stuff. They had some heated discussions, which seemed to drag on for weeks. Schorsch, obstinate like his mother-in-law, stopped at his mother's to avoid dinner at Oma's kitchen. Aunt Klara was pregnant and tired of their bickering. She would have liked to move somewhere else, but housing was still a big problem in Neibsheim.

A Christmas to Remember

For good reasons, I remember Christmas 1948 quite vividly. We left the uncomely room at the Strobels and waded through deep snowdrifts, navigating our way to my grandparents' house to celebrate Christmas Eve. The smells of "Schnitzel" and cinnamon apples from Oma's kitchen tickled our noses as we entered the house of Frau Martin. A small, sparsely decorated tree stood by the window, with several wrapped presents underneath. Aunt Klara laughingly said, "I dare say, but you just missed Christkindl again." I acted the part, although I no longer was convinced about these stories of Sankt Nikolaus, Knecht Ruprecht, and Christkindl. In school, some kids bragged about seeing their parents decorate the tree or finding presents in a closet and then again neatly wrapped under the tree. When I mentioned this to my mother, she replied, "Erikale, it is better to believe in the wonders of Christmas than not to believe," and I left it at that.

After a festive meal made possible by Frau Martin, Opa lit the candles on the tree. My father took out his violin, which he kept stored at Oma's house in fear of Barstel Strobel's threats of setting the instrument on fire. The violin had not seen any action in quite some time and needed tuning. Once the strings had the proper pitch again, he played familiar Christmas tunes with us chiming in, and he ended with Händel's Messiah; "Hallelujah!" Then Oma opened the door to the mystique of superstition. She cited a few myths, while all held their breath, relieved when she was done with those irrational beliefs.

The time had arrived to open the packages from under the tree. Opa proudly stated that he had made the house slippers for me from dried cornhusks. He added that he lined them with blue-checked gingham, the same material Oma used for sewing a dress for me. Oma rolled her eyes at Opa. He had mistakenly claimed credit for the slippers, when it was Christkindl who brought them. With the slippers came a long, warm nightgown. Another box contained a new thing—a muff, a tubular fur or cloth cover, open at both ends, for the hands to be placed in for warmth. Mine was a knitted one and was lined with rabbit fur. Along with the new muff came a knitted scarf and hat, made of the same color yarn. *All these wonderful gifts,*

I thought. *Surely only Christkindl had such magic to bring them*, and I was a believer again.

Frau Martin suggested for all of us to attend Midnight Mass at St. Mauritius. It still snowed, and Opa once more prepared the oil lamp for us to take on the way to church. As always, church had no appeal for him, and he stayed behind.

It was pitch black as we stepped out on the street. The lamp's unsteady flame provided a glimmer of light, and we could hear the muffled voices of other churchgoers. The church was all lit up, and many pews already occupied. Frau Martin took my hand, and we walked up front, where her reserved seat was in a third-row pew. There was no name on the seat, but the congregation, out of respect to this devout, generous woman, granted her a special seat. I squeezed in next to her. From my spot, I was able to admire the life-size manger, surrounded by tall, green spruce trees, decked with white candles and lustrous tinsel. Several altar boys, holding long-handled lighters and snuffers, lit each one of the many candles. A huge pipe organ started with vibrant clamor, leading the congregation into song. Small clouds of myrrh incense poured out of a brass censer, swung back and forth by an altar boy to create the heavenly scent. Father Göpfrich in his regal robe said Mass, and the whole atmosphere gave the feeling of a divine afflatus. The bells started to ring as we left church, and I felt such warmth and happiness in my young heart. Starting with that night, Midnight Mass became a part of my life.

First Communion

In 1949 I turned nine years old and was finally a candidate for First Communion. In school, catechism class prepared me for the sacrament. I was excited, and as early as March I began to work on the decorations of my two-foot-tall communion candle, which my parents had to buy. This, too, was a competitive matter—and not just for the kids. Parents wanted to outdo each other for their communicant to have the most beautifully decorated candle on that special day. My entire family put their touches on my candle, and it turned out quite nicely, but not the best by comparison. There was no prize to earn, just looks and comments by the congregation.

My mother saw a fine white fabric in a general store in Gondelsheim and bought it. She and my grandmother designed and sewed my Communion dress. Oma's Pfaff had a feature to sew ruffles, and my dress flaunted ruffles galore. It was a very pretty dress, accented by white shoes, ribbed cotton stockings, and thin gloves with a lace edge. My mother curled my hair, and I wore a small floral diadem on my head. I never felt closer to being a princess than on my Communion Day. Our families celebrated my First Communion and Aunt Klara giving birth to a baby girl, all at the same time.

Both my parents had entered the job market. My father and Uncle Schorsch worked for the same railroad construction company replacing damaged rail tracks. Together they rode their bicycles to Mühlacker every day, rain or shine. My mother landed a part-time job in a new cigar factory. She always smelled of tobacco, although she herself never smoked. Opa started a job as a forest conservation worker with the forestry service, initiated by Bürgermeister Göpfrich. Oma cooked for all of us and took care of the new baby, while Aunt Klara helped Frau Martin in daily peasant routines. Sometimes after school, I played with and babysat my new baby cousin, Helga.

In the spring of that year, the municipal council of Neibsheim allotted some fallow land outside the village limits for garden development to interested Flüchtling families. My parents and most other families signed up, but there were not enough plots to go around. A lottery was established. We were lucky to win a plot for lease, with a one-time fee of five DM.

On Saturdays, the three of us spent most of the day working the land, preparing the soil, planting, and weeding. My father became somewhat of a self-proclaimed master gardener with a green thumb, while my mother took care of the invasive snails, a pest from the nearby creek. She used a cheap beer, which they liked and drowned in. My job was to provide the fertilizer; that meant collecting "road apples and cow pies" from the streets of Neibsheim. During the week, we Flüchtling kids went on the hunt for manure, a serious business, and sometimes we would literally fight over the easier-to-shovel horse dung.

Since the establishment of these community gardens, Neibsheim experienced an unforeseen benefit; never were the cobblestone streets more clean. We kids removed every pile of manure left by the cows and horses pulling through the streets. The Flüchtling gardens, as the locals called them, became a model of garden cultivation. Our thriving garden grew into an immense food source for us, and we shared our good fortune with the rest of the family.

National and Local Elections

On May 23, 1949, the Western Allies merged their occupied zones to form the Federal Republic of Germany, while a few months later the Russian-occupied zone became the German Democratic Republic. Informally, there was West Germany with Bonn as provisional capitol and East Germany with East Berlin as its capitol. People in West Germany freely elected their first chancellor, Konrad Adenauer, though the Allies continued to militarily occupy the country. Our subsequent schoolbooks reflected on the two-state solutions as an artificial status quo. Many times, my parents spoke of their timely escape from the Soviet-occupied zone, just eighteen months prior to the division of Germany.

With the birth of the Federal Republic, state and local governments followed the same democratic process of free elections. In 1949, the city of Bruchsal became the county seat of at least nineteen surrounding villages and communities, and Neibsheim was one of them.

My father showed an active interest in politics and joined Adenauer's popular, conservative CDU Party. He decided to run as county representative for Neibsheim. At the same time, elections for mayor and the municipal board took place in September of that year. Bürgermeister Göpfrich and his board were prominent candidates of the party. Most of Neibsheim's citizens voted for CDU, which stands for Christian Democratic Union, and without opposition, my father easily won the election. His official title, *Kreisrat* (county commissioner), had a term of four years and was mostly an honorary position. He traveled to Bruchsal by train twice a month for evening meetings and always came back pumped up with ideas and with many papers. Still, without fail, he complained with every trip about the half-hour walk from Neibsheim to Gondelsheim to catch the train to Bruchsal and thence back again in the dark of the night.

Disappointments and Regrets

Finally, we moved out from the weird Strobels. The Westermanns, where Tante and I had a small room once, offered a big furnished room for five DM a month. My parents painted the room, and we settled in immediately. What an improvement over that previous hell hole.

During our stay at the Strobels', my father was unable to play his violin. Barstel told my father that he would smash or burn the instrument if he heard a sound out of it. To avoid Barstel's unpredictability, the violin was stored at my grandparents'. My father was always grateful to my mother for grabbing his precious possession when the Czechs evicted her from our house in Komotau. He started playing again after we moved to the Westermanns', and he played anything from classical to modern.

My parents decided that I, too, should learn the violin, and my father began to teach me. Instinctively, I held the violin bow in my left hand, since it felt right for me. It drove my father crazy to make repeated corrections for bow and violin to be properly situated. He demanded complete attention. The slightest distraction on my part earned me a hefty tap of his bow on my head. I did not enjoy these sessions and quickly lost all interest in learning the instrument.

I had finished third grade with an excellent final report card and took the entrance exam for Gymnasium (academic high school). Mr. Ruf, the school principal, had a serious talk with my father about my future education. He agreed that I was bright but claimed that success could be achieved without going the academic route. He impressed upon my father, "Girls who choose Gymnasium and continue studying need financial support until they are twenty-four or twenty-five years old. Then they get married. Most likely, they abandon their career and raise a family. Who needs to study for that?" He mentioned, "If she was a boy, there would be no question for a higher education, but a girl?" Mr. Osang, my teacher, encouraged my father to let the principal have his opinion but not take his advice.

Mr. Ruf and my father were avid chess players. Together they took bicycle trips to nearby villages to play in chess tournaments. During those events, the two men came to know and respect each other. My mother labeled Mr. Ruf a lousy educator whose gender decision discriminated against girls. But in the end, my father shared Mr. Ruf's personal view, and there was no more talk about Gymnasium. I was deeply disappointed and never quite forgave my father for denying me the opportunity. Years later, he sincerely regretted that decision.

Panic and Tragedy

One hot August day the approach of roaring thunder and an eerie-looking sky gave me the fright of a lifetime. I was by myself and kept looking out the window, where the elements seemed out of control and in all their fury played tricks on my mind. The story of Judgment Day from my catechism class came to life in my mind. I had not prepared for the Rapture. I crawled into my bed and pulled the covers over my head, sweating and waiting for the call of my name. Suddenly, someone pulled back the cover, and I stared into my mother's face. The bad dream or fever, whatever it was that put me in such panic, was over. I gratefully kissed my mother and thanked her for rescuing me. That day, a severe storm unloaded on Neibsheim and left the village square flooded with two feet of water.

On that ill-fated day in August of 1949, a most shocking catastrophe unfolded in the house of the Bürgermeister. Mrs. Göpfrich did not return from the field in the evening. When her husband and some people went looking for her, they found her drowned in the rapids of a violent Talbach creek. This horrific tragedy affected everyone, locals and Flüchtling alike. The community shared their grief with Maria, pregnant at the time, and her sorrowful father for years to come. Every anniversary of that cursed day, people visited the cemetery and put flowers on the grave of Klara Göpfrich.

The New Decade

As a new decade began, I turned ten on January 16, 1950. My parents bought a used, all-black bicycle, and my father, the impatient teacher, taught me to ride it after the snow disappeared. I learned quickly, and he seemed pleased. Every day for at least one hour, I rode back and forth on Main Street and eventually all over Neibsheim.

My responsibility was to keep it clean and stored properly after each ride.

The age of motorization slowly meandered its way to Neibsheim. Some people sported a new motorcycle, or its cheaper version, the moped, which was an oversized bicycle with a small motor attached. In addition, there was talk of a vehicle-manufacturing company in Northern Germany starting to produce a car affordable for all Germans, the Volkswagen *Käfer* (beetle).

Bürgermeister Göpfrich and his council members invited my father to their planning meeting when the necessity for road improvement was on the agenda. Such a project needed authorization and funds, and my father, as the Kreisrat for Neibsheim, was to present the request to the county commission in Bruchsal. However, his plea did not fall on many open ears at the commissioners' meeting. They rebuked my father adamantly that Neibsheim, like other villages, had no war damage. Upgrading cobblestone streets could not have priority over removing piles of rubble and destroyed thoroughfares. Indeed, their arguments had validity, and my father used the diplomatic route by putting the undertaking on the back burner. He lent his vote to the assembly's priority projects and ultimately gained favor for his road proposal.

Some years later, Neibsheim enjoyed an extended tar-paved Main Street, including a sidewalk starting at the church and leading to the village square. The overjoyed locals organized a parade to christen the newly paved road and to honor Bürgermeister Göpfrich and my father for their accomplishments. They sat on a horse-drawn wagon, decorated with flowers, flags, and streamers and followed by Neibsheim's pride, a brass "oompah" band.

The first of May arrived, and Germans all over West Germany celebrated the holiday, and with good reason. After ten years of living with ration cards, on this day in 1950, the cards were abolished and became part of a nonglorious past. The new decade finally closed the chapter of the horrific forties. A well-functioning democratic government with a great leader, Konrad Adenauer, had been established, and the beginning of an economy, which some years later enjoyed world recognition, became known as *Wirtschaftswunder* (economic miracle).

During the early days of May, we kids still collected road apples from the street, arguing as of old over who reached the spot first. The time had come for our garden to get plenty of natural fertilizer before preparing the soil for the planting season. Like in the previous year, there was no waste of precious land; each inch contained a plant or seed in the hope that something useful would grow. However, this year we treated ourselves and allowed a small area for flowers. In addition, we built a scarecrow from cans, straw, an old shirt, and dingy-looking long underwear to keep those annoying birds away. By June, we were able to assess the efforts of our gardening attempt. All indications pointed to another rich harvest, assuming no natural disaster would destroy the good-looking crop.

A Colossal Acquisition

We moved again. Through our landlord we made the acquaintance of the nice Gerweck family. They were building a new house, and it had reached completion. We wanted to rent their second floor. On a beautiful, Indian summer–like autumn day, we gathered our few belongings in the one room at the Westermanns' and moved to Upper Mill Street. The new domicile was close to our garden plot but quite a distance from the activity of the village and my school. We had so much space and hardly any furniture, only some donations made to St. Mauritius Church. I liked living in a new house, but best of all, I had a room of my own and a bathroom just for the three of us.

Our first big-ticket acquisition was a kitchen stove, and it took all the money my parents had saved so diligently. When the store delivered the stove, it required four men to carry this monstrosity of cast iron up to our second floor. Indeed, it was a beauty, with multipurpose usage. Besides being a basic wood burner, this modernized style could also accommodate coal. In those days, the kitchen stove was the main source for heating, cooking, and hot water. By hot water supply, I mean the built-in deep oblong water container that kept the water hot long after the fire died out. My parents were happy with their purchase, and they both started cooking again.

It seemed as if more responsibilities became part of my daily chores, and I had less time to play. Since we no longer ate at my grandmother's, it was my job to start the fire in the new stove punctually at 4:00 p.m. On many occasions, I lost track of time. It was on those days when I experienced the frustrations of getting a fire started. My mother usually took pity on me when she came home and saw my blackened face from blowing so hard and gave it her own try. Not my father. He was the disciplinarian and a believer in order and rules. Very seldom did he accept my poor excuses, and without fail, he quoted something like, *"Die Welt will Ergebnisse, nicht Entschuldigungen"* ("The world wants results, not excuses"). Generally, I had my bike-riding privilege suspended for a day or two.

A Mischievous Trio

There were no girls my age living on Upper Mill Street. The Gerweck's son, Hermann—his mother endearingly called him Hermännle—and his friend Paul Schleicher lived nearby. Both were classmates and sometimes playmates of mine. Paul, whom we called Polle, came from a very large family, and his father loved the bottle more than anything else in life. On pretty days, the three of us biked to Büchig, a village next to Neibsheim. My parents would have never approved of my biking escapades to another village; fortunately, they did not find out. If we had money, we stopped at the ice cream parlor. For ten Pfennigs we could treat ourselves to one scoop of vanilla ice cream in a cone. On rare occasions, Polle brought his own money and bought a cone. Usually, Hermännle and I let him have a lick from ours when he agreed to clean his disgusting snotty nose.

Once I shared my peach of an idea with the boys: digging a hole all the way to China. "China!" They were on board instantly. We dug in Hermännle's backyard incessantly until his father shot down the operation and chased us out of the yard. Other times we ran through poppy fields, searching for ripened capsules of poppy seed for our consumption. Farmers did not like kids messing around in those fields, because the plants break easy when they have reached a dry stage, which ripens the seed in the capsule. I vividly remember an irate farmer coming after us with a pitchfork. He screamed and cursed while pursuing us all the way into the village. We ran to the church and hid in a piled position inside a confessional, praying that the farmer did not see us entering the church. Apparently he did not, and the experience taught me a lesson: I stayed away from the poppy fields.

Good Things Do Happen

Although Germany witnessed an upsurge in the economy, unemployment and poverty among the millions of Flüchtling still ran rampant. We counted our blessings when my father received a reinstatement notice from the Deutsche Bundesbahn (German Federal Railway), formerly Reichsbahn. Since his escape from East Germany, he had hopes for reemployment by the railroad. Unexpected, this notification seemed like a miracle to my parents.

During the harsh winter months, my father's job as a laborer replacing railroad ties closed down, and he collected meager unemployment benefits. I recall the time when he was on the dole and managed to cook a daily sapid meal for us. On Fridays he conjured up an *Oblaten Torte* (layer cake), all on five DM a week. My mother could not fathom his cooking magic, and even my grandmother vied with him jealously. There was no waste of a crumb or morsel in his organized kitchen, and the meals showed his inventiveness and innovation.

Christmas of 1950 was our first time in more comfortable living conditions since we became Flüchtling. After bringing the tree home from the woods on Christmas Eve, we decorated with the same home-made ornaments from the previous year. However, this year we covered the tree branches with a thin layer of fluffy cotton ball to achieve the look of snow. In addition, we bought more candles, tinsel, and a few fragile glass ornaments. I kept on admiring the magnificent-looking tree and felt content that our struggle as Flüchtling had mitigated in some way.

Our walk to Oma's house was much longer now. She was again hosting Christmas Eve dinner. Although my grandfather had no woodworking tools to speak of, somehow he made footstools for my toddler cousin, Helga, and me. Besides some exotic fruits of oranges, dates, and bananas, which I had read about but never eaten before, I received the usual home-sewn and knitted clothing and new shoes, still a size larger than needed. That Christmas we had another addition to our family. Aunt Klara had a baby boy in July and had named him Reinhold.

On January 15, 1951, just a day short of my eleventh birthday, my father went back to work as a civil servant with the German Bundesbahn. I figured it to be a turning point in our scanty existence, and we would finally be able to shake off the image of Flüchtling. Quickly did I grasp the reality of our true status. Nothing really changed, other than that my parents were able to save more money and my father had the job he liked so much.

An Extraordinary Teacher

Fräulein (Miss) Schmitt, my fifth-grade teacher, an attractive, dark-haired woman in her early thirties, embodied the dream-girl idol for all eleven-year-olds in my class, especially the boys. After we had had Mr. Osang as a teacher for four grades, Miss Schmitt was like a breath of fresh air, and fifth grade was my most memorable experience in grade school. She made learning fun. She developed interests and promoted potential in all her students. I always had a passionate devotion to reading, but she took me a step further and aroused an interest in writing. It was in her class that I started writing entertaining essays, which not only earned a hard-to-achieve A but were read in front of the class. Even in later years, I found expressing my ideas on paper a gratifying pastime. One more thing Miss Schmitt did for me: she started to teach English, a nonrequired subject, and I became her star pupil.

My fun school year had ended, and my report card was my best so far. In the fall, I advanced to sixth grade, and English lessons with wonderful Fräulein Schmitt continued. I overheard some conversations my parents had with Aunt Klara and Uncle Schorsch about the Liepold brothers building a house in Bruchsal, the county seat. They were saying that more housing opportunities were available and that perhaps they should explore them.

Scrutinizing Home Sites

One sunny July Sunday in 1951, my aunt, uncle, and our family walked to Gondelsheim to board the train to Bruchsal. It was my first train ride since that dreadful trip five years ago in those smelly cattle cars. I barely remembered those days of the expulsion, but my aunt did. The commuter train stopped twice before arriving in Bruchsal. Next to the station, I saw a deep hole in the ground, and I was curious about it. My father explained that the hole was a bomb crater, a remnant from the war. By the time we reached our destination, the south side of Bruchsal, we had passed quite a few craters and ruined buildings. When we spotted an area that looked like one gigantic construction site, we knew that it was the place we had come to see. One row of houses—identical, two-story, white stucco doubles covered by red tile roofs—was near completion. A paved road, named Waldstrasse, separated the staked outlines for more houses on the opposite side. The adults liked what they saw and decided on the spot that they would apply together to build such a double.

Back in Neibsheim, my father went to see one of the Liepold brothers to learn more about the housing project in Bruchsal. Victor Liepold, a master painter from Moravia, knew my father from the chess club. He gladly shared his knowledge and advice for gaining consideration with the proper authorities. The basic criteria was being Flüchtling, and having POW status or being a former DDR citizen earned additional points. Furthermore, it was necessary to provide satisfactory employment information with income verification, and each approved applicant had to contribute five hundred hours of labor. Lastly, both parties had to sign a commitment paper to make available one floor for rent at a set price to another Flüchtling family. My father and Uncle Schorsch submitted their applications in the hope to get a quick and positive response.

Almost six months had passed when we finally received word from the Housing Commission informing us of the approval for building our double. However, our permits applied to Phase III, and construction would begin in the spring of 1953. It was good news; my mother and her sister liked the idea of living right next to each other. Poor Oma—she had a difficult time accepting the fact that both of her daughters were moving away from Neibsheim.

Uncle Scrooge

Uncle Schorsch was a loner and a tightwad. He never talked much or socialized, and he worked all the time. After the birth of his children, he seemed increasingly agitated and moody, and I felt uncomfortable around him. By trade, he was a carpenter and an excellent artisan in furniture making. He constructed a beautiful buffet, which stood in my aunt's kitchen, and Mrs. Martin was his best advertising tool. She invited all her Neibsheim friends to look at the pieces he built, stained, and polished. His craft earned him substantial extra income, and being the parsimonious fellow that he was, he became obsessed with money. He hid the money and allotted a sparse allowance to my aunt for running the household. He finally built a bedroom suite for him and my aunt, after she threatened to leave him. My parents put an order in with him for kitchen and bedroom furniture, to be ready for the new house in Bruchsal. The price of one thousand DM was not negotiable, and he told my father, "Take it or leave it." My father took it.

Uncle Schorsch never changed jobs either. He kept working hard for the same company in Mühlacker. One day he was up for promotion to supervisor in their added road-construction business. Nothing changed; he still wrote his bike to work, rain or shine. After thirty-three years of loyal service, he retired in 1981. After his death in 2005, my aunt decided to get a new bedroom suite and do away with the one he had reluctantly built so long ago.

Village Living

Mauritius, the patron saint of Neibsheim, had a birthday, also called *Kirchweih*, or "*Kerwe*," in Neibsheim dialect. This was one big event in the fall of 1951. During the war, the church discouraged Kirchweih celebrations, and in the years immediately after the war, people had no money for frivolous things.

A few days before Kerwe Sunday, traveling gypsies came in trailers to the village square, where they set up amusement rides. Prior to their arrival, they had obtained permission from Mayor Göpfrich to use the square, and 20 percent of the generated gross income had to be paid to the church rectory. The main attraction was the small

Ferris wheel, and it cost twenty Pfennig to get a five-minute ride. The other ride, the chain carousel with flying chairs, was my favorite, and I spend most of my money there. There were peddlers selling all kinds of goods from bed sheets to boot laces, and sometimes they doubled as performers and fortunetellers. Neibsheim had never seen a livelier crowd in recent years, and we kids had the time of our lives. It was a tradition for people throughout the county to attend each other's village Kerwe, and they happily complied after such a long Kerwe hiatus. In the evening, two of the four Gasthäuser had live bands, and Neibsheimers danced and celebrated, in true Kerwe fashion.

My parents appeared happy with each other. My father played the violin whenever he had a free moment. Sunday mornings, we attended mass. Afterward, we stopped at my grandparents' house for a visit or a meal, if the smells gave away a pig roast in the oven. In the afternoon, we worked crossword puzzles for hours or joined my father in one of the Gasthauses, where he played chess or participated in a tournament match. When it was not chess, he played *Skat*, a card game similar to bridge. My mother usually met some other "straw widows," and they got into lively discussions about cooking, children, and juicy gossip; my mother was always just the quiet listener. I disliked going to those boring games, but I had no other choice. My father's flamboyance captivated me at times, but it also turned me off, especially on Sundays like these.

My year of bad luck began in September, when I started sixth grade, and Herr Ruf, the former principal, was now my teacher. I still held a grudge against him advising my father against my going to Gymnasium. Worse yet, my friend Gretel, my "nemesis" in class, did not return to school after the Christmas holidays. Her father had taken a job in Backnang, a town near Stuttgart, and the family moved there in the middle of winter.

With Gretel gone, I had no competition for the rest of that boring sixth grade, but most of all, I missed my friend. Instead of showing empathy to my feelings of dejection, my father reiterated another one of his famous wisdoms: "That's life; you'd better get used to it." He expressed disappointment in my report card, and with a stern face and raised finger, he let me know that my performance was not good enough and that I needed to have more self-discipline.

9

Two Prisoners of War Reminisce

The Famous Architect

A black Mercedes stopped in front of the Gerweck's house. Alone, I played a game of hopscotch on the unpaved Upper Mill Street. The vehicle stirred my attention, as I had never seen such an elegant car, except in pictures. A well-dressed man stepped out, walked toward me, and inquired about Rudi Veit. I told him I was Erika Veit, Rudi's daughter. He stretched out his hand for a greeting, smiled, and followed me into my house.

My father and the stranger definitely knew each other, as they fell into each other's arms. When they lifted from the long embrace, both had tears in their eyes. My mother could only guess who the visitor was. When introduced, she was pleased to finally meet Erich Schelling, the fellow who escaped with her Rudi from a British POW camp in Normandy, France.

Oddly enough, Erich Schelling, professor of architecture at Karlsruhe University, and my father hardly had a thing in common other than being soldiers in the war. But each possessed a survival instinct that paved the way for an extraordinary journey from Normandy, France, to the Rhein River in Germany. They trekked close to 1,000 km (621 miles) through enemy country during the late summer of 1944, and it took many weeks of sheer madness and determination to make it to safety.

The two men had not seen each other since 1944, when they parted at Erich's house on Riefstahlstrasse in the city of Karlsruhe. Then the war was still raging, and much had happened since. Finally now, in the fall of 1951, they had a chance to reacquaint themselves and reminisce about their arduous journey. Even though I had heard their story numerous times from my father, I was all ears again, as the two key players stepped back into the past to recall their ordeal.

Escape from Caen, France

Rudi and Erich did not know each other until after the invasion of D-day in June of 1944, when they both ended up in a prison camp in Caen, France. There were hundreds of captured German soldiers squeezed into an open camp enclosed by a makeshift fence and guarded by British chaps with machine guns. The POWs were about to be shipped out to POW camps in Great Britain. Rudi decided to escape before he was on a boat crossing the English Channel. There were eight guys who barely knew each other, one of them Erich, and all wanted to join Rudi's venture. However, his plan called for two people only, him and one more. Of all the desperate men, he chose Erich, a man slightly wounded in the leg by a grazing bullet and walking with a limp. Rudi shared his escape route with the rest of the gang and recommended that they make their attempt in pairs only.

One warm July night, with the help of the little group of six, who by now had plotted their own escapes should their two friends succeed and not be captured, brought back, and shot, Rudi and Erich crawled through the hand-dug hole underneath the fence and inched past the napping guards to a nearby barn. Rudi figured that the search for them so close to the camp would not be as intense as further down the road. Early the next morning, they heard the searching Brits running up and down the wooden stairs, hollering out directions to here and there, passing the silos and the bins where the two were hiding in. One of the soldiers was about to lift the heavy cover of a bin when his comrade urged him not to waste time with these silos; they were for grain storage only. After such a narrow escape, Rudi and Erich left the barn that night en route to Paris.

Before Rudi's capture, while barricaded in a school during an assault by American troops in the battle of Cherbourg, he had helped himself to a map of France. This folded-up paper would serve as their precious guide from the westernmost to the easternmost part of France and to the way home.

In Slow Motion

Normandy in those days was exclusively an agricultural province, and the automobile was somewhat of a supernal machine to glare at, not fit for unpaved country roads. Therefore, traffic consisted of horses, cows, and wagons and an occasional herd of sheep. Road signs were scarce, but usually at the entrance of a municipality, a small sign displayed its name. Rudi and Erich, still dressed in German uniform, could only travel at night, alongside railroad tracks. During the day, they hid and rested in high grain fields or in the thickets of the forest. While one slept, the other kept watch for possible intrusion by people or animals. At daybreak, they looked for a cow pasture and filled their army canteens with milk, straight from the udder. Other times they helped themselves to vegetables from fields and remote gardens. They ate until their bellies ached. The province had a reputation for its delicious apples, and the early crop, still green and sour, was nevertheless a juicy abundance to the two hungry wanderers. Their involuntary vegetarian life-style caused a few intestinal problems, but at night, when they came upon a body of water, they went skinny dipping, and that took care of their hygiene.

Six days had passed since they left the POW camp. A sign on a crossroad read "Lisieux." According to the map, that was a disappointing 60 km (38 miles) they had traveled, and, at that rate, they would be walking for three months for ten hours a day. Erich had more swelling in his upper thigh, and moving it provoked a painful facial expression, but he did not complain. Taking a second look at the map, they saw that Paris was approximately 170 km (105 miles) away. Once there, they would be home free.

In 1940, Germany had invaded France, and per the armistice agreement by the Allies, the German army occupied designated areas in France, including Paris. That arrangement changed when Allied forces landed on D-day in Normandy and the liberation of France began. The two friends fantasized being welcomed in Paris by the German occupation authority with open arms, maybe even celebrated as heroes. There would be a brief recuperation period and issuance of back pay, as they would need money for sightseeing and exploring Paris by night. Erich insisted on a must-see visit to the legendary cabaret, Les Folies Bergère, and the can-can dance revue at the Moulin Rouge. Finally, they hoped to receive their duty dismissal papers and then board a train to Karlsruhe, Germany.

In reality, the two agreed that so far everything had gone well and they needed to continue their routine but to speed it up and thereby reach Evreux in five days, a 70 km (43 miles) hike. Unfortunately, Erich could not keep up with their set goal, and at times Rudi had to carry the friend on his back to gain a few more meters. Rudi himself experienced weakness due to their diet, and travel became a slow and difficult process.

After eight days instead of five, they reached Evreux, exhausted and distraught. Erich insisted that Rudi let him meet his fate, right there in the wheat field outside of Evreux, and move on without him. Rudi told Erich that he was a psycho and that not even the French farmers would want to waste a bullet on a lunatic like him. Both men needed to relieve their stress levels by insulting each other, but they knew that each was dependent on the other to have a chance for survival. When their quarrelling subsided, they shook hands and decided not to set time goals anymore. Their biggest desires were a decent meal and riddance of their uniforms. They saw a sign with large letters that read "Ile De France," which meant they were at last in the same province as Paris, and it boosted their spirit.

A Venerable Frenchman

The sun was beginning to rise over the horizon when they spotted a somewhat isolated farm with several barns scattered around the main house. They had passed many farms so far, but this one had an appeal like none other, and they had twisted thoughts of stealing food and clothing and maybe a bicycle. First, they both wanted to get a good day of sleep, in a barn with a hayloft to get lost in. Second, they needed time to observe the farm's activity and then make their move. Any imprudent conduct could jeopardize their safety and freedom, and Paris was just 35 km (22 miles) down the road.

It was no bad dream but a real dog barking and going crazy on the barn floor that awakened the two men *"tout de suite"* up in the loft. When they cautiously leaned forward to see about the ruckus down there, they stared into the eyes of a tall, slender man who stood on the ladder halfway up the loft. Rudi and Erich, in a state of bewilderment, did not know what to do but held their arms over their heads, just as they did when taken prisoner in Caen.

The man on the ladder unflinchingly said, "Bonjour," and made a motion for them to come down while he secured the seemingly vicious dog. For a moment, the three men stood silently looking at each other; then the man stretched out his hand to Erich, then to Rudi, and introduced himself: *"Je suis Marcel."* Erich had a good knowledge of the French language that he had acquired from school and during a summer apprenticeship in an architectural office in Strasbourg. Rudi had two years of French while attending the Bürgerschule in Komotau. Now both men had a chance to put forth their best French and explain to the man Marcel their identity and the reason for their sleeping in his hayloft. They begged him to let them go and not alert anyone. Marcel smiled and explained that he was the only human on this farm, and that they were free to go—whenever. However, he thought that they could use a hot meal and perhaps a change of clothes. Rudi and Erich looked at each other, hardly believing what the man had just offered them.

Marcel Boulanger was a lively Alsatian and proud of his German heritage, although he could not speak a word of German. His ancestors came from the Alsace, and when his grandfather married a girl from outside that region, he broke the tradition for good. Marcel was born outside of Paris in 1902, the illegitimate son of a dancer from Montmatre. He never knew his father, and his mother died from tuberculosis when he was three. His grandparents raised him, and when they passed away, he inherited a little money, which afforded him this farm. He had never married but was always looking for the right match, which he had not yet found. He had been exempt from the draft due to an accidental hearing impediment and his slight limp, caused by a foot deformity at birth.

The three men sat in the clean, spacious farmhouse kitchen and devoured a hearty breakfast of fried potatoes, eggs, and bacon, which Marcel had prepared. Rudi and Erich floated still in a daze of unbelievable good fortune, having chosen this place and met a Good Samaritan like Marcel. Was it a trap? Perhaps he is working for the Underground? All kinds of valid questions flashed in front of their eyes while trying on some clothes from a cedar chest. Even the clothing sizes of the three men were almost identical, except for the shoes. Marcel might have had an inch on the two Germans' heights. Erich and Marcel were one year apart in age, forty-one and forty-two respectively, with Rudi a young whippersnapper at thirty-one. Additionally, both were unmarried and had a problem with their leg. The similarities kept on coming, to the point of being creepy.

It was the middle of August, and Marcel expressed that he could use some help with the grain harvest. Erich's wound had started to show improvement, and he had better use of his leg. He and Rudi decided to hang out a few more days and give Marcel a hand. One day, a neighbor riding on a bicycle came up the dirt road, yelling some news of the liberation of Paris from the Germans. Rudi and Erich were hiding and devastated as they listened to the man's excitement, "*Libération de Paris par les Allemandes.*" Their plan to go to Paris and all the other illusions they had just went sour. Instead, they must choose a different route and avoid Paris. Marcel, an apolitical man, concurred and suggested that they travel from Gargenville, where they were then, in the direction of Cergy, north of Paris, bypassing Reims, and then on to Metz. The three studied the map and agreed that this would be the best route. It avoided major cities and highways and cut through the dense forests of the sparsely populated outskirts of the Ardennes Mountains, which could only be of benefit.

In late August, an appreciative Rudi and Erich said their good-byes to Marcel. Equipped with an old bicycle, dated street clothing, and some food, they left the farm and continued their journey homeward. They had burned their uniforms, soldier books, and anything that could reveal being German soldiers, except Rudi kept his photos. They still liked to travel at night using the train tracks as a guide. With most grain fields harvested by now, their hideouts became densely wooded areas. Someway, somehow, they needed another bicycle to make better time and travel during the day. Three days after leaving Marcel, they arrived in the city of Cergy. Saint Marcel, as they called their mentor, had given them a few francs to buy at least bread and cheese. One day, they saw a farm that had the looks of another overnight stay in a hayloft. As they approached the farm, four, maybe five dogs came charging toward them. It was clear to the visitors that those barks were not of welcoming nature. Rudi quickly turned and got on the bike, while Erich hopped on the back carrier with his legs dangling on both sides, and away they sped. How fortuitous that the ride was downhill …

Pedaling toward Home

The two walkers averaged 16 km (9 miles) in a twenty-four-hour period, and, though they realized it was not a great accomplishment, they kept on moving east, toward Metz. At times, they heard the thumping sounds of artillery fire in the distance. It seemed to come from the direction of Metz. Both men were infantry and had experienced combat firsthand in Normandy; they had no interest to be involved in another conflict.

Early one morning, mushroom hunters surprised them in their forest hideout. Erich told the group of seniors that he and his friend had the same idea. Rudi kept quiet. The seniors looked at the duo rather questionably but continued with their search for mushrooms. Rudi and Erich followed, pretending to do the same, but maintained a distance. Once the opportunity arose, they ran back to the bicycle and quickly left the area. When they reached the edge of the forest, they could not miss the two bicycles that leaned against a tree. Without a word, Erich took one of the bikes, jumped on it, and rode off. They were convinced that luck was on their side.

With the newly acquired two-wheeler, they traveled during the day, oftentimes using bumpy field roads, trying to avoid main thoroughfares. They were able to pedal 40 km (25 miles) per day, stopping for the last time to buy a small loaf of bread. The money was gone, and they contemplated their shortage of food. Nature still supplied some variety, especially the sweet grapes in the vineyards, to their bland diet of bread and cheese. Finally, a sign appeared that listed the distance to about four towns and one big city—Metz 38 km (23 miles). They have been on the road for nine days, pedaling and sweating in the summer heat, and now, in one more day, they would be home free. They hugged, laughed, and danced around, but could not ignore the more intense thumping noises sounding like roaring thunder as they drew closer to their destination.

At last they reached Metz, a city on the Moselle River and capital of the province of Lorraine. Neither Rudi nor Erich was involved in the battle of France in 1940; they knew, prior to the Treaty of Versailles in 1918, that Metz was a German city. After the fall of France, Hitler immediately annexed the city as well as the regions Alsace-Lorraine to the German Reich.

The two men, exhausted and exhilarated at the same time, pushed their bicycles through downtown Metz. There were German soldiers everywhere, and armored vehicles rolled down Main Street. Oddly enough, Rudi and Erich seemed to be the only civilians in the midst of this maneuver-like movement. Someone called, *"Arréter"*—"stop" in French. A lieutenant stood behind them asking in French why they were in the area and not obeying orders to stay off the streets. Rudi smilingly told the officer that he can speak German to them and proceeded to tell him in brief their situation. The lieutenant was more suspicious than impressed and walked them to his army headquarters.

A major with a few ribbons on his chest sat behind the desk gazing questionably at Rudi and Erich on the opposite side. He listened to their story and in the end said, "Indeed, perfect German, but show me one thing that identifies you as a member of the Wehrmacht. Where is your *Erkennungsmarke* (dog tags), *Soldbuch* (pay book), or *Wehrpass* (draft card)? A German soldier is required to carry these identifiers at all time, and if you were a German soldier, you would know these rules and obey them." He continued by accusing them as members of the French Underground, working for the Americans, who had reached nearby Verdun and already attacked Metz on several occasions. Rudi and Erich pleaded their innocence and gave names of their units and superior officers before their capture in Normandy, but to no avail.

What irony—escaping from the claws of the enemy and ending in the tentacles of one's own people, a military regime Rudi and Erich were part of. They were detained and interrogated daily. During their involuntary stay in the stockade, General Patton's advancing forces heavily shelled Metz. By the middle of September, the German military was engaged in grueling ground fighting with oncoming American troops. The Germans prepared for a major offensive, and by doing so paid Rudi and Erich little or no attention. They toyed with the idea of escape but knew that without the bikes, money, and the intimidating Frenchmen's clothing, their chances were slim to none. The act of escape could have lethal consequences. As their last recourse, they chose to approach the major once more. Erich took charge of that conversation, pointing out that he had opened an architectural office in Strasbourg in 1942 and was instrumental in the planning of the "New Strasbourg." He revealed that he had been a member of the NSDAP since 1937, which came as a shock to Rudi. In addition, he was the lead architect for building the largest publishing house in Karlsruhe, one that printed propaganda newspapers and the popular magazine "*Der Stürmer.*" Erich urged the major to make a phone call to Karlsruhe or Strasbourg and verify the information he had stated. Two days after that chitchat, the two men were free to go but were warned of repercussion with their units for not being in possession of proper identification.

The calendar indicated September 20, 1944. Rudi and Erich were at the Metz train station, tickets in hand to board a train to Hagenau and on to Karlsruhe. When the train rolled into the Hagenau station, they found out that it was the train's end station; they had taken the wrong train. During the battle of France, a nearby bridge over the Rhein River suffered heavy damage, and all rerouted traffic had to either go north or south from Hagenau. Erich knew Strasbourg well and was sure that most bridges over the Rhein there were intact. They had their tickets changed, and the following day, a short train ride took them to Strasbourg, over the Rhein to Kehl. From there it was 80 km (50 miles) to Erich's house in Karlsruhe. Rudi spent a few days with his friend Erich before he boarded a train to set forth the

600 km (373 miles) journey home to the Sudetenland. He wanted to surprise his wife on her twenty-fifth birthday, September 28, 1944.

Enchantment

It was late evening when Erich Schelling left our place on his first visit to Neibsheim. He returned several times and always brought a bar of Lindt chocolate for me. On one of his visits, he told me I should call him "Onkel Erich." He made my day with that request, for I was so proud to have an uncle like him with such a beautiful car—a Mercedes. I could not wait to let everyone in my school hear about my rich uncle.

The day my new uncle Erich invited the three of us for a ride in the black Mercedes to his house in Karlsruhe, I will surely never forget. My father sat up front, and my mother and I in the back, sinking into the soft, black leather seats. I did not dare to move during the ride; just my eyes peered around the interior and to the window on my side, hoping someone would see me. It was my first ride in a car, and a luxury automobile at that. When we arrived at his house, a friendly woman opened the door, and welcomed us in. Erich introduced her as his housekeeper. She led us to the dining room where an already beautifully set table waited for guests to indulge in *"Kaffee und Kuchen"* (coffee and cake) time. She addressed Erich as *Herr Professor* and inquired if she should start serving. As if hypnotized, I sat at the long table in a heavy, high-backed chair, carefully slurping *heisse Schokolade* (hot chocolate)—something I had never had in my life but liked instantly. After Erich had shown us every room in his large house, furnished with massive, antique furniture, satin couches, huge mirrors, and chandeliers, he drove us back to our place. He told my father about the car's velocity and immediately stepped on the pedal to demonstrate his point. My mother, alarmed by the sudden acceleration, reached over and held my hand. It did not matter that she did; I was in a trance the entire visit and did not snap out of it until we came back to our drearily furnished apartment.

Two years later, in 1953, Erich Schelling achieved international fame through a one-of-a-kind architectural design: the *"Schwarzwaldhalle"*, a kidney-shaped convention hall with a suspension roof in the middle of Karlsruhe. Besides his masterpiece, he designed theaters, soccer stadiums, banks, and government buildings in Germany and throughout Europe. He died in 1986 at the age of eighty-two in his beloved Karlsruhe. The established Schelling Foundation has immortalized his foresight and contribution to modern architecture by awarding a biennial prestigious architectural prize to keen visionaries in the field worldwide.

10

Moving to the City

ᘯ ᘯ ᘯ ᘯ

New Experiences

Another birthday, and I was twelve years old. The year was 1952, and an old German book-publishing house, Bertelsmann, had reinvented itself by creating the Bertelsmann *Lesering* (book club). My father signed me up, and I could choose two books every three months. It was my birthday present, and I was ecstatic to receive this membership. For mail ordering, we had a catalog listing all the titles, including a very short synopsis of each book. Miss Schmitt, my former teacher, lent me a book once with the title *Das Fliegende Klassenzimmer* (*The Flying Classroom*) by Erich Kästner. The book club featured many of Kästner's books, among them *Das Doppelte Lottchen* (*The Parent Trap*) and *Emil und die Detektive* (*Emil and the Detectives*). Another book that caught my attention was a translation of an exotic Arabian world with the best-known tales of *1001 Nacht* (*1001 Nights*); I was in book heaven.

An unexpected opportunity uprooted our Neibsheim life earlier than anticipated. Victor Liepold approached my father and offered to let him rent the second floor in his new house in Bruchsal. My parents jumped on that proposal without hesitation, and by the middle of July 1952, we had moved to Bruchsal. Sadly, we had to leave our beautiful new kitchen stove behind. The kitchen in Bruchsal could not accommodate such a monstrosity, so we sold it to the Gerwecks. The move had obvious advantages, especially to my father's employment station in Karlsruhe. The trains conveniently ran several times a day between Bruchsal and Karlsruhe. In addition, my parents were able to put in the required labor hours at their convenience and oversee the building of our home, which would start the following year.

The new housing development had the name *Waldsiedlung* (forest settlement). The surrounding large tracts of forestland gave appropriateness to the name. Furthermore, every street bore the name of a tree, with the exception of the very first street, which was called Waldstrasse (Forest Street). Besides learning about my new neighborhood and life in the city, I started seventh grade in a new school. The building looked more like a medieval castle sitting on a steep hill. During the war, the German military used the building as a garrison. It was a good twenty-five-minute walk from the Waldsiedlung to the *Kasernen Schule*. For the first time, my class consisted of only girls, a new concept of gender separation. This method was in the experimental stages while I was a student there.

The Rhein valley stretched to the Waldsiedlung on the southwest side of Bruchsal. Here the land was flat and ideal for bicycling and roller skating. Many Sundays, some adults and we kids rode the easy twenty-two km on our bikes to the Rhein, the biggest river in Germany. While hanging out on its rugged right bank, we folded sheets of white paper into miniature boats and followed with eager eyes whose boat floated furthest down the river. Another one of our pastimes was sending a message in a bottle, always hoping for a response from someone in northern Germany or even the Netherlands, where the Rhein disembogues into the North Sea. We never heard from anyone, but that did not discourage our enthusiasm.

A Mutilated Christmas Tree

It was our first Christmas in Bruchsal, and my father and I searched in the nearby woods for just the right spruce for a Christmas tree. As in the previous year, we used cotton for a snow effect, and we added a few more store-bought ornaments. My father removed all the extra little twigs between the main heavier branches, assuming that the decorations could hang freely and be more visible. In the end, the tree looked scrawny and barren, and he admitted that his pruning was not such a great idea after all. I had wished for a new coat and roller skates, and my packages, now wrapped in bright Christmas paper, contained just that. In addition, two more books from the book club had arrived, and someone laid them under the tree. I could hardly wait to use my holiday vacation for some serious reading of Karl May's American frontier tales of *Old Shatterhand* and the Apache Indian chief, *Winnitou.*

Waiting up for Midnight Mass, we played games in the Liepold's leaving room until it was time to bundle up and walk a half a mile to Abele's abandoned factory. There, in a metal building, St. Antonius Church had found a temporary home. One of the priests from St. Paul Parish in Bruchsal read Pope Pius's Christmas message and held mass in this austerely furnished and freezing large room. I wore my Christmas gift, the new, hooded brown coat (bought with another year of usage in mind). I trembled from the cold like everyone else in the unheated building. My thoughts wandered back to the dazzling Christmas tree lights and warm atmosphere of the Midnight Mass in Neibsheim. Suddenly, I realized that it was my first Christmas without my grandparents and my aunt and their traditions and superstitions and all the familiar aromas and busyness. Overcome with sadness, I tried to suppress the swelling of tears in my eyes. I yearned for the little village with the rolling hills, wondering if our move to Bruchsal was really a great idea.

The Ice Pond

In January of 1953, shortly after the Christmas holidays, school started with a teacher-parent conference. Miss Leppert, my teacher, told my parents that I was a pleasure in her class and an outstanding student. She also told them that I would have been well-suited for an academic environment like the Gymnasium; unfortunately, it was too late. My father did not elaborate on her remark and seemed rather uncomfortable discussing the matter. I continued to be the good student she talked about; I also became a full-fledged teenager on January 16, 1953. Since "teenager" is an English word, it had no special relevance in German. Therefore, I just had another birthday and turned thirteen.

Although I had received roller skates for Christmas, I now had a wish and need for a pair of ice skates for my birthday. Every day on the way to school, I passed by a frozen pond where kids of all ages ice skated after school and on weekends. With my new skates, I started my ice-skating career on my thirteenth birthday. That day, I spent most of the time falling and crawling on the ice, but I was committed.

The *Eisweiher* (ice pond) gained more popularity as the winter months lingered on. Some days the crowds of little people made it difficult to skate, especially for an unsteady beginner like me. There was an older girl—someone said she was sixteen—and her name was Heidi Griesheimer. Nobody dared to invade her large area of needed space to perfect her figure eight. I watched her from a distance, not for her skating capabilities but for her chic and fancy outfit. She wore a short, flared red coat, red tights, white boots, and a red bonnet. Around her neck hung a twisted, shiny rope holding a white fur hand muff. I was in awe of her coordinated costume, wishing I could look just like her. Other kids shared my envy, and they talked about her rich father, a bank director of some big bank in Bruchsal. Uncle Erich came to mind, a man who also had reached fame and wealth, and I concluded that being Flüchtling had ruined my life.

Sweat Equity

After the last major frost in the spring of 1953, the Bruchsal Housing Commission launched Phase III of the Waldsiedlung building program. The building site was a bustling place cluttered with cranes and machinery I never had laid eyes on before. Contractors tagged the outline of each lot along the newly paved street, called Eichenweg (Oak Lane), our new address-to-be. My parents, Aunt

Klara, and Uncle Schorsch spent every free minute on their designated lots, numbers eight and ten, where they diligently put in many hours of hard labor, digging out the basement for the double. On weekends, neighbors and people we hardly knew who were already living in the Waldsiedlung showed up with pickax, shovel, and wheelbarrow to offer their help. Some days, the site had twenty or twenty-five people digging, moving soil, and hauling rocks. It was like human machines working on a community project. By the end of the day, these volunteers, dirty and tired but still smiling, shook hands with my father, who thanked each and every one for their helping hand.

Within two months, the dug-out basement met specifications and was ready for the construction crew to lay the foundation. After that, we saw the house growing block by block and wall by wall. After each completed section, a building inspector appeared, to the disdain of the contractor, and marked his stamp of approval or disapproval on the finished job. By November, a small fir tree with wafting streamers, defying icy winds, appeared on top of the roof rafter, indicating the shell of the house was completed and the house had passed its final inspection. This is an old tradition honoring the builder and the workers for their accomplishments. Just before winter set in, the installers of doors and windows worked overtime while the roofers hung the red roof tiles, also determined to beat the first snow. They all met their time goals, and our house, protected from the weather, had time to settle over the winter.

Distant Relatives

Tante Hilde, a distant cousin of my mother and aunt whom I had met frequently on her five-minute stops when traveling through Bruchsal had repeatedly invited me to her home in Kaufbeuren. My overprotective mother finally agreed to a one-week visit during the summer of 1953. Wearing my Sunday dress and carrying a small suitcase, my parents accompanied me to the train station in Bruchsal, where I boarded an *Eilzug* (fast train) to Munich, all on my own. My white clutch purse contained some money, my ticket, and a list with instructions pertaining to my itinerary. When the train arrived in Munich Hauptbahnhof, I needed to change trains. As instructed by my father, I searched for a conductor who could direct me to the platform where the train to Kaufbeuren would be. Overwhelmed by the size of the large bomb-damaged hall swarming with people, I wriggled through the crowd looking for a uniformed railway employee. In a matter of minutes, a nice woman took me to the designated platform and put me on a waiting commuter train.

The train stopped in every little village until it reached Kaufbeuren. Tante Hilde waved a white handkerchief, and I recognized her instantly. The girl with her had to be the daughter, Christine, I had heard so much about, and I could hardly contain my excitement to meet her. We were the same age and size, only her short-cropped hair was extremely blonde, and mine, also short, was dark blonde. She wore pale yellow Capri pants and a matching blouse, and I immediately liked her in-fashion look.

I remembered my instruction to buy a postcard and write to my parents that I was in the safe hands of Hilde Hausmann. A tramline and two changes later, we reached their apartment house. There I met the rest of the family. Mr. Hausmann, Tante Hilde's husband, a tall, friendly man, reminded me of my father; he even had the same name, Rudi. And, there was Günter, a ten-year-old boy with a mischievous smile; his mother adoringly called him "Günterle." I fell in love with the whole family and could not wait for what was in store in the days ahead.

The next morning, everyone got up early. I was told that we would take Günterle to a weeklong boy's camp at Lake Staffelsee, spend the day there, and have a picnic. The Hausmanns owned a green VW bus that showed age and usage. It had a few dents and scrapes, but Mr. Hausmann drove at steady speed through the hilly and curvy countryside. For the first time in my life, I saw the snow-topped mountains of the Alps looming in the background, and I swallowed the scenery in big gulps. After an hour drive, we arrived at Staffelsee and signed our young camper in, although he stayed with us most of the day. We searched for a nice spot close to the lake and set up a table and lounge chairs. Despite a bright sunny sky, the air was vigorously cool. Christine and I stayed inside the bus while Tante Hilde tried to get the small kerosene burner going so she could prepare the promised hot chocolate. The waterfront filled quickly with cars, and people readied themselves to soak in the sunshine or drop off a young camper lad. I was amazed by all the cars parked along the lake, something so totally new and foreign to my world. I inquired, "Did everybody in Bavaria own a car?" They all laughed, and the answer was, in unison, "No." However, Mr. Hausmann did mention that more people owned cars now than ever before in the history of Germany.

On our way home, Mr. Hausmann took a short detour to show me nearby Garmisch-Partenkirchen, an idyllic alpine town. Nestled at the foot of Germany's highest mountain, the Zugspitze at seven thousand feet, the city's fame came from hosting the Winter Olympics before the war.

Like Sisters

The following days, Christine and I hung out by ourselves. She took me around in her neighborhood, and we stopped by the Hausmanns' jewelry store, where both her parents worked. We compared notes of likes and dislikes: school (she attended Gymnasium), friends, clothes, and pretended to be sisters. One hot afternoon, we took bikes and rode to the city swimming pool in Kaufbeuren. I did not own a bathing suit, but Christine had several, and she let me choose one of hers. She demonstrated her swimming abilities to me and even jumped off the diving board. I had never been at a swimming pool before, nor did I know how to swim, and I was afraid of the water. She wanted to teach me, but I was not ready. That did not stop us from having fun: fooling other kids with our very limited English vocabulary, speaking in a fake British accent, and claiming London as our home.

Tante Hilde was pleased that we hit it off so well, and she had a surprise lined up for us. She knew the owners of a dairy farm a short distance from Kaufbeuren, where she bought her fresh milk and butter. Every second or third day, someone from the farm would hike up the mountain, where their cattle grazed in succulent mountain pastures during the summer months, and pick up the collected fresh milk. Our surprise was to accompany the young milk runner to the *Alm* (Alpine meadow) and spend two nights in the care of the *Sennerin* (dairy woman) with whom Tante Hilde had prearranged our visit. It sounded exciting, and we each saw ourselves as little

"Heidi," the main character from the world-famous children's book with the same title.

An Alpine Meadow Experience

From the dairy farm to Schönhenger's Alm was quite a hike. Although a scorching summer sun kept most people sweltering in the valley; we were told to bring along warmer clothes. Also, we had to be at the farm no later than 8:00 a.m. or we would miss our guide. Seppl, a sixteen-year-old boy, leaned against a hand wagon with two empty milk containers waiting for us. He never spoke a word but just pulled the wagon as Christine and I followed him up the winding path. Suddenly the fog was lifting, and a bright sun sent inviting rays from an azure sky. After a short rest, Seppl indicated that we could help push the cart from behind, since the trail led up a steep incline.

Finally, we reached the green, lush meadows of the Alm. A middle-aged woman and a teenage boy stood on the porch of a weathered cottage, seemingly awaiting our company. Christine knew the dairy woman, Frau Bachmaier, and introduced her to me. She welcomed us both and turned around looking for her son, Hannes, but he had quietly disappeared. She excused his behavior as being bashful, especially with girls.

The gray cottage was a one-room wood building, and the Bachmaiers only spent the summer months on the mountain. Besides milking the cows, they churned butter and produced a soft cheese called *Bauernkäse*. While we chatted away, the milk runner, Seppl, with the help of Hannes loaded his wagon with the earmarked dairy products. After a proper snack, he tackled his way down the mountain.

Frau Bachmaier was a heavyset woman with rosy cheeks, and a thick braid of blonde hair framed her jolly face. She wore a dirndl that could have used a good washing. The inside of the cottage gave a functional appearance, and the ruffled, blue-checkered curtains and a tablecloth of the same material added a touch of coziness. Behind a small wood stove lay the outstretched bodies of two sleeping calico cats. A large wooden barrel for butter churning and a table cluttered with cheese-making utensils occupied one corner, while the other provided sleeping accommodations with a sturdy bunk bed. An overwhelming cheese odor made Christine and me look at each other in disgust. Frau Bachmaier smilingly ignored our nose wrinkle. In her jovial way, she pointed to the bed and assured us that we three girls would occupy the bunk. Her son did not mind sleeping in the shed with the goats; they kept him warm. She informed us of the outhouse behind the shed and a bedpan underneath the bunk bed. For a moment, I had a flashback to the rickety outhouse at the evil Strobels' in Neibsheim. Christine looked at me and shook her head. I understood: no bedpan or outhouse. What alternative was there—a tree, a bush, with Hannes roaming the mountain?

Once Is Enough

The tasty *Pfifferling* (chanterelle mushroom) and Speck omelet Frau Bachmaier prepared made for a plain but substantial late lunch. We drank lukewarm cow milk but preferred the cool water from the mountain stream, which looked like a band of quicksilver. In the afternoon, we sat on the porch admiring the beauty of untouched nature and tried to count the brown cows scattered all over the place. The sun slipped away early, and a cool breeze coming down from the mountains made us shiver. Once the sun disappeared, dusk set in quickly and we moved inside. Frau Bachmaier lit a kerosene lamp and made a fire in the stove to take the chill off. She focused her attention toward me, asking lots of questions about my family and background. I felt compelled to tell her that we were Flüchtling, just like the Hausmanns. She ignored my comment and kept repeating her wish to boat down the Rhein River, though she had second thoughts, since she could not swim. It was the cue for Christine to join the discussion about fear of water, swimming, and diving. We talked and laughed until Frau Bachmaier excused herself, picked up the kerosene lamp, and left the room. With the lamp gone, we sat uncomfortably in the pitch-black room guessing if she went to the outhouse or to check on her son, who had vanished when we arrived. She returned a while later and offered us the lamp, which we gladly took and headed for the outhouse.

The next morning, Frau Bachmaier got up at dawn and started her routine of milking the cows. They were already grazing, and we could hear them by the jingle of their cowbells or the mooing in the pasture, which had a resounding echo effect in the mountains. Christine made us soft-boiled eggs, and I slathered the butter on the home-baked bread like never before in my life. All tasted scrumptious!

Secretly, we were hoping that Frau Bachmaier had no chores for us, but we had to ask for politeness' sake. When we stepped outside of the cottage into the chilly morning air, we noticed the mist rising up from the valley. What a spectacular sight, and we had forgotten to bring Christine's camera to capture it! For now, Frau Bachmaier had no work for us, but maybe later, she suggested, we could help with the butter churner. She forewarned us not to pick Edelweiss, should we see any, as the flower was protected under strict nature conservation laws. Her son, Hannes, definitely avoided Christine and me, and privately we called him *Geissenpeter*, the rascal character from the book *Heidi*. Geissenpeter, a lad of fifteen, was tall and blond and a very shy shepherd.

There was little to do for us girls, other than soak in the sunshine and play with the cats, and when we spotted Edelweiss, we broke the rule, plucked the precious flowers, and hid them in our clothes. Christine said, "You know, down in the valley, they would call us Edelweiss pirates," and we had a good laugh. We listened to the echo of our yodeling and Geissenpeter's laughing at it, also coming back as an echo. In the evening, we sat outside wrapped in a blanket and watched the brilliant colors of a perfect sunset disappearing behind majestic mountains. Christine and I were glad; it was our second and last night on the Alm. We agreed that life in this isolation was not as appealing as we anticipated or heard described in the Heidi story, but we would tell Christine's mother otherwise. When Seppl showed up, we were anxious to join him on the descent from the mountain station. Neither of us had the desire to return to Alm life anytime soon, after catching a glimpse of its monotony and struggles.

Such Magnificence

Time flew, and it was my last day in Kaufbeuren. Tante Hilde took the day off and had one more surprise in store for us. She readied the picnic basket and kept us guessing. Eventually, she loaded blankets, picnic basket, and the two of us into the VW bus and positioned herself in the driver seat. I was aware of Tante Hilde's driving capabilities from her solo visits to Bruchsal, driving the same bus. She created quite a furor in the Waldsiedlung; a woman driving a small bus—that was sensational!

Again we passed picturesque mountain scenery and stopped in the city of Füssen. By now, we had figured out that we would picnic on the banks of the green river Lech, near the waterfalls, and visit Neuschwanstein, the fairy-tale castle of King Ludwig II. In history class, I read about the House of Wittelsbach reigning as Bavarian kings, and of Ludwig, the eccentric ruler who spent a fortune building extravagant castles equipped with technologies far advanced of their time. His own cabinet declared him mad and placed him under arrest. He drowned under mysterious circumstances at Starnberg Lake in 1886.

We hiked the steep path up the craggy mountain and found a mixture of German and foreign tourists waiting for the castle tour to begin. The setting was magical. The palace building set with towers, turrets, and spires gave the appearance of a medieval castle. Most impressive was the Hall of Singers and the two-story Throne Room in Byzantine style, with colorful arcades and mural paintings inspired by Richard Wagner operas. Every room had splendiferous chandeliers and exquisite touches throughout. The king's bedroom displayed a hand-carved, four-poster oak bed with a cathedral tower canopy and a sink in the form of a swan with running water. What nostalgic elegance. What insane splendor!

The next day, Saturday, I wanted time to stand still, but it kept on ticking. Günterle needed to be picked up from camp, and I for the last time sat in their green bus while the Hausmanns brought me to the train station. Christine and I had divided the illegally harvested Edelweiss as a memento of our friendship forever. We made plans to visit soon but in the meantime would write each other everything that happened in our lives.

I was in my seat when the train slowly started to leave the platform, and some people stood waving good-byes to the passengers on the impelling train. Leaning out of the window, my extended arms waved vigorously back at the Hausmanns' hand motions and white handkerchief until they became tiny dots and disappeared. My entire visit was a fairy tale in itself, and my mind raced over the many new impressions and experiences and their impact on my feelings. I compared the Hausmanns to my family but could not find a parallel, and it gave me reasons to contemplate and question some things. They were Flüchtling just like us yet were so different in their attitudes and life-style. I had a real need to discuss that observation with my parents. All that thinking and confusion in my head made me hungry, and I dug into the brown paper sack Tante Hilde had sent along on my trip.

Not long after my memorable visit, school started and I entered the eighth grade. My thoughts wandered to Christine, who was starting her fifth year of Gymnasium. I felt somewhat melancholic and wished I could do the same. We wrote each other once a week and always ended the letter with "friendship forever" sealed by a drawing of an Edelweiss.

Much Ado about Hair

A fat letter arrived in the mail; it was a birthday present from Christine. She sent a nice note along with several photographs of my visit in Kaufbeuren. I was elated to have wonderful memories of her and my visit immortalized by these pictures. Over the years, they have served as pleasant reminders of an extraordinary experience at the impressionable age of thirteen. Like many sincere plans or promises in life, Christine and I fell prey to human failure; we never saw each other again.

On January 16, 1954, I turned fourteen and felt more grown up, especially since my solo trip to Kaufbeuren. Just before I visited there, I had my braids cut off. This was no easy task, since my mother and Oma disliked the idea of Erikale without her long braids, regardless of how thin and straight the hair. Unfortunately, I was not blessed with thick hair like my mother and grandmother had; mine had the texture of my Aunt Klara's and my father's feathery tuft. It took some whining and pleading to change their minds, and finally the forced support of my father and aunt helped my cause.

To me, riddance of the braids with colorful ribbons was the symbolic finale to my childhood years. For my age, I was a tall, slender girl, and people told me I had a beautiful smile. Thanks to my grandmother, I had a perfect set of teeth. It was not always that way. When I was much younger and we still lived in Neibsheim, some of my front teeth overlapped. Oma demonstrated to me what to do to straighten them. At least five times a day, I pushed my fingers hard against my crooked eyeteeth. Oma would not let me forget my absolute commitment to my then-little choppers.

11

The New House in the Forest Settlement

❧ ❧ ❧ ❧

Our Own Four Walls

As soon as the temperature reached above freezing, my parents worked on the interior of our new house. They painted, wallpapered, and varnished the wood floors. Uncle Schorsch had completed the highly polished bedroom set and buffet/hutch for our kitchen. We went modern and bought our first electric appliance—a kitchen stove. On a good weather day, the house exterior received the final touch, a white stucco finish.

By April, we packed our things at the Liepolds' and moved one street over into our completed home on Eichenweg. We chose the second floor for our quarters while another Flüchtling family, whom we had not known before, rented the first floor. Their name was Zeigler, and they had two daughters. Inge was my age, and we became best friends. Aunt Klara and her family moved into their side of the double at about the same time, and they, too, chose the second floor. The Frankels and their four children lived on the first floor.

With the house came a one-story *Anbau* (annex), separated by a paved, open courtyard. It housed a good-sized wash kitchen, where a "copper," a large kettle, hung over a specially designed fire pit. On washdays, a well-lit fire boiled the white laundry in the kettle filled with soapy water. We let the Zeiglers use the wash kitchen for their laundry on agreed-upon days of the week. Another room was a storage area for bikes, garden tools, and wood for heating. A small area leading to a spacious backyard was perfect for raising small domestic animals, like a pig, chickens, or rabbits. We decided on a pig, which we called Sugel. The time was just right when my father and Uncle Schorsch prepared the backyard soil to put in several fruit trees, berry bushes, and a vegetable garden.

In late fall of 1954, we had a *Metzelfest* (butchery feast). Mr. Dworshak, a certified butcher and the owner of the Waldsiedlung's butcher shop, came to our house early in the morning and spent the whole day in the wash kitchen, where he processed the slaughtered pig for our consumption. He brought his utensils, grinders, herbs, and skins for sausage making. His fee for the nasty job was half of the pig. I was told that Sugel went to hog heaven, and I was not allowed to step into the Anbau while Mr. Dworshak was there. I found the explanation silly, as I had some good idea of what a Metzelfest entailed.

A few days after our Metezelfest, Uncle Schorsch had Mr. Dworschak in his annex to whack their fattened pig and do the butcher's task. Aunt Klara was nowhere in sight that day. The night before the "Metzeltrauma" as she referred to it, she took the children and went for a two-day visit to her parents' in Neibsheim.

Almost every homeowner in the Waldsiedlung raised a pig, and when old Mr. Dworschak died, rumor had it he was a wealthy Flüchtling from the Sudetenland. He also left behind an unmatched reputation of being the best butcher in Bruchsal and beyond. His son took over the operation, and he, too, established quite a name for himself. In later years, as the Waldsiedlung grew, a new ordinance ruled against keeping pigs and chickens, and the Metzelfest became an old-fashioned practice of days bygone.

Not Just a Game

On July 4, 1954, the Waldsiedlung, Bruchsal, and all of Germany was glued to a magical box, a *Fernseher* (television), to watch the final game of the World Cup in Bern, Switzerland. For the first time since before the war, and with an aura of controversy, the German team was admitted to participate in the World Cup, They were the underdog playing an unbeaten, legendary, and heavily favored Hungarian team. The Germans beat the Hungarians 3-2, and history coined the game the "Miracle of Bern."

My father left our house early, as he was most eager to secure a front-row seat at the Gasthaus Zur Waldsiedlung, a tavern owned by the Dworschaks. Theirs was the only television in the entire Waldsiedlung. Every man and boy, soccer enthusiast or not, was there to get a glimpse of the match that made Germany the World Cup champion. My mother never showed much interest in *Fussball* (soccer). She and I listened to the game on our radio via a commentator overtaken by his emotions when Germany scored the winning goal. My father came home with tears in his eyes. He depicted the emotional reaction of the crowd at the Gasthaus after Germany's win, and television cameras showing the playing of the German national anthem for the first time since WWII. It was a defining moment, and the victory symbolized more than just a win of the World Cup. It gave Germans hope and the beginning of a feeling of success for a beaten nation still living and suffering the aftermath of war.

A Place for Entertainment

Gasthaus Zur Waldsiedlung not only had a big television but also live entertainment on Saturday evening. The trio of musicians consisted of various talents. My father, employed as train conductor, played the violin. Mr. Gröbner, a shoe repairman, was master on the accordion. And Mr. Klunker, a teacher, added his musical flair as the flute and clarinet player. They played their hearts out, with hits from the thirties and forties. The Gasthaus had a very cozy atmosphere and always a packed house of satisfied patrons. My mother and I would go there and sit with the families of the other two players. Usually we had a choice of a free meal, and Mr. Dworschak provided food, beer, and wine to the three entertainers, as much as they could consume. He had ample help from his elderly mother, wife, daughter, and son, Adolf III, who was my age, and I did not like his ogling after me. However, in his father's Gasthaus, young Adolf felt important. He generously offered me, as well as other kids, shot glasses of egg liquor, free of charge, when his parents were too busy and not watching their son promoting the spirit of charity.

My father was the organizer and lead of the happy music makers, who played pro bono anywhere. Mr. Dworschak did pay my father a few DM to cover some expenses in instrument upkeep and sheet music. While watching the entertainers play and people dance, I discovered that women adored my father, and he did not mind. On the contrary, he played silly eye games with them. Surely my acquiescent mother had to be aware of it, but she never gave him as much as a look of reproach or a mention at home. She was content to be there, listening to his intoxicating gypsy music on his sighing fiddle, and he was her Rudi.

A Change of Plans

By the end of July, I had completed primary school and graduated with honorable mention. My parents supported my idea to attend a private *Dolmetscher Schule* (interpreter school) in Karlsruhe. I was excited when my father and I stepped on a train to Karlsruhe in order to visit the language school and meet with its dean. It became clear in the beginning of the interview that this school's curriculum was over my head. I had studied English for four years but had no knowledge of French, one of the requirements. The letter from the institute did not specify these qualifications, but I was an unqualified candidate. Again, a reference to Gymnasium came up by the dean's comment on his school's preference for students from a Gymnasium background. Glancing at my father, I knew that he did not want to hear that, and we left the office in a hurry. Perhaps my father felt guilty; it did not appease my anger and disappointment. He suggested lunch in an outdoor café, which reduced the tension between us. Afterward, he wanted to stop by the office of estranged Erich Schelling. We had not seen the renowned architect since we lived on Upper Mill Street in Neibsheim. I no longer felt comfortable calling him Uncle Erich but addressed him as Professor Schelling. He didn't correct me, and I still felt intimidated by this man's opulence. After that visit, I never saw the famous architect again.

Now I faced a real dilemma in the continuance of my education. My first choice, the language school, was an upsetting failure, and my second choice, the *Höhere Handelsschule* (business/commercial college), was impossible too: due to my first choice, I had missed the date of the entrance exam for the coming school year. Determined to continue a formal education, I refused to enter into a vocational training situation just to satisfy the German education requirement.

We found a new type of school with a one-year program in home economics. Not exactly my cup of tea, but its curriculum offered a variety of studies, from nutrition to community services to family relationship. The schedule included cooking classes, and I remember the modern equipped kitchen, where I ostensibly created delectable dishes. I must have been in a fog, slept through, or played hooky in those classes, since I did not know how to cook when I started a family.

I do remember the handicraft class, where I learned how to knit, but there I refused to apply myself. In my frustration, I became a class clown and a disruptive troublemaker, and I had to sit on a chair outside of the classroom most of the time. However, I needed to get a complete for the class and present my project, a sweater, using two colors of knitting yarn. Aunt Klara had pity on me and knitted most of the violet and black sweater. The few rows I completed on my own stood out like a dark spot of mangled and dirty yarn. The teacher suspected the help of an adult, and I denied it. I received a D, barely passing.

Summer Vacation at Gustel's Bakery

During the summer of 1954, Uncle Gustel and Aunt Linde invited me to Neunburg vorm Wald, Bavaria. I was excited to visit, even though I did not know them. Equipped with good advice and instructions, my parents put me on the train in Bruchsal. It seemed I was the only one in our family using my father's perks from work, the long-distance train vouchers. This trip took me east, very close to the Böhmerwald, and the travel time was the same as going to

Kaufbeuren in the previous year. When the train reached Nürnberg, I vaguely remembered our train stop here in 1946. It looked all different now. The mountains of rubble had disappeared, and the main station had been completely rebuilt. Loudspeakers made announcements of arrivals and departures. People were in a rush to catch their train on an extensive track system going in every direction. To be on the safe side, I asked for help and was directed to the right train. I needed to make two more changes. A little worried about missing them, I kept asking passengers, as they were coming and going every time the train stopped, and followed their advice. Finally, someone said that the next station was Neunburg vorm Wald, and I got my suitcase down from the overhead compartment.

In our letter correspondence, we had agreed that Aunt Linde would be waving a white handkerchief for me to recognize them. The last time they saw me was in 1942; I was two years old. Leaning out the window, I sighted a woman waving a white something, and I felt relieved. We met up immediately; they showered me with endless compliments and made me feel most welcome.

Uncle Gustel was my mother's half-brother, but she and Aunt Klara never used the term. He was their brother! He, on the other hand, had some animosity toward my grandfather, really his uncle, who raised Gustel and his brothers like his own sons. His wife Linde came from Poland, and she and Gustel had married during the war and moved to Neunburg vorm Wald in Bavaria, just thirty-five km from Franzelhütte. He never came to visit nor showed any interest in his family's well-being. Gustel was a baker by trade, and after the war, when the opportunity presented itself, he bought the bakery where he had worked for several years. He and Linde had no children, and they spent all their time working. Gustel, with the help of an assistant, did all the baking and delivering, and Linde stood behind the counter and ran the store. In the evening, they cleaned the shop and prepared for next day. Their days started at four in the morning, and by nine p.m. all was quiet in the house.

My uncle's bakery refreshed my faint memory of the Veit Bakery in Komotau, with its steady stream of customers in the morning—mainly women jabbering idle talk with each other while waiting in line. Aunt Linde's awful pronunciation of German could be compared to a vandal mutilating a painting. However, she always smiled a factitious smile when accepting the money from the customer. I helped her in the store on the days when no deliveries were made.

Twice a week, Uncle Gustel drove a white station wagon loaded with crusty breads, hard rolls, pretzels, and all sorts of yummy pastries to remote villages in the *Bayrische Wald* (Bavarian Forest), a wooded mountain chain that runs parallel to the Böhmerwald in the Czech Republic. I accompanied him on these trips, since I enjoyed the car ride in the boondocks and took a fancy to helping sell these fine baked goods. Usually, the women were waiting by the side of the road for the familiar station wagon. Uncle Gustel had a hearty and playful relationship with them. Sometimes he would drop a pretzel or a *Berliner* (type of doughnut) in the bag of a pretty woman and just nod and smile at her. The first time I came along, he introduced me as his favorite niece to everyone. In his interaction with people, I observed his qualities as a jokester.

We headed back when the station wagon was empty and stopped for an ice cream before going home. In addition, my uncle squeezed two DM into my hand for being such an efficient and cheery helper, as he put it. He asked me not to mention it to my aunt, nor his charitable actions with some customers, since she was a bit stingy and jealous and kept a strict account.

My two-week visit hurried by in a flash, and on Sunday morning my uncle and aunt walked me to a rather deserted-looking train station. I opened the window in my compartment and noticed tears on my uncle's face as the train took me away. I pondered over his motive and concluded that he was already missing my youthful enthusiasm on his delivery route. We relished our time together talking, laughing, and telling funny jokes. Without realizing it, I got an education in selling and handling money. Due to the generosity of my uncle, I had about twenty DM more in my pocket when I left Neunburg vorm Wald than when I arrived. On the long train ride home, I had time to think about all my acquired experiences in Uncle Gustel's business, and the idea of continuing to earn money stirred my interest.

A New Church and Parish

St. Antonius Church finally moved from its temporary housing on the Abele property to a new, contemporary-style church building with a tall bell tower. The diocesan archbishop from Freiburg came to Bruchsal specifically for the dedication of the newly built church. It was a beautiful, warm, and blue-skied summer Sunday. For days, the parishioners had prepared food and drink and set up for this grand occasion. Finally, the Waldsiedlung, a fast-growing community, and its nearby vicinity had their own parish, St. Anton, and a new priest, Father Kluge.

For reasons I don't know, our new parish of St. Anton fell under the aegis of St. Paul Parish, with *Pfarrer* (priest) Menzer in charge of the two parishes. Each parish had its own priest and office, but all major decisions came from St. Paul Parish. In later years, both parishes were incorporated into the Parish of St. Peter, due to ever-increasing shortages of Catholic priests.

After school was in session, our church parish started a youth group, and we met every Wednesday evening. The gathering enabled teenage participants to join various groups of interest, guided by adults. Since I loved to sing and had a good voice, I wanted to become a member of the church choir. However, that group of older women and men was hard to penetrate, and they gave the feeble excuse that I was too young. Another interest of mine was being a lector, reading aloud scriptural passages and announcing the songs during worship services. Pfarrer Menzer took his time but finally decided on me to be lector and lead singer in the Wednesday evening service before youth group meeting. Father Kluge, our young parish priest, chose the songs and prayers, and I carried out his instructions. I felt slightly important within the congregation, but I truly enjoyed my involvement in the Catholic Church.

One day, Pfarrer Menzer approached me with an opportunity to earn some money. The diocese strongly recommended the reading of the *Feuerreiter* (Fire Rider), a newly published magazine for the Catholic family. My job was to knock on doors, sell subscriptions of the monthly magazine, deliver it, and collect the money, which I then had to send to the diocese in Freiburg, a city in the Black Forest. At one point, I had thirty-eight customers, all in the Waldsiedlung, and

I earned over five DM per month. In 1954, that was good money for a fourteen-year-old kid. I kept the job for almost three years, but toward the end, deficiencies in collecting the premiums gobbled up my commission. Subscribers were hard to catch at home or they had no money on collection day, or any other day. In addition, my time was limited, and I could not devote the necessary efforts to the project. I regretfully turned the route back to the parish office.

More Acquisitions

Just before Christmas in 1954, our family took the train to Karlsruhe and visited a large furniture store. My parents decided to buy living room furniture of a simple but new fashion design. The set consisted of a sleeping couch with green and gold cloth upholstery and two matching armchairs, a three-piece wood cabinet unit with built-in mini-bar, and a low rectangular table with inlaid black glass panes. The table had the most interesting features. It could be cranked up to the height of a regular dining table. The wooden panes hidden underneath the black glass could be pulled out and folded over the glass. We used this table on many occasions for dining purposes. My father paid cash for every piece, and the store manager promised to deliver the furniture before Christmas. The merchandise arrived by truck two days before Christmas Eve.

The day after Christmas is the day of Saint Stephen—*Stephanstag*—another holiday. It's not a family day, like Christmas, but a day of visiting friends and exchanging gifts with them. Our good friends the Liepold brothers and their families came to our house on this Stephanstag. As in the past, we exchanged homemade Christmas cookies. Our new living room furniture was the focal point of conversation, and the words of admiration just kept coming. My parents beamed with pride, and my father opened up the black glass-enclosed mini-bar for everyone to see and removed the one bottle of cognac that he had bought for an occasion like this. The adults proposed one toast after another, first to each other and then our new furniture, our improved lives, the Sudetenland, the Waldsiedlung, and whatever silly thought came to mind. When the last drop was squeezed from the bottle, everyone went home in a very happy mood.

Dancing to the Danube Waltz

Right around my fifteenth birthday, in January 1955, the Rhein River at Karlsruhe had reached its highest water levels in 140 years and flooded large areas on both sides of the river. For several days, the front page of the local newspaper showed pictures of the swollen river, and many people had to evacuate. Since the Waldsiedlung was in the flatlands, every homeowner had concerns about the floods of the Rhein River reaching the south side of Bruchsal. Fortunately, the waters receded and we were spared from disaster. However, that summer we experienced an unforgettable mosquito epidemic.

My birthday present that year exceeded all expectations and was a complete surprise—a brand new three-speed bicycle. What a beauty of chrome on a black and green glazed metal frame. In addition, this one had front and back lights, a requirement by law to ride a bike at night. I could hardly wait for the snow to melt so I could show off my latest in bicycle fashion.

Though I never asked, I wondered how my parents were able to afford such big-ticket items of late. Indeed, my father's job and my mother's part-time work in Siemens, combined with their frugality, made it possible to save for the things they needed or wanted most. Sometimes I heard my father express his dream to own and drive a car one day. Perhaps to him, a car portrayed the ultimate in having achieved success.

Some Sunday afternoons, dressed in our Sunday best, the three of us strolled to the Café Kull for a good cup of coffee and a slice from their assortment of delicious tortes. Besides the huge terrace for outdoor seating, there was a large room for indoor dining, with a sophisticated ambience achieved by extensive decorations and luxurious amenities. The Kull was Bruchsal's finest, and their regular patrons came from the old *"Brusler"* elite. Occasionally, they had a three-man band for entertainment. Once while we were there, they announced a dancing contest, and anyone could enter it. The dance was a waltz, and I encouraged my parents to participate, but my reserved mother declined. My father, without saying a word, took my arm and led me to the dance floor. I protested, but he said, "Don't worry; just be limber and let me do the leading." He and I waltzed and floated over the dance floor like an experienced dancing couple to the tune of the Blue Danube Waltz. We competed against five couples, and when the music stopped, we received the most applause and scooped up the first price. I could not believe it but liked the feeling of a moment in the spotlight, and, of course, the ten DM gift certificate that came with it.

Beginning a Formal Education

In 1955, the newest and most modern school building in Bruchsal was that of the *Höheren Handelsschule* of Bruchsal. On my first day there, I could smell the newness of the building and admired the wide hallways flooded by the light of penetrating sunshine through the glass wall of windows. It was a sort of orientation day, and I met some of my teachers, who were to be addressed as either Doctor or Professor. I no longer was Erika but was Fräulein (Miss) Veit. My class was the HHCI, and the cultural ministry still scrutinized gender separation. The boys had their own building within the maze of the impressive complex. More than one-half of all students came by train or bus from surrounding towns and villages. I did not know anyone in my classes, other than occasionally running into an upper classmate at break or in the hall. Everyone had a student picture ID for entrance to lecture halls, lab use, and reduced admittance fees for almost any event.

After several weeks of classes, it was time to select a class speaker. The rule was simple: three candidates; majority vote wins. I do not recall my motivation for signing up as a candidate, but I did, and I received the most votes, which made me class speaker. It was my job to bring grievances or student needs to the attention of the administration, or sometimes to a professor. I found out quickly that this was a thankless job, and I never ran for another office again.

Moments of Discontent

That first of May, the morning dew, still waiting for pervading sunrays sucking up the moisture in the air, promised to make it a perfect picnic day. Our large group hiked up the Eichelberg, a steep wooded hill bordering the Waldsiedlung to the east. Through Mr.

Klunker, a teacher and musician friend of my father, my parents had made the acquaintance of some people about their age. These people, classified as DP (displaced person) came from *Preussen* (Prussia), a state belonging to Germany before the war but annexed to Poland by the Allies in 1945. Under a new government program, individuals with DP status and proof of a certain education level could qualify for retraining and continue studying to become much-needed educators. Mr. Klunker himself came from such background. He invited the group of three men and one woman over to his house almost every weekend. Mrs. Liepold, Mrs. Klunker, and my mother were not too fond of that group, but Mr. Klunker insisted on bringing them along to the First of May picnic at the top of the Eichelberg.

The very last day of July 1955, a much shorter school summer vacation started, due to major changes in the start and end dates of the school year. I was hoping to see Christine over the summer, but Bavaria had a different vacation schedule than Baden-Württemberg, where I lived. Besides, the Hausmanns had plans for a beach vacation in Italy. Christine wrote a letter, passionately conveying her excitement at riding the waves and sunning on the beach of Rimini, a city on the Adriatic Sea. She sincerely wished for me to be part of this dream vacation. Disappointed, green with envy, and angry with my parents for never making any plans for a family vacation like the Hausmanns or other families we knew, I confronted my mother on the subject and accused my father of being a miser. She reprimanded my conduct. Moreover, she reminded me, we were saving toward a car, and it would take several years of sacrifice. Again, my father's fantasy took precedence over reality. As I saw it, a car was not a necessity, but I held my tongue. At this point, Uncle Gustel's letter arrived inviting me to Neunburg vorm Wald, and spending the entire school vacation there became an attractive option. However, four weeks was too long to be away from home and some of the commitments I had. I wrote back and agreed to two weeks.

Formative Experiences

By mid-November, first-semester report cards came out, and some students did not return to classes. My grades were not tops, but I had tried hard and kept a B- average. I had learned how to study and how to discipline myself. The school's curriculum prepared students for an entrance into the business world, accompanied by studies in the humanities and liberal arts.

Dr. Hoffmann, my history professor, very much encouraged his students to read the newspaper to keep abreast of current events in Germany, Europe, and the rest of the world. He was the reason I knew of the Cold War, a tense relationship between the United States and the Soviet Union, and the fear of nuclear threat by the two superpowers. I read about the Hungarian Uprising, when Soviet tanks rolled into Budapest, killing and injuring several thousand people, and the spread of Communism in Southeast Asia. Headlines of espionage made the front pages of newspapers, as well as stories of secret agents from the US agency, the CIA, and the USSR's infamous KGB spying on each other behind the Iron Curtain—the European border of East and West.

I was going on sixteen and had never been to a movie house or seen a movie. Bruchsal had one cinema, and it was showing an older black-and-white movie, "*Über's Jahr wenn die Kornblumen blühen*" ("Next Year When the Cornflowers Bloom"). Movies did not have ratings then, and this one was a gushy love story set on a farm in the mountains of Austria. My parents finally consented for me to see it on a Sunday afternoon. Maria Heller, a new friend I had met in school, was joining me. It was her first movie experience as well. We both left the theater puffy-eyed and were overcome by the powerful emotions inspired by the schmaltzy film. In those days, Germany's film industry fell under the auspices of American scrutiny, and the few movies produced were either comedies or homegrown love stories.

Early in December, Aunt Klara, with the help of a midwife, had her third child, a girl. She named her Barbara, like my grandmother; Oma was ecstatic. Since the birth of the baby, Uncle Schorsch was usually in a morose mood. He blamed Aunt Klara for the additional mouth he needed to feed. My grandmother told him off whenever she had a chance, and he locked the door when he saw her coming. She stayed with us when she came from Neibsheim to help and see her daughter.

For Christmas that year, our family decided on tailor-made clothing for the three of us. Our good friends, the Liepolds, had a relative who was a custom tailor. His wife was Mrs. Liepold's sister, and they lived in Heidelberg. Every so often, they came visiting in the Waldsiedlung. Their last name was Schlegel, and we all called him Uncle Schlegel. On every visit, he brought candy, sample pieces of cloth, and big pattern books with the latest fashions. Uncle Schlegel always had a measuring tape hanging around his neck, which he used for his detailed measuring procedure. While making recommendations in choosing the right materials for a desired garment, he quoted the exact price.

My father chose a light brown and light gray gabardine for his two suits, and my mother and I liked a cashmere wool fabric for our coats. Once my mother heard the price for one coat, she no longer had a need for it. My father persuaded her to get the coat and insisted she also choose a nice light material for a spring suit. As I witnessed my father's generosity, I took everything back in my mind that I had thought about my father. I was ashamed to have painted him as a miser to my mother.

The following week, Uncle Schlegel came on his motorcycle with a sidecar and brought the preliminary assembled garments for the first fitting. A week later there was a second fitting, and by the end of the third week, he delivered the final product. If something did not look or fit right, he took it back and made corrections until it met his approval. He took tremendous pride in his work, a true master of his trade.

A Backfisch at Last

Another birthday rolled around, and in January 1956, I reached the age of sixteen. I was now what Germans considered a teenager—for girls, *Backfisch*, and boys *Halbstarke*. That winter, I retired my ice skates and sold them to one of the Liepold boys. The pond did not freeze well; several kids broke through the ice, and the area for skating was even smaller than before. The ice princess, Heidi Griesheimer, and her entourage of admirers no longer showed up, and I was unable to master the "figure eight."

My interests shifted to movies, pop songs, and popular novels, especially romance novels, which I read by flashlight under the covers. A new singing star, Catharina Valente, and her number one hit *"Ganz Paris träumt von der Liebe"* ("All of Paris Dreams of Love") made an impression on any sixteen-year-old girl, and I wanted to be a singer just like her. One of my other aspirations was to be a flight attendant when I turned eighteen. I had seen publicity pictures of young women in high heels dressed in chic blue uniforms, white gloves, and pillbox hats, standing in front of Pan Am passenger planes, which flew all over the world. It looked so exciting and adventurous, and I wanted to see that world.

My father rarely listened to contemporary music coming from our small Grundig radio; he liked the classics. He knew I favored the new hits, but we had no record player to satisfy our preferences. One day the doorbell rang and two men delivered a *Musikschrank*, a highly polished console with a radio and phonograph, manufactured by Blaupunkt. Included were three 45-rpm records of my favorite *Schlager* (hit songs). I never expected my parents, who had toiled and moiled, saved and skimped in the past eight years, to consider such a frivolous acquisition and concluded that it was I who needed an attitude adjustment.

The Blaupunkt is still in my possession today, and when I give it a glance, I enjoy good memories of being sixteen and hearing my favorite hits of that time.

First Family Vacation

For the first time in my life, my parents made plans for a family vacation. They decided on Lake Königssee by Berchtesgaden in the German Alps. My father booked a two-week reservation for the three of us at the Hotel Königssee. I could hardly wait for my summer vacation from school. My mother borrowed two suitcases from our renters and started packing them as soon as she saw the three complimentary train tickets my father brought home. One beautiful August morning, we sat in a second-class compartment on a fast train to Munich. There we changed to a slower-moving commuter train while soaking in the spectacular mountain scene until we reached the city of Berchtesgaden. It was early evening when we arrived at our hotel near the lake. My father told me that Hotel Königsee has offered specially discounted vacation packages to employees of the Deutsche Bundesbahn and their families. Now I understood why my parents chose this particular corner of the German Alps, but I was very happy they did. In the next few days, we hiked, rented bikes and rowboats, and took a boat trip to the chapel of St. Bartholomä. We walked along the waterfront of the mystical, blue-green lake surrounded by rugged mountain or sunned in striped lounge chairs on the hotel terrace. We enjoyed hearty breakfasts and relished an array of savory dinner dishes, served in the cozy dining room, where an open fireplace and low-key lighting created a delightful ambiance.

Some evenings, the hotel offered entertainment with a *Schuhplattler* (dance) group or a band of zither players making alpine music. My mother observed that one of the young players seemed to show more interest glancing at me than his zither. I was not sure if she approved. At a given opportunity, the young man dropped a note in my lap that read, "I am coming *'fensterln'* tonight." I knew what it meant and discouraged him by shaking my head to the grinning zither player. By 'fensterln,' he had in mind to climb up on a ladder outside my room and for me to come to the window and reward him with a kiss in the dark of the night. And he did. What he didn't know was that I slept in the room with my parents, and when he so bravely knocked on the window late that night, my father opened it and greeted him with a friendly, "Oh, you came to see me?" reaching as if he wanted to kiss him. The baffled lad jumped off the ladder into the bushes. We got a good laugh from that incident, but we never saw the eager suitor again. He was unhurt—just embarrassed—and joined another zither group.

The hotel had vacationers from all over Germany. One day in the dining room, we met a woman and her son from Koblenz on the Rhein. She was a widow, and her deceased husband had worked for the Bundesbahn. Roland, her only child, was seventeen. So far, I had not been too interested in boys, and Roland was no exception, although I did not mind his company. He had completed three years of an accelerated trade school and was in his last year of training with a national insurance company. When his mother extended an invitation to Koblenz for a Rhein River boat cruise to me, I happily accepted. She had discussed it with my parents before mentioning it to me. I had never been on a river cruise but had heard that the Rhein near Koblenz was one of the most beautiful and romantic sections of Germany's mightiest river.

Two weeks after our fabulous vacation in Berchtesgaden, I was on a train to Koblenz. Roland picked me up from the train station, and we met his mother at the dock. The boat took us down the river into the part that is steeped in myths and sagas, past medieval castles to the famous Loreley Rock. There, the legend tells of a beautiful maiden, Loreley, who committed suicide by jumping off the rock, after she found out about her unfaithful lover. She then became a siren who lured sailors to their death with a hypnotizing song. The sound of the murmuring waters is said to be her voice. Our boat had reached its destination, and after passing the narrowest passage of the river, it turned around and the cruise ended an hour later. I thanked Roland and his mother for a lovely sightseeing tour, went back on the train, and headed for home. Our pen-pal writing soon fizzled.

12

Adolescent Years

❧❧❧❧

Shattered Lives

In late fall of 1956, my mother did not feel well, and the doctor treated her for a cold that kept lingering. She and my father acted rather strangely to each other and had heated arguments about money. She also accused my father of having an affair with the woman who came with the Klunkers to the First of May celebration atop the Eichelberg. I had never seen my mother so highly indignant toward my father, or anyone, and I was stunned that she had it in her to express anger. What proof did she have against my father to insinuate allegations of infidelity? I disliked their marital quarrels. I was convinced that my mother's persistent illness was the cause of her irrational behavior. When the opportunity arose, I told her that she could not be serious about an affair of my father with that nondescript woman, Irmgard, who lacked the physical beauty and finesse to enchant a man like my father.

Apparently, I was too young to understand marriage, the meaning of love, or human relationship. One day, I came home from school and found that my father had left a short note on the kitchen table saying, "Irmgard needs me, and I have to go to her. I am sorry for leaving you; please forgive me." He had removed all his clothing and his violin. In a matter of speaking, my mother died that day.

At Christmas, my father sent me a letter. It contained some money and love poems he had written. Supposedly, people told him that he had talent in poetry writing. Those insipid poems meant nothing to me, and I had only contempt for him and the people who praised him. He lamented about his job transfer from Karlsruhe to Waldshut, two hundred km south and very far from the woman who needed him desperately. The letter was the reflection of a man who had no concern for anyone but himself. I could not share my sadness with my mother, who cried most of the time and was feeling poorly physically. It was not a Christmas to remember. Everyone in my family hated my father for his callous action and the effect it had on my mother and me through gossip. Although they had a right to feel angry, being around that constantly condemning verbiage, I silently rebelled against my family as well as my father, who had caused the emotional turmoil. I decided then that I would not stay in the Waldsiedlung once my education was completed.

On January 16, 1957, I turned seventeen, and I did not feel like celebrating; I was in a state of upheaval, and my life was not the same since my father left. I felt abandoned by both my parents, and there was no one with whom I could share my heartache. Outwardly, it was difficult for me to keep smiling and be that friendly, carefree girl who most people knew me to be. I was in my last semester of business college, and my final grades reflected the distress of the preceding four months.

During the previous fall, before my life entered a sphere of abnormality, I had joined a social club called the *Naturfreunde* (nature friends), a group of young people who loved bicycling, as I did. The club owned a small cottage nestled in the woods of the Eichelberg, and once a month we met for planning and social gatherings. A weekend trip to a sister club in Herrenalb in *Schwarzwald* (the Black

Forest) was on the agenda, and I was looking forward to my first big overnight tour.

My mother's health condition went from bad to worse. Her doctor in Bruchsal recommended a hospital stay at the university clinic in Heidelberg for a series of tests. The clinic kept her for three weeks. On weekends, I took the train to Heidelberg and stayed with her. She was in a room with three women, and their camaraderie had a therapeutic effect on her mental suffering. Finally, she received a diagnosis: multiple sclerosis, an autoimmune disease that affects the central nervous system. Who had ever heard of such an illness? I could hardly pronounce it, but the doctors concluded their findings as such, based on her past and present symptoms. There was no medication to take, and no cure. I brought my mother home on the same weekend the bicycle trip to the Black Forest was scheduled.

Shortly before my mother went to the university clinic, I had graduated from business college. During those years, it was not customary to have a party for a degree from any educational institution. However, prior to graduation, the school arranged job placements for students who were eager to enter the giant firms of Siemens, SEW, Reis, or Ihle. Some students chose a route of continuing their education in conjunction with work-training programs. I was offered an apprenticeship with the Volksbank in Bruchsal, a most desired placement. I think that Dr. Gerling, my tough and most disliked accounting professor, had something to do with me getting the spot at the bank. Aunt Klara cleaned the Gerlings house once a week. They trusted her with the key to the house when they went on vacation. My aunt casually mentioned to Mrs. Gerling that her niece was a student of her husband and told her of the worry of landing a well-paying job after graduation.

A few days before finals, Dr. Gerling called me into his office and alluded to my falling grades. I used my home situation as an excuse but promised to concentrate for the final exams. He continued by giving me the advice that I should consider to further my education. I agreed and left his office. By then my idealistic mind was made up in how to escape the Waldsiedlung. I would be searching for a job as a bookkeeper not in Bruchsal but in a big city like Karlsruhe.

Soon after the discussion with Dr. Gerling, I received a letter from the Volksbank Bruchsal asking for an interview. My mother had no knowledge of my wacky plans but was very happy for me to have this opportunity with the bank. She gave me encouragement and made suggestions about my conduct during the interview. She was pleased when I told her that I got the apprenticeship and accepted it. Indeed, it was not an easy decision to forfeit an appealing salary for a trainee allowance plus two more years of studies.

An Unforgettable Journey

Between graduation and the start of the bank apprenticeship, I had some time off, and I really wanted to visit my great-aunt, Luise, in Vienna, Austria. She was the half-sister of my grandmother and was married to a musician with the Vienna Volksopera. My mother emboldened my intention, and Oma wrote letters back and forth with her sister to set up a visit on my behalf. I despised contacting my father, but I needed a free train ticket to Vienna, and he complied.

I traveled to Munich and changed to another fast train, stopping only in larger cities. I had a window seat in a second-class compartment and felt happy to be sitting on this train, away from the emotional distress of my gloomy home life. In Salzburg, a young man stepped in the compartment, and we immediately struck up a friendly conversation. His name was Martin. He was a schoolteacher in Bozen, Tyrol, and was on his summer vacation. He, too, headed for Vienna to visit his brother.

When we arrived at the Vienna Hauptbahnhof, the immensity of this train station overwhelmed my rather put-on "savoir-vivre." Martin knew his way around Vienna, noticed my apprehension, and volunteered to take me to the address of my great-aunt. We jumped on a tram, changed to a different tram, and several stops later reached the nearby apartment. I found their name on the entrance directory and rang the doorbell once and then again and again, but there was no answer. Someone leaned out of the window on the third floor and shouted, "Stop ringing the bell to Luise and Karl's apartment; they are not home but on tour in America." I could not believe what this person was saying and felt tears welling up in my eyes but tried to suppress them in front of Martin. He was a few years older than

I was and obviously viewed my lack of worldly experience as naïve charm. My thoughts circled around my grandmother and her sister and their incompetent communications skills.

Martin interrupted my cogitation and suggested that I make the best of the situation and take advantage of a beautiful city like Vienna while I was already here. From my grandmother, I had heard much about the Schönbrunn castle and her grandfather Wonger, the royal carriage maker. Indeed, I was curious and anxious to walk the grounds where once my titled great-great-grandfather helped assemble carriages for the emperor's use. I wanted to see the grave of my great-grandmother Katharina, who died in the late 1920s and was buried in Vienna's central cemetery. Surrounded by such nostalgia, Martin was right; I should stay, perhaps in one of the very reasonably priced youth hostels. A good choice seemed to be the Kolping House Hostel, and they had plenty of beds available.

I engaged in a nonstop sightseeing tour with Martin as my coy tour guide. The most unforgettable place for me personally was the Prater, a busy amusement park near the Danube Canal. The Prater featured the world's highest (at that time) Ferris wheel as its main attraction. Martin and I sat in one of the gondolas as the giant wheel slowly brought us to the top, where the view of Vienna usually had an unforgettable, thrilling effect. But then, the wheel stopped moving, and we were stuck. The fear of such height crept into my bones, and I could never shake it afterward. It took over an hour to fix the mishap and bring us back down. By then the Prater had lost all its appeal to me. Leaving quickly, we went to the *Stephansdom*, the most famous cathedral in all of Austria. There, I could thank God for being alive. At this point, I needed something to calm my nerves. We stopped at the nearby Café Sacher and I ordered a slice of the world's famous *Sachertorte* and a Mocha. By the time we came to the *Staatsoper* (national opera), the sun was casting its last shadows of the day on the opera house, also known as Vienna's First House.

I concluded that Martin, the knowledgeable stranger, was an accommodating and helpful person, but as time passed between us, I felt that he took on the role of *Verehrer* (admirer), and it made me uncomfortable. At twenty-four, he was too old and too serious for my sprightly personality. We parted in a cordial manner, and in my naïveté, I told him of my plans of leaving the next day, but not before a morning visit to the Schönbrunn castle.

The rooms in the Kolping Haus appeared neatly kept, and three girls, part of a student group from Switzerland, slept in the same room with me. We shared one bathroom, and breakfast was included in the price of twenty-one Schilling (three DM) per night. The front desk let me use the phone, and I made a train reservation to Bruchsal for that evening. I figured that if I left Vienna at 4:00 p.m. in a *Schnellzug* to Munich and caught the connection to another Schnellzug to Bruchsal, I could be home around 10:00 p.m. My mother would be shocked to see me, since I was to stay one week in Vienna. She would not believe the story I had to tell.

As I was wandering through the groomed gardens at Schönbrunn Palace, a castle modeled after Versailles and once the summer residence of the Habsburg monarchs, I saw an arm-waving, tall figure coming closer—Martin! I was truly annoyed but tried to control my agitated impulses. He seemed chirpy and eager to share his knowledge of Schönbrunn and later of the Hofburg, another castle and the winter residence of the royals. Also housed there was the Spanish Riding School, with its highly trained Lipizzaner stallions. These horses were world renowned for their beauty and grace, and we watched a public training performance.

Besides being adventurous, I was slowly running short of money, and a visit to the central cemetery did not fit in the time schedule. I had a train to catch and needed to pick up my suitcase from the youth hostel. Martin insisted on accompanying me to the train station, and I did not object, since using the tram kept me in a state of confusion. We said good-bye, and I thanked Martin for his time and tremendous help. Once I sat on the train, I was glad to be rid of Martin but satisfied to have left on an amicable note.

My mother was in sheer disbelief about my ordeal and fairly upset with my grandmother and her sister. I assured her that my experience turned out to be a positive lesson. This conversation did not end here but became a full-blown mother-daughter feud between my grandmother and mother. As it revealed itself, Oma and her sibling in Vienna wrote to each other in May, using only the day for my arrival, but not the month. One meant July, the other June, and my plans were for June.

A Grand Fireworks Display

Heidelberg was famous for many things, among them "The Burning of the Castle," a spectacular fireworks display featuring the Heidelberg castle and the bridge over the river, Neckar. The event took place in early July. My old friend Hanni Liepold and I were determined to see the event everybody talked about. We took the train to Heidelberg. Once there we found a place in the grass on the bank of the river, where thousands of expectant spectators were waiting for darkness to set in, and for the lavish show to begin. It was a two-hour extravaganza, and the masses oohed and aahed, exclaiming their admiration. The train that took us back to Bruchsal stopped in every little hamlet, unloading people just like us who were coming from the Heidelberger *Schlossbeleuchtung*. It was midnight when we arrived in Bruchsal. We hopped on our bicycles and peddled home.

During the train ride home, Hanni and I caught up on our personal happenings. I knew of her asthma problems and regular trips to a clinic in the Black Forest for treatment. She told me about her boyfriend, Erich, who had joined the French Legion and was fighting the National Liberation Front somewhere in Algeria. He received a bonus of five thousand DM for signing a two-year commitment. Before he left, he had bought her a gold locket with his picture in it, and she pointed to the necklace around her neck. She had not heard from him in over five months, and neither had his family. Erich's family feared the worst, since the legion had a reputation of sending inexperienced, untrained young men into war situations. No one ever heard from Erich again.

A New Chapter—The Apprentice

On July 15, 1957, my apprenticeship with the Volksbank Bruchsal started, and I signed a contractual commitment for a two-year program. The bank director, Mr. Griesheimer, had the obligation to let me train in each department for a minimum of four months under the supervision of the department head, who would document my successful completion and review my performance. Furthermore, I would be given time off to attend the banking academy in Karlsruhe two days a week. In addition, I would receive a monthly allowance of sixty DM in the first year and eighty DM in the second year.

In the first few days, the chief secretary briefed me on the dos and don'ts of the bank's procedures. I quickly learned the names of all the bank employees and the jobs they performed as well as their importance in the institution. The name Griesheimer rang a bell, and, yes, the director had a daughter—Heidi, the ice princess! I did not dare to ask about her whereabouts or reveal my past envy of her prominence on the ice pond.

Indeed, everyone exuded his or her importance to the new trainee, even Wilhelm Zipperle, the former apprentice in residence. In a short time, I became familiar with the use of manual office machines, the telephone, and a variety of forms.

My first assignment was in bookkeeping, where Mr. Schmitt, a wounded war veteran with a limp, ran the department with an iron fist. Everyone addressed me as Fräulein Veit, and sometimes that became a problem, since another Fräulein Veit worked there. Her first name was Waltraut, and she was single like me and hence also a Fräulein.

Wilhelm and I clicked from the beginning, and we stayed friends through the years. He was two years my senior, came from a background of butchers, which he hated, and was the youngest in an affluent family. His grandfather owned half of the village of Untergrombach, nearby to Bruchsal, and was the Volksbank's biggest account holder. I would describe Wilhelm's personality as frolicsome, with a touch of roguishness, and he loved classical music. Because of him, I became very interested in opera and operetta, and for a short time, we both took singing lessons with a passé opera star in Karlsruhe. When my voice reached the high C but could not hold it long enough, I was told, in so many words, that my talents may lie somewhere else. Wilhelm, with his husky voice, received the same verdict. There went our pipe dreams of performing on the big stages of European opera houses.

One Day at a Time

Meanwhile, my home life adapted unwillingly to an uncomfortable situation. My mother went back to work after an extended sick leave, although she did not feel much better. There was little anyone could do for her except to be patient and supportive when she was in the dumps. Sometimes I wanted to shake her and wake her up from her self-imposed penance, but she still loved the man who caused her torment, my father. She hung on to a glimmer of hope that one day he would come to his senses and return to his family, even though he had asked her for a divorce. I strongly encouraged her to give him the divorce, but she could not do that.

One fall day, my father showed up at the Volksbank on a brand-new motor scooter. I was not happy to see him but needed his signature on various papers. When I saw his motorized acquisition, I immediately informed him of our financial dilemma at home and my mother's continuous health issues and demanded that he take care of his obligation. He gave me his version of his life's discord and begrudgingly agreed to pay the mortgage on the house, but my books from Bertelsmann book club he could not afford. He no longer reminded me of the father I once admired but rather of a lovesick adolescent. I lost all respect and wished him out of my life.

I was still active in the church as a lector on Wednesday evenings and Sundays on a rotating basis. Pfarrer Menzer pulled me aside one evening after church. He came straight to the point and offered me an opportunity to attend a Catholic teachers college to study toward a degree in religion and become a teaching sister. The idea of teaching religion spoke to me, but when I asked him if I still could get married, he said no, because I would have to take a vow to God. I declined the proposal instantly and told him that I never desired to be a nun but hoped to get married one day. The priest meant well, and I was flattered by the gesture. Ironically, our parish priest and youth leader, Pfarrer Kluge, a real heartthrob, left the priesthood and married a former teaching sister.

A Culinary Nightmare

Wilhelm invited me to a French restaurant after we enjoyed seeing the "Merry Widow" at the Karlsruhe Opera House. He suggested that I order the specialty of the house, *escargot*. I had no clue what it was, but I wasn't about to ask. After all, I was "sophisticated." When the waiter brought a plate with shells and special utensils to eat the snail right out of the shell, I wanted to die. With a knotty stomach, I watched how Wilhelm ate his snails, and I dug in to do the same. There were three left, and I could no longer maintain my composure. I ran to the restroom to rid myself from escargot and its garlicky sauce. Alone, I could crinkle my nose and make sounds in disgust. Feeling better, I returned to the table and expressed how wonderful everything was, but I was too full to eat the rest of the escargot. Wilhelm Zipperle just smiled and offered me the plate with tiny drumsticks. Due to my announced plenitude, I could not accept one of these luscious-looking legs, even though I wanted one. In the course of conversation, I gathered that these cute little legs belonged to frogs and not chickens, as I had assumed. More "eews" raced through my mind. On our way home I admitted that my experience in restaurant visits was rather limited and that I desired more exposure to exotic foods. For some reason, Wilhelm never invited me to any foreign restaurant again. We usually stopped at the Wiener Wald, a new-style, spit-roasted chicken place, when in Karlsruhe.

While the weather was good, I rode my bike to the bank, and most of the time I had lunch at home with my mother. One day a letter waited for me from Martin. Before I opened it, I was mystified and could not imagine how he had obtained my address. As I was reading, he solved the puzzle and admitted taking the address off my suitcase tag in Vienna. He wrote about his work as an eighth-grade teacher in Bozen, Tyrol. Tyrol was a province in Austria where Oma's first husband fought in WWI and lost his life. Like the Sudetenland, Southern Tyrol was awarded to Italy by the Treaty of Saint Germain after WWI. When Hitler annexed Austria to Germany in 1938, he incorporated the State of Tyrol. After WWII, the Allies returned Southern Tyrol back to Italy. Martin grew up bilingual. His family spoke German at home, but Italian was the official language, also taught in school.

I actually liked the letter Martin wrote and read it to my mother. For a while, we exchanged letters, and we met in Munich once, for just a day. I told him there that I was looking for a pen pal, not a relationship. He sent one more letter, telling me that I was cruel, and his tears caused the smudged ink. After the tear-marked letter, I wanted no further contact.

The Black Cat at Carnival

It was the end of November, and Advent season was about to begin. My mother and I were ready to embrace our favorite time of the year. The Advent wreath decorated the living room table, and the Advent calendar hung on the kitchen wall, waiting for countdown. When December 6 came, I still received a shoe filled with chocolates and candies from my godmother, Aunt Klara; it was her Nikolaus to me. In turn, my mother, who was godmother to Cousin Helga, did the same for her.

I was pleased to see my mother in a perky mood, a much welcome change from the last twelve months. She even suggested that we bake Christmas cookies and plan for a festive holiday. She dug for the Böhmerwald recipes Oma had copied for her and my aunt, and we baked cookies for two Saturdays in a row. In the past, my father did the baking, and she and I were helpers only. We chuckled about having been scolded by the master baker when basting egg yolk or applying sugar sprinkle not the way he wanted it done. Those were blithe, happy hours with my mother in our warm kitchen, scented with the pleasant smells of gingerbread.

Aunt Resl and Uncle Bepp announced their visit for the holidays. Resl was my mother's cousin, and Bepp was her husband. They had no children and lived in Ladenburg not far from Heidelberg. Resl was a daughter of my grandfather's musician brother, Karl, and was born in Franzelhütte. She, too, had to seek employment at a young age to help her family survive tough times and went to Komotau before the war broke out. Resl was instrumental in convincing my mother to come to Komotau where she had job connections, and my mother needed work. After the expulsion from Sudetenland, Resl's family landed in Bavaria. There she met and married Bepp and they moved to Ladenburg, where he found work. We did not see them very often, but when they visited, they divided their time between Aunt Klara and us. They gave the appearance of an old couple, happy with each other, and with wisdom galore. Both of them always came loaded with lots of news about people who once lived in Franzelhütte and vicinity. They knew of their fortunes or misfortunes, marriages, deaths, and births. My mother and aunt sat in attention listening to their cousin and her husband unpack all the stories and gossip. Uncle Bepp never failed to ask me if I had a steady boyfriend yet. He seemed disappointed when I told him there was no boyfriend, and I asked him to quit asking me the same question.

Time seemed to fly. My birthday was approaching, and I turned eighteen in January of 1958. The legal age in Germany at that time was twenty-one. However, the law did not apply to drinking alcohol or smoking tobacco products, and I did neither. *Fasching* (carnival) season was in full swing, and I read about an upcoming Fasching ball at the *Schwarzwaldhalle* in Karlsruhe, the structure that made Erich Schelling famous.

After Christmas break, classes at the banking college resumed, and since I was in Karlsruhe, I excused myself before the morning session ended and went looking for a costume. A metropolitan city like Karlsruhe had big department stores with great selections in everything, and for every taste. I found a slinky, black cat outfit with ears and a long tail, which fit perfectly. I got my money's worth from that purchase, wearing it to several Fasching balls.

It was freezing cold that Saturday in January, but Hanni, Inge, and I went to the event at the Schwarzwaldhalle anyway. They both were dressed in vibrant gypsy outfits, and I was the black sleek cat. After we paid an entrance fee of two DM, a waiter showed us toward a small table where three girls were already sitting. He brought three more folding chairs, and all six of us squeezed around the table for two. His pad and pen were ready to take our drink order, and he became agitated when one was slow in deciding. He threateningly announced for us not to leave this table until he had returned with our drinks and we had paid for them.

There must have been a thousand costumed people either dancing on a huge dance floor or sitting like sardines at tiny round tables. The Schwarzwaldhalle was packed. For a moment, my thoughts reflected on the man who designed this oddly shaped building, and I took pride in knowing him. A big band played German top songs and American hits by Elvis Presley, Bill Haley, and Frank Sinatra. The three of us danced to every tune, and when the band went on break, we'd talk and giggle about the guys we danced with, what we liked or disliked. Hooking our pinkies together, we renewed our solemn promise: "Came together—leave together; no male escorts on the way home."

Aunt Klara prepared vigorously for her daughter Helga's First Communion. For the first time since his wedding ten years ago, I saw Uncle Schorsch in a suit and actually smiling. Even Uncle Gustel and Aunt Linde traveled for many hours in their station wagon to be a part of the celebration. Aunt Resl, Uncle Bepp, and my grandparents together with Frau Martin all attended. Uncle Schorsch's side of the family, the other Gerbers in Neibsheim, had some lame excuse for not coming. Aunt Klara welcomed their absence, as Schorsch's mother insulted her deeply when she came on a rare visit after baby Barbara's birth and made the scathing remark: "This child is no Gerber; I wonder whose it is."

Learning the Banking Business and More

At the bank, I was in the investment division, and Mr. Heft, a genius in high finance, took me under his wings. He was the grandfatherly type, very laid back, just the opposite of the previous boss, Mr. Schmitt. He should have been a broker at the Frankfurt Stock Exchange, given his knowledge and reliable instincts in buying or selling the right stock at the right time. Only a few people I knew gambled in the stock market. Wilhelm confided in me that he "borrowed" money from his grandfather's account and invested it in securities Mr. Heft had recommended. Fortunately for Wilhelm, he made money for himself and returned the "borrowed" capital with interest to the account of his grandfather. When the bank director found out about these funny business dealings, he kindly asked Wilhelm to stop.

In spite of his manipulative money schemes, everyone in the bank knew of Wilhelm's wealthy family, which gave him status and security, but his coworkers really liked him. His training and his clout at the Volksbank were a benefit to me, as he cautioned and advised me about the idiosyncrasies of the bank's key people. He was a good friend, funny and always upbeat; I enjoyed his company. He seemed imbued with idealism and adventure, and we shared many interests, except romantic ones. I found it odd but never asked him about the fact that at almost twenty-one, he did not date or show excitement when a good-looking girl or woman entered the Volksbank.

One day, Mr. Griesheimer called me in his office. I expected the worst. Usually, trainees had very little contact with the director— unless something big was up. He made me feel at ease by starting to tell me what a dependable and good worker I was and discussing the satisfying reports he was receiving from the department heads and my grades in school. I tried to suppress an audible sigh of relief and was all ears to hear the reason why I sat in this plush office across from the man employees had such reverential awe of. He continued talking about the banking college's curriculum in his days, in contrast to today's course of study, and the change of the industry as a whole. Finally, he came to the point and proposed for me to attend a three-week seminar at the WGAH, a bank academy jointly owned and managed by all the Volksbanks of Baden-Württemberg. Its location was Hohenheim near Stuttgart. I could hardly contain my excitement while I was thanking him and leaving his office backward, bowing.

In early July, I was on a train to Stuttgart to participate in a banking seminar in Hohenheim. The bus dropped me off on the grounds of Hohenheim castle, and I made my way to the school, a brand-new two-story building. The lobby resembled that of a four-star hotel. After checking in, I went to my assigned room on the second floor, and to my surprise, I had my very own bathroom. I thought of my mother, my aunt, and my grandparents and wished they could see my fancy accommodations. They would say, "See Erika, being Flüchtling must never stop you from reaching goals, and it looks like you are on your way."

Every morning at 7:00 a.m., my merciless alarm clock tossed me out of bed. I was in class before 9:00 a.m. The instructors changed with the topics, and the sessions started out with a history of European banking systems, leading the timeline to present-day functions of the institutions. Punctually at 5:00 p.m. classes were dismissed and each student's time was his or her own, except some days when additional reading materials were handed out. Nobody had a car, since all forty of us were under twenty-one, the minimum age for a driver's license. We stayed on campus grounds most of the time. Cliques started to form, and, somehow everyone found a group to fit in.

Disastrous First Love

One evening somebody made a campfire and we sat around telling stories and jokes. A young man named Peter had brought his guitar, which he played wonderfully while we sang along. He made an ardent impression with the new American hit "Melody D'Amour." During the course of the evening, I asked him several times to play that song again. I was not sure what was so inspiring: the guitarist, his playing, the song "Melody D'Amour," or all three; I was bewitched. Those gatherings around the fire sparked some romances. By the end of the first week, it was easy to observe who wooed whom, as the paired couples made no secret of their alliance.

I, too, experienced my first romantic encounter when Peter and I sat by the fire one night long after everyone had left. He knew he had cast a spell over me with his "Melody D'Amour" and whispered softly into my ear that it was our song while passionately placing kisses on my lips. I went to bed that night floating on clouds, my stomach fluttering with anticipation. I did not brush my teeth, for it could interfere with the thrill that numbed my lips. This had to be love!

The next day, I dressed especially nice and waited for Peter in the dining room. He strolled in, acknowledged me with a wave of his hand and a faint smile, and sat down with his usual group. He seemed impassive and acted as if the previous night had never happened. I had not experienced romance before, but his demeanor prompted a rude awakening in matters of love. Tears filled my eyes, but this was not the place to give free rein to the emotions. I remembered my mother crying after my indifferent father, and it made me angry. Indeed, Peter was undeserving to cry after, but I was crushed.

In no time three weeks flew by; our departure day had arrived. Before I left my room that morning, I decided to ignore Peter and not bid him farewell. It was the last time we all had breakfast together, and the dining room was in a state of confusion. A few of the lecturers gave short speeches, while some students exchanged personal data with each other. Everyone agreed that it was a great learning experience, professionally and personally, in a beautiful setting and would always qualify as an unforgettable memory of our youth.

Back in Bruchsal, Mr. Griesheimer requested that I write a detailed report and give my assessment of the WGAH facility and the value of the seminar's curriculum as a learning tool. He needed that critique for the purpose of his bank's continued investment participation in a rather new concept. I complied with a positive evaluation on many handwritten pages. Wilhelm was glad to see me back and told me that he felt bored in the last three weeks.

Besides having completed my first year of training, I started to first observe and later work in the large front office where, behind high mahogany counters, bankers transacted business and exchanged money with the public. After the bank closed in the evening, the tedious tasks of balancing the receipts to the money with the help of big, black, hand-operated adding machines took place. No one left until the department supervisor, Mr. Schimmel, was satisfied with the checks and balances and gave the okay to transport the bundled money to the monstrous in-house vault.

Peter still consumed my thoughts, and I told my mother about him. The idea of getting a guitar and taking lessons had preoccupied my mind for some time. As I was revealing my amorous encounter, it would be the right moment to make the request. My mother, a little skeptical but sympathetic to my profound disappointment, agreed to the purchase of a guitar, but the lessons I had to pay for myself. Right away, we visited the Musik Haus Konrad and bought an inexpensive but nice-sounding guitar. They provided us with names of people who gave lessons, and we arranged for one lesson a week. I was happy, and once again I had found my true calling.

A Death in the Family

One September morning in 1958, Frau Martin called the little post office in the Waldsiedlung. It sounded important, and they sent somebody to bring my mother or aunt to the phone immediately.

Both went and listened to Frau Martin's broken voice telling them that Oma had died during the night. My mother called me at the bank, and in a daze I got on my bicycle and peddled home. That same morning, crushed by sorrow and disbelief, we went to Neibsheim.

Opa sat in the kitchen motionless, staring into space, when we walked in the door. My mother and her sister went to the bedroom, where their mother lay lifeless in her bed. Frau Martin had called Dr. Stofer to the house earlier that morning. He told her and my grandfather that Oma died sometime during the night, most likely from a deep vein thrombosis, which could have caused pulmonary embolism. Oma had seen Doctor Stofer for her varicose veins and the swelling and pain in her legs. He treated her with medications and recommended some minor changes in her life-style. Whether she had heeded his advice, nobody knew, not even Opa.

My beloved grandmother was gone, and I could not stop crying. Her life flashed in front of me, and all the fond memories kept reminding me how lucky I was to have had her as my grandmother. She experienced tremendous losses in her hard-dealt life and always wore black, but she managed to be a pillar for her family. She certainly was my anchor, and I relied on her in so many ways. She was only seventy-two, not that old, but the expulsion from her beloved Franzelhütte had literally broken her heart.

Once the funeral was over, everyone went back to their responsibilities and routines. Our mourning period began, and every Sunday afternoon, we visited the cemetery and sat by Oma's grave where two conifers swayed gently over her resting place; she had to be pleased. I took a brief vacation from the Volksbank to spend time with my mother, who, in her poignant grief, also was suffering physically. The pain in the right side of her body had returned, and it was obvious that she had less control over her right leg and therefore dragged it behind. I felt helpless and sorry for her, and we went to the doctor again. He knew of her condition and suggested heat and gave her some pain pills.

Before Christmas, Aunt Klara picked up Opa and his belongings from Neibsheim and moved him permanently into her house. Frau Martin had assured my aunt and mother that she would see after Opa and he would have a home in her house till he chose otherwise.

After Oma's passing, my grandfather expressed a desire to stay in Neibsheim, but my aunt would not hear of it. My mother sided with her father and insisted that we let him be. She and my aunt had a few disagreements on the subject, although each had my grandfather's best interests in mind. It was not a memorable Christmas, with Oma gone, the two sisters not speaking to each other, and Opa just sitting listless in a chair.

Eventually Opa took long walks in the woods of the Eichelberg, and sometimes he stayed there all day. He ate very little, and his frail body had a ghostlike appearance. Only the reddish-brown mustache added a little color to his pale face with the sad brown eyes. Opa never complained and hardly ever said a word, but one year when Oma hosted her Christmas Eve gathering in Neibsheim, he revealed his secret.

In November of 1938 after the annexation of the Sudetenland to the German Reich, the prevailing *Sudetendeutsche Partei* (SdP) (Sudeten German Party) fell under the jurisdiction of Hitler's NSDAP, and they held some cockamamie endorsement election. Other parties were no longer tolerated, and their members were persecuted. A large number of Social Democrats were sent to the Dachau concentration camp. In Franzelhütte, all sixty-eight votes, mostly out of fear, pledged to the SdP, except one vote. It was Opa's, the lifelong Social Democrat. That one vote caused a never-before-seen furor in Franzelhütte. NSDAP election officials from thirty-five miles distant Marienbad came to interrogate the village people and, under threat, demanded the identity of the traitor, but they did not know. No one suspected Johann Gerber, not even his wife, who did not vote. Finally, the investigators left empty-handed, and the one odd vote became a much-talked-about mystery in Opa's hamlet. He disliked Hitler long before annexation and thought of him as a dangerous, power-obsessed, cunning Austrian who could send Germany and the Sudetenland to its doom. Opa had it right.

Another Phase Completed

I was anxious for 1959 to arrive; I would be nineteen, finish my education, look for a job, and make real money. While my training wound down at the Volksbank's foreign exchange department, the IHK- *Industrie und Handelskammer* (Chamber of Industry and Commerce) in conjunction with the banking college set a date at the end of June for me to take the state exam.

In the meantime, I had feelers out for a position at a big bank in Karlsruhe. Unlike Wilhelm, who stayed on after completing his apprenticeship, I was sure, I would not continue with the Volksbank in Bruchsal for various reasons. The word "Flüchtling" never came up during my two years at the bank, but living in the Waldsiedlung was enough of a giveaway, and based on that indicator, I concluded, my chances of advancement would be rather slim. Besides, the bank's key people were in the prime of their lives and not going anywhere in the next twenty years. In addition, both the Volksbank and the Sparkasse (savings bank) had reputations of paying less in salaries than, let's say, the Deutsche Bank or other larger institutions.

Wilhelm had passed his state exam two years earlier, and I was soliciting his help. In return, I had to make some infantile prank phone calls to flower shops in Karlsruhe, ordering flowers for certain opera singers and charging its cost to the account of rival opera singers. We both got a kick out of this juvenile conduct until Mr. Schmitt caught us using the bank's phone booth for private long-distance calls. Without hesitation, he reported it to Mr. Griesheimer. The whole ordeal ended as an embarrassing reprimand.

The day of the state exam approached quickly, and one morning at eight o'clock sharp I sat in a room at the IHK and put down my knowledge of what I had learned in the last two years. It was a four-hour exam, and I felt confident that I had passed.

By the middle of July of 1959, the bank formally released me from my two-year trainee contract. In addition, I received a letter and diploma from the IHK, signifying that I had passed the state exam and had joined the professionals who call themselves *Bankkaufmann* (qualified bank clerks). That was good news, and my mother beamed with pride. I felt a true sense of accomplishment, quite on top of the world. This diploma was my ticket to a brighter future in the banking industry.

All seemed to fall into place. My colleagues at the Volksbank gave me a champagne party for completing my training successfully and passing the state exam. Wilhelm congratulated me but gave me his imitation of a sad face; he knew that I was leaving. Prior to the gathering, I expressed my gratitude to Mr. Griesheimer and my interest in seeking a job at the Zentralkasse, in Karlsruhe. It was common practice after completion of the apprenticeship to pursue employment elsewhere. Besides, the bank had committed to a new trainee, Pius, and they needed the space for him. The director shook my hand and wished me good luck, and we agreed that July 31 would be my final day.

A Real Job

The name of my new employer was Zentralkasse Südwestdeutscher Volksbanken AG, a central reserve bank for all Volksbanks in southwest Germany. Its location was on Karlsruhe's busiest street, Kaiserstrasse, and it was housed in one of the city's historic buildings, the Margrave Palace. The classical Greek-style structure stood under protection of the State Preservation Act for Historical Sites. Thus, its front façade could not be altered.

Every morning at 6:45, I jumped on my bicycle, raced to the train station, and caught the 7:00 train to Karlsruhe. There I hustled my way into a trolley, and by 7:50, I was sitting at my desk. I shared a sun-drenched office overlooking a bustling Kaiserstrasse with several other people. Our section was a branch of bookkeeping that specifically handled drafts, a preferred payment document due on a specific date. It was not the most exciting job. I was under the assumption that my diploma as certified Bankkaufmann should count for something more important. Quickly I found out that my coworkers had diplomas as well, and some had more education than I had and a few years' experience to boot. I was just a beginner and had a lot to learn.

I was delighted to have landed a position with a prestigious institution like the Zentralkasse and to earn a decent salary. My initial purchases were some much-needed professional clothes and high-heeled shoes. In the first two months, I went wild and spent every penny I earned, some on trendy, silly accessories. My mother watched my self-indulgence for a while, but then came the speech about modesty being a virtue and frugality having its merit. She and I had a few disagreements on money matters. She was quick to remind me of a few senseless purchases in the past, like the must-have guitar, abandoned after four lessons, or my ice skates, a dream good for one season. Being on the defensive, I argued back that I had matured and that my banking background qualified me more as an expert in money issues than her. She found those comments amusing, and we never stayed annoyed at each other for long.

An Interesting Group

A colleague told me about a new two-year study program at Karlsruhe University to make up the Abitur. Under normal circumstances, the Abitur was the final academic exam, after eight years of study in Gymnasium, and thus entitled to university studies. The German education system started to unfreeze some of their ancient structures and made concessions for adults to have a second chance at obtaining university degrees. For admittance to the newly offered program, a certain level of previous education was required, and I qualified. It was a hectic schedule of three evenings a week from six to ten with loads of homework. Without hesitation, I signed up at the registrar's office and bought the books on the list they handed me. There was no fee, as all schools in Germany were tuition-free, including university attendance. When I told my mother of my plan, she reluctantly expressed her support.

Our little group of four met at evening class. Wolfgang, twenty-two, a scion of the Moninger Beer Brewery and Restaurant in Karlsruhe, boldly flaunted his wealth anytime, anywhere. He owned a red British MG sports car (absurd for the time) and thus was very much in demand for the car's sake. Dieter, twenty-one, Wolfgang's childhood friend and a Gymnasium dropout, wanted to be a writer but was not sure if he had the talent. And Helmut, twenty-four, my coworker, was married to a sweet country girl who strongly disapproved of his attending evening school and studying with our group. Over just a few weeks, we all became good friends, supportive of each other. Wolfgang and Dieter both tried to strike up a romance, but neither stirred any such feeling in me. It was the time in my still-immature life when looks prevailed, and those guys did not qualify. However, I did have a crush on a fellow student, Dietmar, with whom I studied some weekends at his small flat. One day, out of the blue, he told me that he would not date girls, much less become involved with someone, while working toward his goal: the Abitur. Somewhat embarrassed, I got the message and quit studying with him.

One evening after class, our foursome stopped at our favorite hangout, a hole-in-the-wall café where one could sit for hours, sip on a cup of coffee, and not be asked to leave. As I casually looked around, I saw my friend and former classmate, Edeltraud, walking through the door. She was accompanied by some older guy whose overpowering scent of aftershave tickled some nostrils. What an unexpected occurrence, but a pleasant encounter for both of us! We had over two years of catching up to do. She worked for a national insurance company in Karlsruhe and lived with her married sister around the corner from the café.

The man who escorted Edeltraud was her boyfriend, Mummay. He was a successful salesperson of French lingerie and owned a Vespa scooter and a VW Karmann Ghia sports car. Mummay, a bon vivant in the truest sense, loved a party and the nightlife. He claimed to be a thirty-year-old Berliner, but he looked more like forty. Taking into account the stories he told, the latter seemed closer to the truth.

An Official First Date

Karlsruhe University had a reputation as one of the finest technical schools in Germany. Students from all over the world studied there, and the Middle-Eastern male students most definitely made up the majority of foreigners. Their aggressive behavior toward the opposite gender was somewhat of a nuisance. They loved dating German girls, especially blonde ones, showered them with expensive gift, and became quite serious and possessive by the second date.

Scores of young German women married Middle-Eastern men, as they appeared worldly and rich, and followed them blindly in love to their home country after these men obtained their degree. Once there, Western women found out that their life no longer belonged to them but fell under the dominance of the husband's family. The clueless bride might be wife number two, three, four, or five, depending on the family's social status. Plenty of horror stories appeared in German newspapers about some of these women who, if lucky enough, could escape and tell of their barbaric ordeal. I never had an interest in dating Arab men, but I was curious listening to conversations about their culture. They reminded me of the mysterious stories of *1001 Nights*.

One evening I had entered the student cafeteria to get a quick bite before class started when someone in line behind me whistled "Melody D'Amour." I could feel myself blushing, and with a spasmodic move, I turned to face the whistler, whom I took for Peter, my first and disappointing love. To my amazement, it was not him but was a total stranger. I had the urge to tell this person that his whistling reminded me of someone. We had a good laugh, and he introduced himself as Carsten. He was a third-year architectural student. I volunteered the reason why I was there, and we made a cafeteria date for that next day, at the same time. During class, I felt distracted and found myself preoccupied with my next day's wardrobe, when I would meet Carsten again.

A few days later, on a Sunday afternoon, I had an official first date with Carsten. I wanted to look casually chic and chose a white pleated skirt, a dark blue blazer, and blue leather pumps. He picked me up in his father's Mercedes, and we drove to Wildbad, a sleepy small town in the Black Forest, where his family owned a beautiful vacation home. The family was not there, and we had the house to ourselves. While Carsten had the stereo going full blast and fixed refreshments, I snooped around and admired the tastefully furnished home and the manicured garden. For me, it was another experience of a utopian dream, and I wished it to go on forever but kept the feeling to myself.

It was a lovely day in Wildbad, and on our way back to Bruchsal, Carsten indicated that he had enjoyed his time with me. When the car stopped by my house, we sat for a moment and engaged in some trivial conversation. I thanked him for the delightful afternoon. He did not ask for another date, but in a pleasant voice, he conveyed his preference for casual dating, at least until his studies were completed. I had no valid response, as I felt inferior, knowing that our backgrounds were worlds apart. At times we ran into each other, but we never dated again.

The Joy of Independence

The first snow arrived in early November, and it was bitter cold. With my mother's approval, I had decided to take a room in Karlsruhe and stay there during the week. With Edeltraud's help, I found the ideal location in a new apartment house just five minutes from the Zentralkasse and another few minutes from my evening classes at the university. The apartment proprietor, Frau Finger, had two furnished rooms for rent, including limited kitchen use and sharing of one bathroom. Since I showed up at the landlady's door before the engineering student from Hamburg did, I could choose the larger of the two rooms for the same price. Frau Finger, a very skinny widow with short silver gray hair, spoke with authority when she verbally cited the rules of the house, and we both understood completely.

Life was good; I cherished my independence and did not miss the traveling back and forth to Bruchsal. Free time became a precious commodity, but now and then I caught a movie or met a colleague for a drink. Edeltraud and Mummay loved the nightlife, and sometimes I tagged along to a nightclub for a live show and dancing afterward.

At work, I completed the probationary period and had a good rapport with my coworkers. The first semester of evening classes was almost over. I found myself contemplating whether I should continue this crazy schedule. My three pals had problems of their own. For encouragement, Wolfgang and Dieter dangled a fake Abitur diploma in front of me, with my name in extra-large print on it.

I told my mother that I needed to study for a big test and could not come home on the weekend. I never was good at lying, but this explanation seemed convincing and reasonable to me. Our little clique planned an early semester finals party, and I was to arrange it with Frau Finger. As expected, her first reaction was a definite "no." However, with some coaxing, she finally agreed to not more than ten people and an invitation for her daughter, my namesake. Wolfgang, as usual, provided the alcohol and played the bartender. Helmut's wife came with exotic appetizers, and Mummay handled the music. Frau Finger contributed snacks and seemed pleased that her twenty-one-year-old daughter, Erika, was having a good time with Torsten, their student renter. There was laughter and clinking of glasses after silly toasts and cheers aplenty; it was a fun party. No one heard the doorbell ring until Frau Finger stood in the doorway with my mother next to her. *"Ach du liebe Zeit!"* ("Oh dear!") Nothing else escaped my mouth.

The unsuspected and out-of-character visit of my mother made me feel awkward and ashamed in front of my friends. She wasted no time in letting me know how disappointed she was in my untruthfulness toward her. There was nothing I could say in my defense other than to apologize. She left Karlsruhe as quickly as she came and wanted me home next day, which was a Sunday.

Tired and guilty, I went to Bruchsal early Sunday morning. As anticipated, my mother had spent all night preparing moral lectures and accusations, and they were endless. She reminded me that I was only nineteen, not of legal age, and still in her custody. She strongly suggested for me to quit this highfalutin' life, cancel the short-term lease with Frau Finger, get rid of my weird friends, and travel to work, as other people did. Furthermore, I should date some of the nice boys in the Waldsiedlung; "Franz, down the street, asks about you all the time," she said. That was a terrifying thought, and I tried to calm and win her over to my side of thinking. Once the anger subsided, my mother was her old self again. We were able to discuss our controversies over some subjects, including my dreams and desires, and Franz, who was not my type.

13

Casual Encounter

❧❧❧❧

A Stranger of Interest

Semester finals came in a hurry, and our little group diligently met at the café, where we studied and helped each other in problem solving. I lacked facility with the sciences and felt lost in the chemistry lab. Wolfgang and Dieter, both smokers, would offer me a cigarette for relaxation, as they put it, and I joined them, mostly blowing smoke and obstructing my windpipe. Once I had taken a cigarette from a pack and held it between my fingers when all of a sudden a lighter clicked and a flame slowly lit the cigarette as I was putting it to my mouth. I looked up at the gallant lighter-person; our eyes met for a moment, and I quickly said, *"Danke"* ("Thank you"), and turned away.

While waiting for my study group and going over some French vocabulary, I had the distinct feeling of being watched. There, in the back corner of the café, sat a neatly dressed young man whose eyes were definitely focused in my direction. I recalled seeing him; he had lit my cigarette before. On purpose, I started to remove a cigarette from an unopened pack, and in a flash, he stood by my table ready to light up my cigarette. I again thanked him and uttered that I had my own matches. He smiled and glanced at my notes and said, "*Tu es très jolie*" ("You are very pretty"). It was the first sentence my future husband said to me, and in French.

He must be a Frenchman with a Mediterranean complexion, I concluded, after the stranger with the ever-ready cigarette lighter paid me the compliment. My knowledge of the French language was that of a beginner, and I did not want to make a fool of myself. Therefore, I asked him in German if he was from France. He hesitated with a no but asked, "Do you speak English?" Thinking that my six-plus years of studying English qualified me to say yes to his question, I said that I did. He felt relieved and confessed he did not speak German well but was enrolled in a German-language course at Karlsruhe University. My interest increased another notch, but my study group had just entered the café, and I excused myself from the table where he had joined me.

When there were no evening classes, our clique met at the café and tried to study for the impending finals. My eyes kept searching the tables for the young man, who had made a pleasing impression on me. Sometimes he was not there, and I was disappointed. Wolfgang noticed my distraction and asked me about it. I blew it off as nothing, until one evening, to everyone's chagrin, when I chose to sit with the mysterious stranger.

His name was Alfred, and he came from the United States. He volunteered that he was born in Italy—Sicily to be exact—and that his parents immigrated to the United States when he was younger. Besides speaking English and French, he spoke his native Italian and knew Latin and Greek. He found German a hard language to learn, but he liked challenges. He admitted that he had seen me in the cafeteria at Karlsruhe University but that I seemed unapproachable there. He mentioned that the owner of the café, Marco, was a friend of his, and besides, he liked the café's milieu. When he saw me walk in one evening, he could not believe his eyes and knew then that it was destiny. Ever since that day, he had tried to find of an inconspicuous way to catch my attention. Alfred appeared relieved after his short speech and added, "Oh, and by the way, I am a student of engineering at Karlsruhe University."

The well-dressed stranger had revealed himself and his intense interest in me, which I took as pure flattery. It was my turn to unveil some of the suspense about me, so I talked of my family, my work, and my goals, which led me to the missed study time at the other table. He offered his help, if I needed it, and I immediately made him a deal. He would tutor me in chemistry and French, and I would teach him German. It sounded okay to him, and we agreed to meet the following evening at the café.

Our little gang still met at Marco's hole-in-the-wall café and attended class, but something had changed. I shared my time between them and Alfred, when he was there, and missed his presence when he was not sitting at his usual corner table. I presumed that he had his own responsibilities studying for semester finals, although he made no mention of them. Dieter and Wolfgang were much happier when "that guy," as they referred to him, did not show up and they had my undivided attention. Helmut did not care; he only joined us when he had a problem understanding something. Otherwise, he went home to his wife. He announced that after finals, he would not meet with us again and was unsure if he could continue with the program, since his wife was pregnant.

After finals, we met once more at the café and celebrated the completion of our first semester. Hannelore, also a student in our class, joined us and sat herself next to Dieter. The two seemed chummy with each other, and I was wondering if I had missed something. We talked about the finals, and each of us hoped to have done well enough to earn a passing grade. "That guy" was not there, and I was glad, since I, too, wanted to take a break from our clique, and now was the time to make it known.

A Bit of International Flair

There were just a few more days until Christmas, and Alfred and I continued meeting at the café. He told me that he had an apartment in Neureut, a small suburb north of Karlsruhe. The trolleys did not go to Neureut, and it was a little complicated to come to Karlsruhe. But he liked it there, because the Americans had built barracks and operated a commissary where he could buy American foods and merchandise. I let him know where I lived in Karlsruhe and the reason why. We conversed in German, English, and French the best we could and had many laughs about silly mispronunciations or when a word or sentence had a different meaning than intended. Sometimes we ordered a bite to eat, and Marco would stop by our table and speak in his native Italian to his "amico." I could usually tell when I was the subject of their conversation, as they used words like "*bella, ragazza, tedesca, fortunato,*" which translates into "pretty, girl, German, lucky." Studying romance languages like French and (to some extent) English, helped to identify similar words in Italian, another romance language.

One evening, Alfred invited me to an Italian restaurant for dinner. I had previously heard from Mummay how excellent the food was there. I dressed for the occasion, and my date showered me with compliments on my looks and attire. When we entered the foyer of the elegant restaurant, I detected a familiar, warm greeting between Alfred and the maître d', who called for a waiter by name. The young man, dressed in a black-and-white uniform, appeared well trained in serving the various courses, drinks, and a flambéed desert. He served our table only, always smiling, and I was convinced that he could read every wish from our eyes. It was an unforgettable dining experience and a memorable first date. As we were leaving, I caught Alfred handing, but slightly concealing, a fifty DM banknote to the maître d' and thanking him profusely. In later years, I found out that the waiter was specifically hired by my date to put on a show just to impress me.

It started to snow as we walked slowly and in a giggly mood toward Kaiserstrasse, where hundreds of lights illuminated festive decorated shop windows. The smooth, sippable wine with our dinner made my body move in slow motion; I felt a tad tipsy. By the time we reached the apartment building where I lived, the biting cold had unnumbed my senses, and I could feel an awakening tension between us. Here was my opportunity to resist those amorous impulses and convey the "nice girl" image to my Italian suitor. I told Alfred that Frau Finger did not allow male visitors and that he could not come up. For a moment, we stood there, in the dark, the snow still trickling down, not knowing what to do or say. Then he stepped closer. I could feel his breath as he said, "Thank you," placed a light kiss on my cheek, and left.

A Little White Lie

After Alfred and I parted that evening, from what I called our first date, I admitted to myself that he had an infatuating effect on me. I liked his manner, demeanor, and intelligence and felt a strong desire to be near him. Based on my almost three-week experience of knowing him, I determined that, besides his admirable qualities, he must come from a rather wealthy background. Based on the fifty DM tip he left at the restaurant, I felt pleased to have attracted this twenty-four-year-old Italian-American's attention.

We met again the next day. I felt myself blushing when carefully inquiring if he had plans for the holidays. I finally asked him, "Would you be interested in experiencing a German Christmas at my house— not minding sleeping on a couch and taking a train to Bruchsal?" Smiling bashfully, he seemed grateful for the invitation and accepted a one-night stay on Christmas Eve. He had a prior commitment for Christmas Day and needed to be back in Karlsruhe late that afternoon. I was pleased with my cleverness using the German Christmas experience as bait to have the interesting foreigner at my house for Christmas. There was one more hurdle to overcome, and that was to convince my mother of my ingenious plan.

We sat on the trolley heading to the train station in Karlsruhe for me to catch an early evening train to Bruchsal. Alfred accompanied me to the station, and with some time on hand, we studied the train timetable for his visit to Bruchsal two days later. He did some planning of his own and told me that he would take a taxi to my house after arriving in Bruchsal.

My mother appeared to be in good spirits and happy to have me home for the holidays. She knew me well and wasted no time asking if there was something on my mind. I had a prepared plan and presented it to her in such way that she could not say no. It started out with my semidecent grades from evening school; then I casually mentioned that some of my classmates were inviting foreign students from Karlsruhe University to their homes to experience a German

Christmas. I was hoping she would not object to my invitation of an engineering student from America. As expected, she did not mind, but a student from America unable to go home for Christmas was puzzling to her, and, frankly, I had not given it a second thought.

Our house was spotless and incensed with the good smells of Christmas. As on past Christmas Eves, Mr. Zeigler, our renter downstairs, provided us with a freshly cut spruce, which he dragged into our living room and mounted on the tree stand. I decided not to decorate the tree but to wait until our guest arrived in case he would like to help with the fun task. A few neatly wrapped packages lay under the bare tree, and I added a small box with a pair of men's cufflinks.

Looking out the window every so often, I noticed a taxi driving slowly toward the house. I needed to calm my excitement and tried to walk instead of running downstairs to open the door and invite Alfred to our house. He looked his dapper self, and I introduced him to my mother, who cordially welcomed him. With my help, he tried his best German on her, and even if he had not spoken one word in her language, I could tell that she liked the young man.

In preparation for Christmas, we had a few unfinished chores, and my mother excused herself to go to the kitchen while Alfred and I busied ourselves with the decorating of the tree. He stood on a stool and hung the ornaments as I handed them to him. The stereo played a German Christmas record, and I hummed along. Suddenly he stepped down, pulled me toward him, and kissed me. I did not object, nor was I surprised, as there was chemistry between us from the moment we met. I could feel the tension every time we saw each other at the café. Since that night of our first date, I had butterflies in my stomach and could hardly contain my anxiety. However, here in my house, I felt somewhat uneasy with my mother in the next room, especially as I had brought Alfred home under a false pretense. Nevertheless, the inevitable had happened, and it felt right.

We enacted every Christmas Eve tradition we could think of so that our guest could gain some insights into a German Weihnachten. I lit the candles on the tree, and after our singing of "Silent Night," we exchanged gifts. Alfred brought two gifts with him: one for me and one for my mother. Mine was the larger box and contained a beautiful turquoise angora wool sweater. I absolutely loved it! My mother's gift was a bottle of white Vermouth, a wine flavored with aromatic herbs. She hadn't expected anything and appreciated his gesture. I gave him the little box with the silver cufflinks, which he kept on admiring. He thanked me in English and insinuated that, at a more appropriate time, he had something else to say.

The next day, Christmas, Alfred had to leave before noon and could not stay for the roast duck. He had arranged with the taxi driver to pick him up, and it was almost that time. He thanked my mother and me for the "best Christmas ever" and apologized for having to leave. As he got into the taxi, he looked at me and whispered, "Can't wait to see you at Marco's, Sunday evening."

I was miserable for the rest of the Christmas holidays but had to be careful around my mother so as not to give her any clues of my being love struck. She had many kind things to say about Alfred, but she assumed he was someone she would never see again. When Aunt Klara and my cousins came over in the afternoon to exchange Christmas gifts, my mother told them that the American student who spent the night was a nice young man with a good appetite for a home-cooked meal.

Young and in Love

Christmas had wound down, and by Sunday afternoon, I was stir crazy and ready to board the train for Karlsruhe. My mother questioned my early departure, though she knew I had to be at work Monday morning. I was anxious to get to Karlsruhe and meet Alfred, who was waiting at the café. We both confessed how slowly the time passed while we were apart. It was exhilarating to look into each other's eyes, knowing that we both were head-over-heels in love with each other.

We made plans for New Year's Eve, and I suggested the newly opened jazz club, the Zigeunerkeller (gypsy cellar), where I had been with Edeltraud and Mummay once before. The last time I talked with Edeltraud—shortly before Christmas, to wish her happy holidays—I briefly mentioned that I had met someone and wanted her to meet him and that she needed to brush up on her English. I kept thinking that New Year's Eve would be an ideal time for the four of us to be together and ring in the New Year of 1960. Helping myself to Marco's phone, I called Mummay and announced our visit. He was one of few people I knew who owned a telephone, a luxury, which he claimed as a necessity in lingerie fashion sales.

Alfred and I took a trolley to Mummay's place, where, in all likelihood, my friend Edetraud had spent her evening. I guessed correctly. After introductions and small talk, we all agreed that celebrating in the Zigeunerkeller was indeed a fantastic plan, and Mummay volunteered to take care of the reservation. To my astonishment, Mummay spoke fluent English, and I found out he had spent some time in London. He and Alfred became quite chatty, while Edeltraud complemented my choice in men—but also warned of consequences in being involved with foreign students.

By now, I was able to convince Frau Finger to allow Alfred to come up to my room and stay until 9:00 p.m. with the door wide open. I had signed up for a new semester of evening classes, and I had to tell my former clique, now consisting of only Wolfgang and Dieter, that Alfred and I were dating and I would not join them in the café any more. Their taunting reaction and dislike for "that guy" was no secret, and I had to listen to their annoying comments during break.

Some evenings, Alfred was not available; he had to meet with his study group, and I fully understood. Between my classes and his commitments, we spent our free evenings together in my room, at Marco's café, or meeting Edeltraud and Mummay for dinner and dancing. We both were addicted to movies, especially epic films like *War and Peace, The Ten Commandments, Ben Hur*, etc., all made in the United States, and most of them dubbed into German. Not only did they help improve Alfred's German, but they also satisfied my cravings as a history buff. In addition, I became an admirer of Hollywood movie stars like Audrey Hepburn and Paul Newman.

My mother really wanted me home for my birthday, which fell on a Saturday. Alfred knew of my discomforting family situation and encouraged me to spend the day with my mother. He and I would celebrate on Sunday. I appreciated his understanding and went to Bruchsal. My mother was in the process of decorating the torte she had baked when the doorbell rang and a florist delivered a bouquet of roses. I counted twenty red roses and a small card that read, "Happy Birthday Erika—Alfred." My mother glanced at the flowers and then at me and raised her hands to a questioning pose. I decided to stop with the charade and tell the truth about Alfred and my relationship with him. Slightly agitated, I said, "I am just dating, not marrying, so don't worry." She paused for a moment and said, "Today is your twentieth birthday; let's make it a good day."

In the afternoon, my aunt, Cousin Helga, Frau Liepold, and my longtime friend Hanni (recently engaged to Herbert Keller) came by the house to congratulate the birthday girl. My mother invited them for coffee and a slice of the scrumptious birthday torte sitting on the living room table next to the vase with the red roses. The first to inquire about the flowers was my aunt, and I again answered truthfully but rephrased the original sentence to "I have met someone in Karlsruhe, and I think he likes me." I could tell that she and everyone else in the room were eager to hear more, but I diverted their attention to the fine-looking torte and started slicing it. In the course of our little celebration, several comments alluded to the beautiful bouquet and the meaning of red roses.

Back in Karlsruhe, Alfred picked me up at the train station and we went to the hotel, where we stayed after welcoming in the New Year 1960. He knew how to suffuse an atmosphere with romance. There were more red roses in the room and a chilled bottle of Henkel champagne ready to have its cork popped. After two glasses of the sparkling wine (I never could tolerate much alcohol, especially champagne), I floated on pink clouds.

The next day, in the real world, I was sitting at my desk day dreaming a little when someone interrupted my thoughts and announced that I had a visitor at the guardhouse. It was Alfred. He seemed to be in a dither and handed me a key and a piece of paper with an address scribbled on it. I was confused, but he briefly stated to meet him at the address this evening and he would explain. A little disheveled and apprehensive, I walked the short distance to the apartment house where he instructed me to go. I knocked on the door; nobody answered. I inserted the key and unlocked the door, and there he stood in front of me. I was not sure what to think of this exercise and was rather annoyed. He admitted that he wanted to test me, to see whether I trusted him and had guts. He untangled the mystery about the room by telling me that he had rented the place, and the room would be beneficial for both of us. Still disgruntled, I told him that I needed to think about this arrangement and left.

The following day, I went straight to the room. Without knocking, I opened the door with my key. Alfred was not there, but I found a note on the table asking me for forgiveness of his presumptuous behavior and saying that he would be back the following evening.

Fashing was in full swing. Alfred and I decided to attend one of many masked balls, again in the Schwarzwaldhalle. I had nothing better in mind than to wear my black cat costume, which I accessorized with a fitted rhinestone choker necklace around my neck. He loved the outfit and enthusiastically accompanied me as my escort in a rented tuxedo, top hat, and walking cane. We were a handsome couple; even the no-nonsense Frau Finger had a complimentary remark. We danced all night until the band stopped playing and disassembled their equipment.

Skeletons in a Closet

A few days before Ash Wednesday, when all dancing stopped for forty days until Easter, we sat at the Café Wien listening to the live band and dancing to slow, schmaltzy songs. Alfred excused himself to go to the restroom, and I kept staring at his fat wallet lying on the table in front of me. The temptation to find out what made it so big took its course, and I opened it. The first item was a valid picture ID of Alfred issued by the US Army. Then a slew of photographs, all of the same girl, Frances, in cheerleader and prom dress pose with inscriptions of "I love you," "Love forever," "Miss you so much," and more lovey-dovey scribbles. In some daze, I put the wallet back in its place and was unsure what to do next. Alfred came back cheery and ready to take me to the dance floor. I wanted to leave, and he realized that I was trying to control my emotions.

It was late, but Alfred asked me to come with him to our room. At first I declined, but he begged repeatedly and pleaded, "I must tell you something important." There was silence between us as we sat at the table with a vase of wilted red roses. He pulled out his wallet, removed the ID card and every picture and scrap of paper and laid them on the table. He then came toward me, embraced my face with his hands, and said, "Erika, I love you, and I want to marry you." He reached for the ID card and told me that he was a student of engineering in his home state of Connecticut, and at Karlsruhe University, he just took a German-language course. However, the real reason for him to be in Germany was to fulfill his three-year US military commitment, which would end in July of 1961.

By now, my head was spinning, but he continued talking about his parents immigrating to America with a written promise from an aunt for his father to take over her clothing manufacturing business and eventually buy her out. The aunt—a sister of his mother—and his father had a major falling out. The aunt withdrew her promise, and his father had no job. Forced out of the aunt's house, his family had to find an apartment, and his father work.

The apartment owner, a widow with two children, a boy in college and a girl in high school, was most helpful and decent to his family. Her daughter, Frances, a junior in high school, wanted nothing more than become his wife after graduation. Living in the same house made the situation convenient, and Frances was a nice girl. He liked her, and so did his family, and when he was drafted into the army, he semipromised marriage to her after his return from Germany and bought her a hope chest.

Alfred stopped talking and started shredding the photographs one by one, except the ID card, placed the paper scraps into an ashtray, and lit the little pile with his cigarette lighter. Before I could say anything, he put a question to me, "Would you have paid any attention to me at the café if I had been dressed in uniform or told you that I was a soldier in the US Army? I think not." His point was well taken; most likely, we would not be having a conversation in this room. I remembered when the Sigmann girls, who lived down the street from the Liepolds, came home on weekends with their Ami boyfriends in those long, wide cars or convertibles. Everyone in the Waldsiedlung referred to them as promiscuous Ami whores, and the neighbors took up a petition to have the entire Sigmann family evicted from their house, but that never happened.

In my mind, I contemplated what to tell my mother, my aunt, my neighbors, and my friends. What will they say and think of me when Alfred's real identity was exposed? He admitted that he owned one of those chrome-studded opulent cars. He used it for transportation from Smiley Barracks in Neureut, his duty station, to Karlsruhe but parked the vehicle far away from the center. My mind concentrated on his car, which he would never park by my house in Bruchsal, nor would I ever be seen in it. I was not anything like the Sigmann girls; I simply fell in love with an intelligent, attractive man, not his background. What a dilemma!

He no longer balked, as he had in the past, when explaining his commitments to me. Alfred described his relationship with Frances as platonic. Prior to meeting me, he had a brief, intimate encounter with a German girl in Rastatt, when his unit was having maneuvers there. He told me that he had written to Frances before Christmas, explaining to her that he had fallen in love with someone else and that she could keep the hope chest but his promise to marry her was off. As of yet, she had not replied. He also wrote the same lines to his parents. They wrote back to him that his amorous adventures had caused great confusion and discord in their good friendship with Frances's mother. They now felt compelled to look for another apartment, and poor Frances did not speak to them. Alfred stared forlornly at the ashtray, thinking aloud, wishing he had discarded the meaningless photos some time ago and confessed his real purpose in Germany. The truth was that he was scared to lose me, and based on that, he had made very bad decisions.

Finally, the talking stopped, and Alfred remorsefully looked at me. Earlier in the evening, I was angry at my gullibility, I felt betrayed, even abused, and I cried. Somehow, I saw myself in my mother's footsteps during a time when my father already had started his affair with Irmgard and kept lying about it. She was angry and sad all at the same time, and that is how I felt now. So many emotions running through my body, I needed distance from this experience. I left the room controlled and calm and whispered, "Good-bye."

More Confessions

Days later, as I was stepping through the main entrance of the Zentralkasse, I saw Alfred leaning against one of the tall white columns. He immediately came toward me and told me how nice I looked. He reaffirmed how sorry he was to have caused such a mess, and asked if I would consider giving him another chance. I had classes that evening but hinted that I would stop at the room afterward and give him my answer.

Dietmar, the student I had a crush on once, seemed unusually friendly during class breaks. He finally asked me if I would like to have a coffee with him after class. Ever since his little spiel about goals, girls, and dating, I felt miffed. I declined his offer and let him know that I had plans.

The room looked different. I noticed a new white bedspread with a flower design covering the German-style down feather beds. I liked it. Alfred said it was made of chenille and was an American-style bedspread. He had bought it in the PX. Also, there were fresh flowers, more red roses on the table. I told him that I must see my mother on the weekend and tell her the secret that had unfolded. He asked if he could come with me, and I agreed, but not in his American car, which I had not seen yet. We took the train to Bruchsal and a taxi to my house.

My mother could hardly believe her eyes when she saw Alfred and me walk through her kitchen door. She scolded me for not letting her know in advance that I would bring him along so that she could have baked a cake or prepared something special. "That's not why we came," I said. Without embellishing the truth, I told her that Alfred was not a student at Karlsruhe University, as I believed, but a soldier in the US Army, stationed in Neureut, near Karlsruhe. Here I paused and decided against mentioning the Frances affair, since it had no relevance to my mother. Alfred in a subdued voice apologized for his deceptive behavior and proceeded to tell my mother his intentions of marrying me.

Visibly overwhelmed, my mother sat down on a chair. She looked at Alfred and me with a sad expression on her face but said nothing. I hated such silence and said, "Mutti, please say something."

She calmly replied, "You always wanted to escape from the Waldsiedlung, but why so far away—America?"

"Dearest Mutti, I never gave thought to where; it just turned out that way," I said.

She then had reasonable questions about his life and family in America, his army commitment, my evening school, and my room at Frau Finger's. She also referred to my father, that his signature of consent would be required if I was to marry before I turned twenty-one. Her inquiries indicated that she was not notably upset with us—perhaps disappointed over her daughter's choice of a non-German husband, but he was Catholic, and that counted in his favor.

Engaged to a Soldier

Spring peeked around the corner; I was in love and in blithe spirits. I maintained my room at Frau Finger's, went to work at the bank, and continued with evening classes. Alfred and I relished our time together. His Signal Corps unit was actually stationed at European Headquarters in Heidelberg, but a small squad of microwave communication specialists was assigned to Karlsruhe. He belonged to the army first, and for twenty-four hours a day. I listened and learned much about the ins and outs of army life, and America in general. He took me to the barracks where his cot and locker with his personal belongings were and where two of my professionally made photographs adorned the inside of his locker door. Not married to a member of the armed forces, I had no ID and thus could not enter the PX or the commissary, which were the shopping centers for the soldiers and their families. However, I could get into the movie theater, where I was introduced to popcorn and Coke and was appalled over the mess people left behind after the movie ended.

In 1960, the American military no longer forbade German-American marriages, as they had shortly after the war. Nevertheless, they did not encourage such unions and made the application process for a permit to marry rather difficult. Alfred suggested that we put our application in just in case the military decided to find reasons to prolong the process. He was still an Italian citizen, although drafted into the US military service; he was not sure if that could present a problem. One day in early April, he drove to Heidelberg and submitted our request for marriage papers to his commanding officer.

Mummay had recently returned from a short business trip to Paris, and we met him and Edeltraud over dinner one evening. His enthusiastic delight for the City of Lights infected all of us, and we decided that the four of us would go to Paris together. When I mentioned our trip to my mother, she immediately objected to such a proposal. She labeled it as inappropriate for two unmarried girls to be in the company of two men in a city like Paris, especially spending the night there, and I was not going. Unfortunately, work schedules and vacation time presented a problem for some of us, and our plan fell by the wayside.

When May arrived, Alfred and I became engaged. We chose two gold rings with a grooved surface and had our names engraved on the inside. On a Sunday afternoon, with my mother present, we slipped the rings on each other's left-hand ring finger, as it was the tradition in Germany, and lifted the waiting champagne glasses to toast our future together. My somewhat somber mother wished us happiness forever. She liked her son-in-law to be; it was just his snatching her daughter away to that vast distance continent that was a problem for her.

Now officially engaged, I found it absurd for my mother to oppose my going to Paris with my fiancé. She obviously had not heard or read of my generation's sexual freedom movements. I felt uncomfortable discussing sexual liberties with my mother or touching on those outdated taboos of hers. As in the past, she avoided discussions about love, sex, or marriage. Finally, she let go of her old-fashioned beliefs and wished us a good time in Paris and a safe journey.

A Trip to Paris

At last we sat in Alfred's two-toned, blue and white, 1952 Chevy sedan and were on our way to the City of Lights, Paris, France. It was my first time sitting in the Chevy, and I was remembering my adamant pledge: I would not be seen in his vehicle. Dismissing that foolish notion, I huddled up close to my fiancé while riding down the Autobahn. It was still a bit cool, but spring had used all its magic and painted a colorful countryside. We figured the 350-mile trip would take us seven hours, but earlier than anticipated, we arrived in a still-sunlit Paris. Our destination was the Latin Quarter on the Left Bank of the River Seine. We found ourselves in a labyrinth of one-way and narrow cobblestoned *rues* not accustomed to monstrous cars like the American Chevrolet. Alfred truly had his hands full maneuvering the vehicle until we found the small, nondescript hotel whose address he had learned from one of his soldier friends.

Our room on the second floor had no view. The floor-to-ceiling windows, adorned with faded curtains, faced the dark-gray plaster of the house next door. The ceiling and walls could have used a new coat of paint, and the tattered rugs covered creaking old wood floors that had seen better days. The modest room contained a metal-framed, full-sized bed, a petit armoire, a little wobbly table, and one chair. In one corner sat a bidet and a tiny sink, and the toilet was next door, to be shared with other guests. Our cheerful, red-headed host made it clear that she needed to collect the money for our four-night stay in advance. In her abysmal English, she proudly informed us that her establishment was a favorite stay for Americans visiting Paris. Maybe she meant American GIs, since rooms could be rented by the hour and only the renter and not his female companion had to show an ID. We were not sure if we were staying in an upscale brothel, but the price was right, and we only were there for four nights. In addition, the Chevy had a permanent parking place nearby, and our hotel was in a most convenient location to do Paris by foot.

The next morning after a *petit déjeuner* (breakfast) in one of the sidewalk cafés, we were ready to go sightseeing. With a map in hand, we whizzed through the grounds of the Sorbonne, Notre Dame, the Tuileries, and the Place de la Concorde, the largest square in Paris, where once the guillotine stood that beheaded Marie Antoinette. From there, we walked down the Avenue des Champs Élysée, which ends at the Arc de Triomphe. Our camera had been clicking away all day long and was out of film. It was evening, and darkness set in quickly. We navigated our way back to the hotel and fell exhausted on the bed's hard mattress.

The following day our program included the Eiffel Tower and Montparnasse. We bought tickets for the elevator ride up the Eiffel Tower to catch the panoramic and breathtaking views of Paris on this clear and gorgeous spring day. By noon, we had reached the hilly district of Montparnasse, with an interesting structure, the Observatoire de Paris, which was founded by King Louis XIV in 1667 and has been used for astronomical discoveries and purposes ever since. The area is a mecca for artists and intellectuals and has several famous cafés that have been hangouts for the likes of Hemingway, T. S. Eliot, Matisse, Picasso, Lenin, and others.

Our last stop of the day was Montmartre, a historic district primarily known for the white domed Basilica Sacré Coeur and its nightlife. Once we reached the summit of the highest hill of the city, we were at the doors of its landmark church, Sacré Coeur—Sacred Heart of Christ. Tourists from all over the world gather on the steps and terrace around the basilica to take in the panorama of Paris. It was another beautiful day and was the perfect time to have a short photo session. Then we walked to nearby Place du Tertre, a small square on Montmartre hill. Artists equipped with easels, palettes, and paints were hustling to paint the portraits of the wandering tourist or selling their completed art works, especially the background site of Sacré Coeur, captured at every hour of the day. Most of these painters were still starving, just like their penniless, famous predecessors, Van Gogh, Monet, and Renoir, to mention a few.

As darkness fell over Montmartre, its nightlife came alive. We found ourselves amid a tourist crowd at Pigalle, the notorious red light district. Alfred and I had seen the 1952 movie *Moulin Rouge,* and now we stood in front of the famous cabaret with its trademark, the red windmill on the roof. Without discussion, we bought tickets for that evening's show and had dinner there. The female performers, dressed in their feathers and very skimpy, glitzy costumes, provided interesting entertainment. Alfred and I compared their dancing and showmanship to the movie and agreed that we liked the film's cancan dancers better. Overall, it was an exciting evening, and for the first time, we took the metro back to our hotel.

Our last full day in Paris, we designated the entire day to the Louvre. At the entrance, we picked up a free map for a self-guided tour and decided which exhibits we wanted to see. Again we had to deal with crowds of people clustering around certain works of art, one in particular, Da Vinci's *Mona Lisa*, considered the most famous painting in the world. We then made our way to the wings with paintings of the German, French, Flemish, and Dutch artists and concluded the day with the sculpture of the *Venus de Milo*. It is impossible to see everything in one day, but our plan worked well for us, and on our way out, we stopped at the museum bookstore and purchased a few souvenirs.

On our final evening, we had a reservation to the renowned cabaret Lido de Paris. It was not required, but we dressed up for the occasion and had a taxi take us to the cabaret on the Champs Élysée. When we got there, Alfred slipped the waiter a twenty-dollar bill with the request for a table up front, close to the stage. At that time, the dollar was a much-desired currency anywhere in the world, and the waiter made certain we were pleased with our seats. We ordered champagne, and while waiting for the show to start, a photographer came to our table and took pictures, which could be purchased before we left the nightclub.

Bright lights illuminated the stage, and out came the sexy Bluebell girl dancers with their enormous headdresses and exquisite costumes of feathers, cloaks, and trains. They were the main stars of the splendid revue, and in combination with the guest stars, the singing and dancing German Kessler twins, the audience could not get enough of the lavish extravaganza. The show projected elegance, style, and was in a class by itself. It was not surprising that the rich and famous, like the duke and duchess of Windsor, Maurice Chevalier, or Salvador Dali, frequented the Lido de Paris.

Before we left the establishment, the photographer presented us with a series of photos, framed, unframed, small, large, and on matchboxes. We liked them all, and the technique of our smiling faces on the matchboxes was especially appealing; we bought the entire package.

The next morning, we packed our suitcases and walked toward the car. There was a piece of paper on the windshield held by the wiper. A hasty scribble in French stated, "Very sorry to have damaged your car; here is my name and address. Please send the bill for the repair." We looked at the dent near the protruding back fender and decided not to worry about it. The Chevy was nine years old and had gone through several GI owners. A few minor dents and scratches and the 140,000 miles on the odometer made little differencc to the old-style vehicle. We got in the car and left Paris with a wistful *"au revoir"* (good-bye), and a definite promise for *"retourne"* (return).

14

Marriage and Family

✿✿✿✿

A Complicated Matter

My mother was glad to see me back from Paris, and I had much to tell about Paris and our marvelous experiences. Also, my colleagues at the Zentralkasse had a curiosity about the much-talked-about city, and I was happy to recommend sites and places—except the dubious hotel! I mentioned that it helped to speak French, as my fiancé did, because nobody speaks German, and English only a few, and even then it was certainly not preferred.

By this time, my aunt and my neighbors knew of Alfred, his origin, and his US military association. They all liked him and accepted him for what he was, including his boat of a car. My cousins Helga and Barbara adored him, even when he forgot to bring candy or gum to them. When Uncle Gustel heard about me getting married to an Italian, he went berserk and wrote to my mother that he would never speak to me again and would not attend the wedding. This grudge reached back forty-four years to when an Italian soldier in WWI killed his father during a battle with Italian forces in the Dolomite Alps.

By the middle of July 1960, I was preparing for semester finals and had to listen to Wolfgang and Dieter hold forth during smoke breaks about my fatal mistake in marrying an Italian-Americano—worst yet, a Sicilian Mafioso. Their inappropriate and constant teasing made me quite irate, and I was glad when the semester was over. I decided not to sign up for more classes but to concentrate on my impending marriage, which had no set date—a problem in itself.

Three months passed, and we had not heard a word from Alfred's commanding officer in reference to our marriage permit. When Alfred put a call in to Heidelberg, he got the runaround, and the captain, his commanding officer, was not available. Two weeks later, the sergeant called Alfred and arranged for me to come for an "interview" with the captain. It was a Sunday afternoon, and I sat for three hours in the captain's office being interrogated about my refugee background, parents, education, and employment, complete with salary disclosure. Based on my good knowledge of English, the captain insinuated that perhaps I had dated a few US soldiers in the past. Appalled by his innuendos, I declined to continue this line of questioning and told him so. He quickly tried to play the part of a mentor by putting Alfred's family and background in doubt. He used some scare tactics by telling me that many German girls marry GIs, and when they get to America, they find out that life is quite different from what their husbands had told or promised them. I wanted to ask if he ever heard of happily ending stories but dismissed the question when I heard him say, "I realize you are not a gold digger, and I wish you well." As I was leaving his office, he mentioned that I was now subject to an investigation conducted by US military investigators.

In the meantime, Alfred and I made a trip to Bruchsal City Hall inquiring about obtaining a marriage license. We knew that legally the marriage had to be recorded at the registry's office, and that certificate was the only document the Catholic Church recognized for marriage in the church. It was important for me to have a church wedding along with the beautiful white dress and veil and all the trimmings that go with a wedding celebration.

Mr. Heim, a short, skinny man with round, rimless spectacles, embodied the perfect specimen of a loyal, longtime bureaucrat. He never smiled as he listened to our situation, and when we finished, he handed us several forms and a list of requirements that supported the completed paper work. He looked at us and blatantly stated that ours was a complicated matter and could take time.

Buckets of Frustrations

In September, I terminated my lease with Frau Finger. I was rather sad, as it seemed like closure of a chapter of my previous life, but it made good financial sense. Alfred maintained his room near Kaiserstrasse; the location was convenient and discreetly private. My mother, her MS somewhat in remission, was elated to have me back home. I resumed my prior commuting habits and made friends with Frau Lichtenberger, an executive secretary to one of our bank's directors. She was a newlywed and lived in South Bruchsal close by the Waldsiedlung. We saw each other every morning on the train and passed the time by chatting about everything imaginable. She confided that her husband, Karl-Heinz, was the son of a wealthy sheep farmer in the next county; he wanted her to quit her job, but she liked her independence. Eventually, Alfred and Karl-Heinz met and clicked immediately when the subject of auto racing came up. Both were avid followers of Formula I races, and a few weeks later, they were on their way to the big race in Monza, Italy.

In America, Alfred's parents were most unhappy to hear of their son wanting to marry a German, not a nice Italian girl like Frances. They could no longer save face with Frances and her mother and had no choice but to move out from the apartment they rented from her. To vent her anger, Alfred's mother wrote that she could not find his birth certificate, which he needed for a marriage license. Later, it was the same excuse with his baptismal certificate, a required document for church nuptials. With his parents being so uncooperative, it seemed as if the whole world was against us to get married.

Some days I had to work longer hours, and Alfred, frustrated as he was, accused me of seeing someone else behind his back. I always knew that he was a little jealous. At first it was cute, and I felt flattered, but his perpetual, nagging jealousy became an unbearable burden. We argued a lot, and one day in the room when he repeated his absurd accusations, I snapped. Pulling the ring off my finger and throwing it at him, I left.

My mother noticed my discontent and the missing ring but did not ask any questions, knowing that I would eventually confide in her. Two weeks went by, and Alfred and I had no contact with each other. Early one Sunday morning he stood at the door of my house with a bouquet of red roses, begging and imploring forgiveness for his abominable behavior. Somewhat hesitant but glad that he came, I agreed to take a long walk. He put the ring back on my finger and swore his love forever to me. We made plans to see my father in Waldshut. I was not twenty-one and needed permission to get married from both of my parents, since they were not divorced.

A Friendly Game of Chess

Waldshut is a town in southwestern Germany flanking the Swiss border, separated only by the Rhein River. My father's duty station with the railroad had been there for the last four years. I did not need an appointment to see him, as he wasn't going anywhere, confined to a hospital bed at Waldshut Hospital and recuperating from a serious motorcycle accident. Both his legs sustained major damage, and there were doubts about him even walking again. He did not expect me, and when Alfred and I walked into his room, his eyes almost fell out of their sockets. There he lay with one leg in a cast from the groin area to the toes. The other leg, an awful sight of blood and oozing wounds, rested suspended in a contraption. I could hardly take my eyes of that leg in the air but managed to introduce Alfred and outline the reason why we were here.

Under the circumstances, my father seemed in good spirits; he was happy to have visitors. We brought him some chocolates and reading material, and he gratefully accepted our gift. After a lengthy exchange of personal details, mainly about my fiancé and me, he challenged Alfred to a game of chess. I was reading while they played, and finally I heard my father's unmistakable "checkmate." He complimented Alfred on a good game and hoped to play him again. He signed the underage permission papers and recited an unfamiliar love poem to us. It was evening, and we still had three hours driving ahead of us. Nine years passed before we saw each other again.

It Smelled like Conspiracy

Another trip to Mr. Heim at the registry office; still our application could not be processed due to the US Army's delay of the marriage permit. Their investigation of me was incomplete, and it would take three more weeks to finish the case. We got the distinct impression that Mr. Heim, the devoted civil servant, enjoyed relating disappointing news to us, and we were not sure if some of his requests were legally necessary.

The calendar showed November 1, *Allerheiligen* (All Saints Day), a federal and Catholic holiday. By now, I was certain that there would be no wedding this year. My white lace and silk organza wedding gown, veil, shoes, and gloves hung in the closet, ready to go down the aisle. A week earlier, Alfred and I went to Heidelberg for a blood test required by the US military for a marriage permit. I had never had such a test in my life. An army nurse roughly stuck the needle in my arm and could not find my vein. After poking around for some time, she left, the needle still in my arm, and engaged another nurse, who finally got the blood flowing to fill the vial; I was about to faint.

Alfred had enough of the red tape from the Americans and the Germans and suggested various options. "We are going to get married in Switzerland," he announced and drove to Basel. Unfortunately, the neutral country of Switzerland had the same requirements as the Germans. Disappointed, we left Basel City Hall and went sightseeing. The following weekend, we tried our luck in Strasbourg, France, and received the same answer.

We learned to be patient and waited to be contacted. It was now the end of November, and an evergreen Advent wreath adorned the table, ready to have its first candle lit. The Christmas season was upon us. The Zeiglers downstairs moved out, and we had the whole house to ourselves. The rule of having to take Flüchtling in a Waldsiedlung house no longer applied. Alfred and I started to furnish the downstairs rooms, our future living quarters. On Christmas Eve we went out in the woods and cut a spruce. As we decorated the tree, we recalled our secret first kisses during the same time a year ago and laughingly told my mother. She smiled back and made the comment, "I know more than you think." The three of us went to Midnight Mass at St. Antonius Church, and I told Alfred that I used to be a lector in this church and that the parishioners knew me well. This evening, they were not shy stretching their necks to get a good look of Erika's fiancé.

Our friends Edeltraud and Mummay wanted us to join them at the Hotel Kaiserhof in Karlsruhe for a New Year's Eve bash. Those two frequented the most chic and exciting places, and we never questioned their choice. Knowing that it was an elegant gala, we dressed accordingly. I opted for my nifty pink designer cocktail dress, which had attracted a few bold looks at the Lido in Paris. Alfred had always been a neat dresser, and he looked fabulous in his dark blue pin-striped suit. The four of us celebrated with several bottles of champagne, ringing in another year: 1961.

Planning a Small Wedding

Finally there was some good news in the first week of the new year of 1961. Several weeks back, Alfred had ordered a brand new Volkswagen Beetle through the military exchange program, and the car was ready to be picked up in Frankfurt. Furthermore, his company commander summoned him to Heidelberg to pick up our marriage permit. In addition, the Chevy was as good as sold to another soldier, and we were just waiting for our VW to arrive.

We wasted no time and went to Mr. Heim's office at Bruchsal City Hall. He looked at the permit and commented that he could not read it and that we needed a certified translation. I wanted to choke his short neck but refrained from showing my anger and implored him to approve the application. He sat down, filled in the blanks, stamped and signed the form, and handed it to us without saying a word. As we were leaving, he said, "You know it's really not quite legal, and your marriage could be annulled; just don't come back to me." We did not care what Mr. Heim's verbiage meant; we went straight to the office of St. Anton's Parish and arranged for a date to have Pfarrer Menzer marry us. Very few people get married in the middle of winter; therefore, the church was available for January 21, even at such short notice. Although Pfarrer Menzer was on retreat during that time, Pfarrer Kluge had no commitments for that Saturday morning.

It had taken nine long, exhausting months to obtain a marriage license, and now we had barely two weeks to put on a wedding. The guest list was short to begin with, and my aunt helped my mother with the baking and cooking. We used an empty room downstairs, and Alfred brought folding tables and chairs and covered them with white tablecloths. The menu had German and Italian dishes to choose from, and Marco was hired to be the chef in my mother's kitchen. We chose a three-tiered wedding cake from a bakery in Karlsruhe, and Alfred bought enough wine, beer, and champagne to get a large platoon drunk.

Some of Alfred's army buddies were invited, and one of them, Ronny Frank, was his best man. Ronny, a fun-loving jokester from Montana, loved German beer and a cold winter. He claimed that his ancestors came from Germany, and after a few beers, Ronny started to speak German. He was married and could hardly wait for his wife, Lorna, to visit him in springtime. Ronny wanted our approval and showed us the cream-colored tweed suit he would be wearing for our wedding. He explained that this suit, although it had a hole from a cigarette burn, had special meaning: it had served as both his high school graduation outfit and his wedding suit when he and Lorna got married. Staring at the dime-sized hole located, of all places, by the fly-front zipper, I felt slightly embarrassed and asked Ronny if he would not mind for my mother or aunt to use a little magic and cover the hole. Of course my mother and aunt were extremely busy with preparations, but that hole needed quick attention, and they knew just how to fix it. We had the suit dry-cleaned, and Ronny looked rather dapper in his repaired and cleaned attire.

In the euphoria of wedding preparations, my long-awaited twenty-first birthday came on January 16 as almost an inconvenience. Nobody had time to fuss over or celebrate my being of legal age, a most special occasion under normal circumstances. The city of Bruchsal had sent me a congratulatory letter for having attained legal age and emphasizing the rights and responsibilities I now had as a full-fledged citizen of West Germany.

Unlike in previous years, the temperatures this January were much milder, with hardly any snow. On Friday, January 20, we drove in our new VW with our witnesses, Ronny and my mother, to the registry office in Bruchsal to be married in a civil ceremony. Our appointment was at 11:00 a.m., and we were ushered into a small room where the mayor's deputy performed the formalities and pronounced us man and wife in less than ten minutes. We signed the document, as did our witnesses, and left City Hall as a legally married couple. By now, it was lunchtime—for most people the main meal of the day—and there was a good reason to celebrate; we invited our witnesses to one of Bruchsal's finest restaurants, "Zum Bären."

Although we were legally married, my mother would not hear of Alfred and me sleeping together in our newly acquired bedroom suite that night until we were married by the church. Perhaps she did not want Aunt Resl and Uncle Bepp, who stayed with us, to get the wrong impression of her daughter's good morals. My new husband went back to his barracks in Neureut and spent the night there.

Saturday, my church wedding day, the sun came out early and promised a pleasant winter day. Alfred arrived with Ronny, his best man, and readied himself in his wedding attire. My mother, who was my maid of honor, looked wonderful in her blue lace-embroidered dress. She appeared a little melancholy that morning and could hardly contain her tears while helping me with my veil. When it was time to go, she told me what a beautiful bride I was and sent me off with affectionate hugs, kisses and many good wishes.

Our wedding had been announced for the last two Sundays during mass at St. Antonius, thereby partially satisfying an ancient church custom: the marriage banns. Besides that convention, we also bought a good-sized wedding announcement in the local paper, *Bruchsaler Rundschau*. By the time we arrived at the church, invited and uninvited people alike were sitting in the pews waiting for us to enter. Alfred in his new black suit and I in my gorgeous white gown, holding a bouquet of long stem red roses, walked down the aisle toward the altar, where my mother and Ronny waited with Pfarrer Kluge, who gave the cue to the organist, and the ceremony began. About forty minutes later, blessed by the sacrament of matrimony, our gold rings now on our right-hand ring fingers, and my veil lifted, we walked out of the church under the shouts of good luck and the throwing of rice.

We drove straight to the Ohler Studio for a photo session. Mummay was supposed to take pictures during the nuptials and had our camera. However, snowy roads in the high elevations of the Black Forest, where he attended a *Dessous* (lingerie) show the day before, delayed him and Edeltraud. They finally showed up, and we were able to take pictures of our momentous day. Marco was in charge of the reception and had created fabulous Italian dishes of antipasti, pasta, and sauce with meatballs as well as an out-of-this-world chicken cacciatore. In addition, we had local German dishes of *Rolladen, Knödel*, and *Kraut*. Late in the afternoon, coffee and tea were available, and delicious-looking tortes and cakes were brought to the tables. We started with the sweets by cutting our beautiful wedding cake, and there was plenty to go around.

During teatime, Alfred left the party for a while so he could listen on the radio in the VW to a live transmission of the inauguration speech by the newly elected US president, John F. Kennedy. He seemed very pleased when he returned, lifted his glass, and made a toast to the new president of the United States of America. It was also the proper time to take a few minutes for Alfred and me to walk over to my aunt's house, where my grandfather lay in bed sick. I wanted him to see us as bridal couple and to bring him a piece of our wedding cake. Opa nodded his head and smiled a little. I knew that he was pleased that we thought of him.

A Long Honeymoon

I held the atlas with our mapped-out honeymoon trip in my hand and quickly shared our extended itinerary with my mother. The weather report forecasted more snow for the German Alps region— definitely for the vicinity of Salzburg, Austria, our first stop. Once we arrived in the city of Mozart, we checked into the hotel. There was still plenty of daytime left to visit the "Old Town," with its baroque churches and towers, and admire the massive fortress of Hohensalzburg looming over the city. It was too late to take the funicular railway up to the medieval castle, and we opted for another time.

After a delicious, traditional Austrian breakfast we left Salzburg and focused on our next destination, Trieste, Italy. Alfred had relatives living in Trieste. His father's widowed sister-in-law, Elsa, and her son, Dario, my age, lived there. They were waiting for us and were very happy to get reacquainted with Alfred and to meet his new wife. I could not speak or understand Italian and was glad to have brought a small German-Italian dictionary with me. His aunt insisted I call her Zia (aunt) Elsa and that we stay in their house and not in a hotel. We met Dario's fiancé, Mariuccia, and her family. Her father owned an *osteria* (tavern), where I tasted pizza for the first time along with some other dishes of the region. Most of the food was tasty and to my liking—except for espresso, a potent type of coffee. I tried to dilute it with milk, somewhat sacrilegious to Italians, but even that made no difference. Eventually I heard of cappuccino, and it replaced my cravings for German coffee.

We had knowledgeable tour guides in Dario and Mariucca and walked all over this Mediterranean seaport city. It was interesting to find out that before WWI, Trieste had belonged to the Habsburg Empire and was—after Vienna, Budapest, and Prague—the fourth largest city in the empire. The grandeur of that time left its marks throughout the city.

Our Trieste relatives made our two-day stay a memorable experience. As we were leaving, Zia Elsa put a little box in my hand, and she whispered, "It's for you—a keepsake of Trieste." It contained an eighteen-carat gold medallion larger than the size of a quarter and embossed with the tower of San Giusto and a palm tree. The medallion represented more than a keepsake after we bought an eighteen-carat classic gold chain and I wore it around my neck. It became an entertaining conversation piece.

Venice was less than two hours west of Trieste. We just wanted to do the one-day tourist thing, including a gondola ride. We were not dressed for the elegant dining room at the restaurant of the world-famous Hotel Danieli, and it was suggested we sit in the Terrace Bar, which had a more limited menu. Still, the experience from the rooftop of this palazzo overlooking the Grand Canal and the Venice lagoon walled by countless flickering lights made for an unforgettable sight.

The fuel gauge on our VW indicated almost empty, and we drove to close by Vicenza for a gas fill-up at a US Army garrison. The gas cost about twenty cents per gallon and was well worth our short detour. As we traveled south and reached Bologna, we hopped on the newly opened Autostrada del Sole (Highway of the Sun), and continued to the capital of the Tuscany region, Florence. Once ruled by the powerful Medicis, this historical city has been a cultural mecca for centuries. Our goal was to see some artworks held in the Pitti Palace and Uffizi Galleries.

Our next stop was Rome, the capital of Italy. There we would stay several days and tour at our leisure. It became obvious that driving around Rome was a hazard to man and machine. Traffic was out of control. Nobody observed posted signs; the only recognized form of traffic control was the wild and crazy hand motions of the hurried Roman motorist. Walking was the best and safest choice, and we did a lot of it. We signed up for a Rome bus tour, a great way to see the major attractions. We devoted one day to the Vatican. It took our breath away to step into the vast space of St. Peter's Basilica with its domes, altars, and statues. We got a close look at Michelangelo's masterpiece, the *Pieta*, and walked by the tomb of St. Peter and those of other popes. We strolled through the Vatican Museum, where priceless treasures collected by popes over the centuries were on display. Adjacent to that immeasurable wealth is the Sistine Chapel with its famous ceiling painted by Michelangelo and its other wall frescos created by the greatest artists of the Renaissance.

Leaving Rome and heading south, we passed the city of Naples, and soon Mount Vesuvius was in sight. Our interests were the ruins of Pompeii, a city buried by the volcano in CE 79. Once we had satisfied our archeological curiosity, we hopped on a ferry that took us to the mountainous but tiny island of Capri. Besides the main attraction, the Blue Grotto, there are the impressive villas owned by the rich and famous. It was a quaint little tourist trap, and we did not stay too long. Back in our car, we drove along the scenic Amalfi coast, a stretch of rugged terrain and picturesque villages ending in the city of Salerno, where we stayed in a rustic *albergo* (inn).

Time ticked away, and we still had not reached our destination, Sicily. Driving south through the long, narrow peninsula of mountainous Calabria, we reached the Strait of Messina. There we took a ferry, which accommodated our car for the two-mile ride, and landed on the island of Sicily.

More Nice Relatives

Driving further south on the eastern coast of Sicily, we finally arrived in the town of Randazzo, where another family of Alfred's relatives lived. They, too, had been waiting for us. The patriarch of this family was the oldest brother of Alfred's father, whom we called Zio (uncle). His wife, Pippa, her mother, Nonna (grandmother), and three sons, aged fifteen to twenty-six, made up the rest of the clan. They lived in an enormous old house, where Zio and his seven siblings were born. Zio inherited the house after the parents died, and he had it completely renovated and equipped with the latest in kitchen and bathroom furnishings and fixtures. Pippa, a quiet woman, made the house an appealing, comfortable home. She was a wonderful cook, and what she called a modest meal, I viewed as a delightful feast. Nonna and she patiently taught me little sentences in Italian, and, by the time I left them, my vocabulary was good enough to make myself understood.

Randazzo is a small town located at the base of Mount Etna, an 11,000-foot active volcano. Over centuries, Randazzo miraculously had been spared from the volcano's many eruptions. Several churches, a castle, and a town square dated back to medieval times. The town thrived on open-air markets and tourism. The enforcer of law and order was none other than Zio, the chief of police.

One day Zio came home with about thirty rings in a small paper bag and insisted that Alfred and I each choose a ring of our liking. I immediately eyed a large, oval-shaped, beveled amethyst in an eighteen-carat gold basket setting. Alfred chose a small diamond in eighteen-carat gold man's ring. Those rings were our wedding gift from Zio and his family, and I wore mine, a much-admired piece of jewelry, for almost fifty years.

During our stay in Sicily, we luckily experienced some mild Mediterranean climate, and there was no better-qualified tour guide than my husband, who was born on the island. We soaked in the warm sunshine as we sipped our cappuccinos on the terrace of the

Villa Hotel Schuler in Taormina. This charming city is perched on a mountainside with fantastic views of the coastline and snowcapped Mt. Etna. The beauty and mythical atmosphere of Taormina has inspired many famous writers and artists and has captivated tourists from all over the world.

Another day, we went to Piedimonte Etneo, a quaint village on the slopes of Mt. Etna, and Alfred's birthplace. We entered the only café in town, and at noon, it was a rather busy place. People kept staring, not sure if they knew or should know us until Alfred approached them, revealed who he was, and made himself available to their endless, curious questions. The news of Alfred from America and his German wife visiting at the café spread like wildfire through the village, and soon there was standing room only. Eventually we had to take a firm leave from these friendly townspeople.

When we reached our parked car, some teenage boys were cleaning the windshield and showed a real interest in the VW. They just wanted a ride in the Beetle, and we squeezed four of them in the backseat and drove around the village square and through the town itself. We made their day.

From Piedimonte Etneo we drove further up the mountain and came to Linguaglossa. Alfred's mother and her twelve siblings came from this community. She still had a sister there who operated a vegetable and fruit booth in front of her house. A brother lived in the countryside and made his living from a citrus grove. The rest of the siblings had immigrated to America as early as 1918. We visited the aunt and uncle, both surprised to see their nephew from faraway America and married to a *tedesca ragazza* (German girl).

Sicilians still remembered the German occupation of Sicily during WWII after their leader, Mussolini, lost control of his people and eventually was ousted. The once-welcomed Teutons became a nuisance by staying in Sicily and thereby drawing the war to the island. Allied forces fought bitter battles against the German defenses. At times, I felt uncomfortable by mere association of being German, but most Italians were quite fond of their northern neighbors, and in Sicily I was treated with nothing but kindness and respect.

After Palermo, Catania is the second-largest city in Sicily. Besides the many churches, we visited palaces, squares, and the largest amphitheater in Sicily—and that just grazed the surface of historic treasures. We strolled through the old town with its bustling, smelly fish market, and there time had stood still. This was an amazing place, so many kinds of sea creatures—certainly a seafood lover's delight.

I loved Catania and Sicily, but my vacation time was slowly ending. I pressed Alfred for our return, but he proudly informed me that he had sent a telegram to my employer, terminating my position in the bank. My reaction to his presumptuous conduct was quite different from what he expected, and we had our first major argument; I was extremely annoyed.

Feeling a Little Queasy

I woke up early feeling poorly and spent most of the morning in or near the bathroom. Later in the day, the dizziness subsided and my upset stomach had settled down. I blamed Alfred for his insidious plan in terminating my job, and he was truly sorry. I had no appetite, and the following morning I experienced the identical routine as I had the day before. We both became concerned, and I told Pippa and Nonna that I must have eaten something that caused such nausea. The two women reassuringly looked at me, and one mentioned, "That's how I felt when I was pregnant with my first child."

Since my condition neither improved nor worsened, I considered Pippa's innuendo regarding pregnancy a likely cause. One fact was certain: I could not make this 1,300-mile trip home in the VW. We pondered over other options and decided to return by train. Alfred's parents did not attend our wedding but sent us money for a wedding gift, and now we had to use half of it to pay for the unexpected expense. Zio helped us with the arrangements for the car to be transported by rail to Germany.

After changing trains several times during the two-day trip and being unable to look out the window due to a feeling of motion sickness, I was certainly glad when the train rolled into Karlsruhe Hauptbahnhof and, a while later, into Bruchsal.

Somewhat bewildered, my mother saw us getting out from a taxi and had to be assured that we were not involved in an accident. I told her I might be pregnant. As expected, my mother ignored that insinuation but blamed the spicy and greasy Italian food and immediately prepared her favorite cure-all: a cup of hot chamomile tea. The tea was soothing indeed, and my mother felt vindicated, though it was early evening, the time when I usually felt better anyway.

A Baby on the Way

Finally I could get an appointment with a doctor at Heidelberg Army Hospital. I had no idea what to expect but quickly realized that the hospital's priority was sick or wounded soldiers and not delicate females who had no tolerance for pain. Two days later, it was confirmed that I was pregnant and that our baby was due at the end of September. They gave me vitamins and a schedule for prenatal care. The so-called "morning sickness," I was told, is common in normal pregnancy, and there was no pill for it.

We were excited to have a baby on the way. Alfred was certain that it would be a boy. It took some time for my mother to believe that her daughter, her Erikale, could be pregnant, but then, one day she told me how happy she was to become a grandmother. In my fifth month, the morning sickness stopped and I felt like a real person again. I had gained no weight, but the doctor seemed unconcerned. We bought all kinds of baby stuff at the PX and German baby stores and prepared the new crib.

Edeltraud was a little surprised over my life's fast pace and chided me for letting Alfred halt my carrier. She had been offered a job as an *au pair* in London and accepted it. Her commitment was for one year, and she really wanted to become fluent in English. Besides, her relationship with Mummay was on shaky grounds, and she needed some distance from him. I envied her independence and wished her the best of luck.

In July of 1961, Alfred's army obligation ended and he would be shipped back to the States. We discussed our situation with the doctor in Heidelberg, and he informed us that I would not get medical permission to fly. With that in mind, we carefully considered all options and concluded that Alfred would reenlist for another three years of military duty. He had assurance that he could stay at his present job for the next eighteen months. It was the best news for my mother, who was fretting over our potential departure from Germany before her grandchild was born.

My mother and my husband had a little business going where he bought American cigarettes dirt-cheap in the PX and my mother sold them in Siemens, where she worked, for the price of German cigarettes. People still loved American-made cigarettes, and the profit on a carton was both obscene and illegal. Luckily, they were never caught. They both justified their dealings, since German smokers could not buy the American brands in the German economy. Indeed, theirs was a lucrative service.

One Saturday in September we invited my mother for dinner and drove to Baden-Baden in the Black Forest, where we knew a lovely mountain restaurant. During that night, I started vomiting and felt sick; I assumed it had to be the food I ate. Sunday morning my condition was unchanged, and we drove to the emergency room at Heidelberg Army Hospital. They could not tell what my problem was but kept me for observation anyway. Late in the afternoon violent pains set in. A nurse said, "They are labor pains, and you need to lie still." The next thing I knew, I was wheeled to a huge room—I heard the words *spinal block....delivery room*—and by 6:42 p.m. I welcomed my Sunday baby, a beautiful baby girl. A nurse brought our baby to the hall where Alfred waited and showed him not a son but a daughter. He had just lost a few bets but was delighted with a little girl.

The US Army hospital, a no-frills, no-fuss facility, had their own way of doing things. I was in a room with three other women and their babies, and the only visitors allowed were husbands dressed in sterile caps, gowns, and face masks. Since mine was a normal delivery, I could leave the hospital after three days and go home, but not before the baby had a name for the birth certificate. Alfred liked Italian names, while I liked German names; we could not come to an agreement. However, we both liked the hit song "Patrizia," and we decided it would be the perfect name for our baby.

Suddenly a Family

Life with a new baby was certainly a big change for all of us. Alfred slept at the barracks in Neureut just to get some sleep. My aunt, who bore three children, was convinced that our baby had problems with colic, while my mother insisted that the baby had her days and nights mixed up. She and I took turns during the night tending to little Patrizia's needs and preventing her from crying. I found it odd that she never cried when she was in our arms. After four weeks of nightshifts, we both felt like zombies, and Alfred suggested I should read about baby sleeping habits. We bought Dr. Spock's *Baby and Childcare* book. I established a different routine, and shortly after, Patrizia slept the hours a baby that age should sleep. Finally, we all got some needed rest.

We prepared for Patrizia's baptism with Pfarrer Menzer officiating and chose Zia Elsa from Trieste as her godmother. She was unable to attend, but cousin Tano from Sicily came by train and stepped in for godmother Elsa. Tano was Zio's oldest son, a tall, handsome twenty-seven-year-old CPA who hoped to meet some German women while visiting us. I thought of Edeltraud; he would have liked her, but she was in London, and I had no other fitting recommendations for him.

Her first, and our last, Christmas in Germany, Patrizia was three months old. She was a happy baby, a good eater, and her round little face with the big brown eyes made her already a beauty. I loved dressing her up, and her wardrobe had the latest in American baby fashion.

In the South of France

Since the erection of the Berlin Wall in 1961 by Communist-led East Germany, the US military in Europe, specifically in West Germany, had been on high alert. Since we lived off base, we were required to have a phone installed in my mother's house. Alfred received many early morning calls to report for duty immediately at the radio station in Neureut. As tensions between the Soviets and Americans escalated, we had to restrict our long-distance traveling, even on Alfred's days off, unless we had special permission. The Army demanded that every member and his or her family have their vaccination record up-to-date. The purpose for this requirement was to keep in readiness in case of evacuation back to the States. The pediatrician at Heidelberg Hospital made sure our baby received boosters and immunization according to infant guidelines. Mine was a different story: I had to catch up on years of required vaccinations in order to comply with US Army regulations.

In June of 1962, Alfred and I left our baby with my mother for a long weekend, and we drove to the French Rivera. Actually, our first stop was San Remo on the Italian Riviera, where we stayed in a charming seaside villa. From there, we made our way to nearby Monte Carlo to watch the Grand Prix of Monaco, a prestigious Formula 1 race through the narrow streets of this tiny principality. The race is known not for its speeds but for the glamour and danger of racing through the rugged mountainside. Alfred and I had our own competition going; he cheered for Ferrari, and I for Porsche. When the race was over, a British Cooper had won.

Before we left Monte Carlo, we went to the roulette tables at Casino de Paris, lost a few francs in a hurry, and had dinner on the terrace of the café de Paris. For decades, Monaco had been a hangout for European royalty; the famous and infamous with their wealth and passion for fame all rubbed shoulders together.

Bypassing the rather big city of Nice, we drove on to glamorous Cannes, best known for its international film festival. It was once a small fishing village owned by monks, and we spent the day on a crowded Cannes beach with the Mediterranean sun pounding down on my fair skin.

Apparently we had not managed our time very well and had to forfeit the city of Saint Tropez, dubbed the playground of the jet-setting millionaires, movie stars, and models—and where French movie icon Brigitte Bardot was discovered.

Having my mother for a babysitter was a true blessing, and when we arrived in Bruchsal, I was overcome with tears; I missed Patrizia so much, even though she had had the best of care. It was our last big trip before Alfred's duty in Germany ended.

A Citizenship Nightmare

We now had to prepare for our move to the United States in November. My mother and I could not talk about; it was too painful for her. I already had a German passport and was good to go. One day, we took Patrizia and her American birth certificate to US Army headquarters at Heidelberg to apply for her passport. The office that dealt with such legal documents told us the baby was not an American citizen and that therefore they could not issue a passport. Although she had an American birth certificate, she was not born in the United States, but on German soil, and her father was Italian citizen. Under German law, a child born in Germany takes the citizenship of the father. (That law changed later.) Back in 1960, Alfred became eligible for US citizenship, but he was stationed in Germany, and US citizenship can only be granted on American soil. A member of the US armed forces was not required to have US citizenship yet was subject to the draft, as in Alfred's case.

Every citizen in Germany, regardless of nationality, had to be registered at City Hall thirty days after taking up residence in the township. After Patrizia was born, I went to the registry office in Bruchsal and had her birth recorded. It seemed reasonable for me to inquire about the legal ramifications of my child's nationality in that same office. The man, another bureaucrat, was certain that the baby was not German. Discussing the matter with his coworkers, they all seemed convinced the child fell under US jurisdiction, since US bases in Germany were the property of the United States of America, a liberty taken by the victors after Germany lost the war. Additionally, it was suggested we make a trip to Stuttgart, where the Italian consulate had an office. Perhaps they could be of help.

In the midst of these complicated nationality issues concerning our child, I felt unwell. My mother reminded me of the time after we returned from our honeymoon, when I was sicker than a dog because I was pregnant. She was right, but this felt different. These episodes were of short durations early in the morning, and riding in the car was not bothersome. Two weeks of nausea prompted a trip to Heidelberg. The army doctor assured us that I was quite healthy and that pregnancy was a strong possibility, but we needed to wait for the test results to come back. The next day, I received a call confirming that I was pregnant. After the initial shock, I felt joyous thinking that this baby may have been conceived on the French Rivera—what nicer place is there?—and little Patrizia would get a playmate.

One day, all four of us, my mother included, drove to Stuttgart to visit the Italian consulate. On the way, we stopped at a photo booth where young people hung out to have funny, grimacing pictures taken. We put our money in and held a frightened Patrizia up to the lens to get a passport-sized, black-and-white photo of her. We were lucky: the consul general was in and listened to our request for a passport for our baby. He spoke some German but was visibly glad when Alfred conversed in Italian with him. When he started smiling and shaking his head, I knew this was another dead end. He advised us to pressure the Americans, as their superiority in Europe could make or break any law and Italy could not possibly recognize the child as its citizen.

This time, we went straight to the JAG office at Heidelberg Military Headquarters and presented the case to them. Again we accomplished zilch, and a legal aid soldier told Alfred, "I am a lawyer, and I am telling you—it's the responsibility of these goddamned Italians to issue a passport; the child is their subject, not ours."

Meanwhile, time was running out; it was already September. Patrizia had four teeth and dark little curls and had been walking since she was nine and a half months old. We celebrated her first birthday and invited my aunt and cousins, our friends Edith and Karl-Heinz, and her mother. I was barely three months pregnant and started to show just a little, so I told everyone that I was not getting fat but we were expecting another baby. People always seem surprised by such news, although it was well received.

Almost at wit's end, Alfred planned one final trip to the Italian consulate. He wanted to go by himself, speak with the consul general in private, and not have any witnesses, as he intended to bribe this man with a bottle of Hennessy Cognac, two cartons of cigarettes, and fifty dollars cash. As Alfred suspected, the consul general was a rather easy target to corrupt, and he asked Alfred if he had a photo ID of the baby. He put the dollars in his coat pocket, sat himself at the old black manual typewriter, took a piece of blank white paper, inserted it, and waited to be told what to write. Alfred told him to start out with the word Passaporto in capital letters and a space between each letter. Most of the information was on the birth certificate, and when the consul completed transcribing the data, he glued the photo from the photo booth in the space he had reserved for the picture. He opened a desk drawer and stored away the cognac and cigarettes. Then he took out the official Italian consulate seal, affixed it to the sheet, stuck on some other stamp, signed and dated the paper, and handed it to Alfred, saying, "Is that what you need?"

When Alfred showed me the paper, I burst out laughing. Looking at this mess of smudged lines, typing errors, holes in the paper from striking the keys too hard, and no official letterhead, I asked, "Who will accept this ridiculous, botched piece of paper as a passport document?" Alfred seemed to think that with a certified translation, the letter could serve as a proper document; after all, it had the seal of the Italian consulate for authentication. Presentation of the paper raised many eyebrows but accomplished its purpose.

The Final Good-Bye

November came in a hurry, and it was an upsetting time, especially for my mother. Regardless of our plans of her joining us in Ft. Gordon, Georgia, Alfred's new duty station, after we had settled in, she was an emotional wreck. All I could do was to emphasize her coming to the States and encourage her to have a passport made. These pep talks helped for the moment, but she cried most days, except when she played with our baby.

For our wedding gift, my mother had bought a modern *Einbauküche* (fitted kitchen furniture), which we used while living in the house. We intended to take the Einbauküche, our new bedroom suite, and other acquisitions with us to America. My mother insisted that we take the living room furniture she and my father had bought in 1954. It was an elegant and timeless style, and I had always liked that furniture. Besides, the army paid for our move to the States, whereas she would have to pay for transportation if she decided to bring furniture with her to America.

The movers came in the middle of November and started packing everything in boxes and finally into three large crates. It took nearly a week to get the job done, and I only had to tell them what went and what stayed. The entire downstairs was empty with the exception of electrical appliances and gadgets, which we could not take since the US electrical system was not compatible with German voltage lines. A friend of my mother wanted to rent the downstairs after our departure, and I was more than pleased to have her and her husband move in.

We arranged rail transportation for our VW to Hamburg, a large port city on the North Sea. From there our vehicle was shipped over the Atlantic to a harbor in New York. We had good-bye dinners with our friends, laughing and crying all at the same time. Our suitcases were all packed, ready to go. The night before our departure, my aunt came over and started to reminisce about the time when I was five years old and came on a train from Komotau with Liesel. We spoke of that Christmas Eve, my desire to leave the farm and find my mother, our expulsion from Franzelhütte, my wait for cookies in Hockenheim, and our little room in Neibsheim. What memories! My heart ached, listening. We sobbed, and tears rolled down our cheeks as we hugged each other good-bye.

The next day, I was leaving the Waldsiedlung forever; my much-desired wish came true. Yet I wanted to reverse everything I wished for, for it no longer felt right for me. Patrizia needed her Oma, and I needed my mother. Looking at my poor mother, I saw a face marked by agony, but there was no turning back. The taxi had arrived. She and I just stood and cried. The taxi driver impatiently tooted his horn for us to hurry up and get in his car. "Time is money," he muttered. He had no clue of our separation anxiety. I felt relieved when the three of us sat in the taxi and drove away from the mental anguish of the last few days.

Overwhelmed with emotions and uncertainty, I walked up the steps of the waiting plane at the Frankfurt airport. Closely behind me followed my husband, holding our child in his arms. As I looked at her, in a brief flashback I saw myself, an innocent little girl rudely exposed to the menace of war and its aftermath. Surviving it, all grown up, married, and a mother, my eyes rose up to the wintry sky, imploring Him to spare this child and the baby in my womb from the terrors of war.

One last glance at the vast space below, and the plane disappeared in the clouds. I was leaving the land of my roots, flying to my future home, the United States of America. The date was November 27, 1962.

Glossary

Alm—alpine meadow
Anbau—annex
Bahnhof—railroad station
Berliner—doughnut
Bierwurst—beer sausage
Brötchen—crusty buns
Bucheln—beechnuts
Bund Deutscher Mädels—Federation of German girls
Bundesland—state, province
Bürgermeister—mayor
Bürgerschule—step up from grade school
Butterbrot—bread with butter
Danke—thank you
Deutsche Bundesbahn—German Federal Railway
Diligence—public stagecoach
Dolmetscher Schule—interpreter school
Einbauküche—fitted kitchen furniture
Einser—one; an A as in grade
Eintopf—vegetable stew
Eisweiher—frozen pond

Fernseher—television; TV
Flüchtling—refugee
Fräulein—Miss
Frau—woman, misses; Mrs.
Freund—friend
Friedhof—cemetery
Fussball Verein—soccer club
Gasthaus—tavern, pub
Gesindel—riffraff
Gestapo—secret police
Glas—glass
Griffel—slate pencil
Gymnasium—academic high school
Hauptbahnhof—central train station
Heimat—homeland
Heisse Schokolade—hot chocolate
Herr—man, mister: Mr.
Hitler Jugend—Hitler youth
Hochzeitschmaus—wedding reception
Hoppi Hoppi Reiter—hop hop rider; game
Hussar—Hungarian cavalry member
Hütte—hut, shack
Kachelofen—tile stove
Kaffee—coffee
Kaiser—emperor
Kastanien—chestnuts
Kilometer (km)—kilometer (1 mile = 1.609 km)
Kirchweih—birthday of a patron saint
Klöppeln—tatting; lace making
König—king
Kreisrat—county commissioner
Kuchen—cake, torte
Kutschenmacher—carriage maker
Lebkuchen—ginger bread
Leiter—ladder
Lesering—book club
Maibaum—Maypole
Metzelfest—butchery feast
Milchhaus—milk house

Misthaufen—dunghill
Modehaus—fashion boutique
Mohnkuchen—poppy seed cake
Most—cider fermented
Mutti—mother
Nationale Sozialistische Deutsche Arbeiter Partei: NSDAP—Nazi Party
Natur—nature
Němci—Germans in the Czech language
Němec —German
Niemandsland—no man's land
Oblaten Torte—layer cake
Oma—grandmother
Onkel—uncle
Opa—grandfather
Ostern—Easter
Papa—father
Personenzug—people train
Pfarrer—priest, reverend
Quarkkuchen—cheesecake
Rathaus—town hall
Ringlo—greengage; type of plum
Rotkäppchen—Little Red Riding Hood
Rucksack—backpack
Schlager—hit song
Schneelzug—fast train
Schoppen—drink; half pint
Schrank—wardrobe
Schuhplattler—type of dance
Schwartenmagen—headcheese
Selige—blessed
Sennerin—dairywoman
Siedlung—settlement
Sparkasse—savings bank
Speck—bacon
Staatsoper—national opera
Stadt Kirche—city church
Stille Nacht—silent night
Strasse—street
Streuselkuchen—crumb cake

Stube—parlor
Tante—aunt
Tanz—dance
Vaterland—fatherland
Verehrer—admirer
Viehwagen—cattle car
Volksbank—people's bank
Volksoper—people's opera
Vollalarm—major alarm
Wagen—wagon
Wagner—wheelwright
Wald—forest
Wanderlust—wanderlust; desire to wander
Weg—lane
Wehrmacht—armed forces
Wehweh—booboo; hurt
Weihnachten—Christmas
Weihnachtsstollen—Christmas loaf, cake
Wirtschaftswunder—economic miracle
Zigeuner—gypsy